Philby

Phillip Knightley was born in Australia but has spent most of his life in London. He was a special correspondent for *The Sunday Times* for 21 years until he left in 1985 to concentrate on writing books. He is married, has three children, and divides his time between Britain, India and Australia.

Also by Phillip Knightley in Pan Books

The Second Oldest Profession:
The Spy as Bureaucrat, Patriot, Fantasist and Whore

The First Casualty:
The War Correspondent as Hero, Propagandist and Myth-maker

Phillip Knightley

Philby

the Life and Views of the
KGB Masterspy

Pan Books London, Sydney and Auckland

First published 1988 by Andre Deutsch Ltd

This edition published 1989 by Pan Books Ltd,
Cavaye Place, London SW10 9PG

9 8 7 6 5 4 3 2 1

ISBN 0 330 30753 3

Printed and bound in Great Britain by
Cox & Wyman Ltd, Reading

For Y.K. who went with me

Contents

List of Plates

1   St John Philby *(Hellis & Sons)*
2   The Philby clan *(Family album)*
3   Kim aged eight *(Family album)*
3a Kim aged twelve *(Aldro school magazine)*
4   Philby aged twenty-one *(Family album)*
5   Litzi Friedmann, Philby's first wife
6   Frances *('Bunny')* Doble, Philby's mistress
7   Philby, *The Times* war correspondent
8   Philby in Washington
9   Aileen Furse, Philby's second wife
10 Philby meets the Press *(United Press International)*
11 FBI 'wanted' notices for Burgess and Maclean
12 Donald and Melinda Maclean *(Associated Press)*
13 Guy Burgess in Moscow *(Peter Keen)*
14 James Jesus Angleton *(Associated Press)*
15 Philby picnics in Beirut *(Family album)*
16 Philby and Eleanor Brewer, his third wife *(Family album)*
17 St John Philby and Eleanor *(Family album)*
18 St John Philby, Kim and his half brothers *(Family album)*
19 Philby in Moscow *(John Philby)*
20 Philby and George Blake in Moscow *(Daily Mail)*
21 Philby in his Moscow study *(Phillip Knightley)*
22 Philby with his Order of Lenin *(Phillip Knightley)*
23 Philby with St John's manuscript *(Phillip Knightley)*
24 Philby and the author at work *(Yvonne Knightley)*
25 Family dinner in Moscow *(Phillip Knightley)*
26 Philby and Rufa, his fourth wife *(Rufa Philby)*
27 Philby's grave *(Yvonne Knightley)*
28 Philby's funeral *(Associated Press)*

Acknowledgements

I would like to thank the following people and organizations: Bruce Page, who first set me on the Philby trail; David Leitch, Hugo Young, Alex Mitchell, Adam Hopkins, Nelson Mews and all the others on *The Sunday Times* who spent the winter of 1967–8 bringing old spies in from the cold, and whose drink-stained notes of that period I have disinterred from my attic. I owe a particular debt to the Australian writer Murray Sayle, the only one of the Philby team actually to meet the master spy at that period (see Appendix), and whose frequent reflections on Philby's personality and motivation kept my interest in him alive over a twenty-year period.

André Deutsch himself and Tom Rosenthal urged me to write the book and offered money, advice and encouragement along the way. My editor, Steve Cox, temporarily abandoned the world of fictional spies for that of real ones, and discovered how closely they intermesh. He understood instantly what I wanted to say and helped me do it, all that any writer needs.

I am indebted to Hamish Hamilton and Grafton Books for permission to quote from, respectively, *Philby, the Long Road to Moscow*, by Patrick Seale and Maureen McConville, and *My Silent War*, by Kim Philby. *The Sunday Times* gave permission to reprint Murray Sayle's interview. Acknowledgement to picture sources is made elsewhere. Any omissions will be rectified in later editions.

Former members of various intelligence services gave me guidance and anecdotes. I sincerely hope they will neither lose their pensions nor be prosecuted under the new Official Secrets Act. CIA officers were, of course, able to speak freely without any such fears.

Finally, I suppose I should thank Mikhail Sergeievich Gorbachev, for without *glasnost*, the KGB would not have allowed me to see Kim Philby and there would have been no reason to have written this book.

Phillip Knightley,
London, August 1988.

Introduction

Harold Adrian Russell ('Kim') Philby was the most remarkable spy in the history of espionage. In nine years he rose through the ranks of the British Secret Intelligence Service (SIS) to become in 1949 the British liaison officer in Washington with the Central Intelligence Agency (CIA) and the Federal Bureau of Investigation (FBI), a position at the heart of the Western intelligence war against the Soviet Union. He was being groomed to take over as 'C', the chief of the British service.

Yet all the while Philby was a serving officer in the KGB, recruited soon after he came down from Cambridge and given his lifelong assignment, to penetrate SIS. This extraordinary deception made Philby the most successful penetration agent ever, a Soviet spy who had special access to a whole range of British and American secrets. True, Philby was exposed before he could become 'C' and he fled to Moscow in 1963, but nevertheless the damage he did to Western intelligence was enormous. When Philby's real role was made public in 1967, Miles Copeland, a former CIA officer who knew Philby, had this to say: 'What it comes to, is that when you look at that whole period from 1944 to 1951 – leaving out anything [Philby] picked up other times – the entire Western intelligence effort, which was pretty big, was what you might call a minus advantage. We'd have been better off doing nothing.'[1]

There have been many books and hundreds of articles about Philby. He himself wrote *My Silent War*, a KGB-authorized version of his espionage career, which was published in 1968. But apart from meeting a *Sunday Times* correspondent, Murray Sayle, at that time – to discuss publication of his book – for the last twenty years of his life Philby studiously avoided all Western journalists.

He lived at a secret address in Moscow. His telephone was ex-directory. He kept away from public places, and when he did go out his KGB security officer checked out all his arrangements. During these years Philby once or twice bumped into a Western correspondent by accident – once at the Bolshoi, for example. On these occasions he left immediately. He never spoke of his work or his feelings, even to his Moscow friends.

Yet shortly before his death in May this year, in the safety of his apartment and in a secure Georgian restaurant, I met with Philby, at his invitation, for some twenty-five hours of conversation. He spoke of his boyhood, his remarkable father (Harry St John Bridger Philby, a famous Arabist), his tragic mother, and his early days in India. He told me of his schooldays, his time at Cambridge, and the origins of his political convictions. He moved on to the so-called 'Cambridge ring' of spies – a source of fascination to both the FBI and the British Security Service (MI5) since the early Fifties. He named for the first time the man who steered him to the Russians – who told him that they had more important work for him than dying for communism on some foreign battlefield.

He discussed the first love of his life, a Viennese girl, and their underground work helping communists and socialists escape from Austria in the dangerous but exciting days of 1933–4, when the Right and Left clashed in the streets of one of Europe's loveliest capitals. He recalled his days in Spain as a war correspondent for *The Times* of London, covering the Civil War from the side of the fascist dictator, General Franco – part of Philby's plan to construct a right-wing façade to hide his earlier, public, socialist stance.

Philby then spoke with some pride of his work for SIS in the intelligence battle against Germany during the Second World War and revealed a scheme he had for assassinating Admiral Wilhelm Canaris, the head of the Abwehr (German military intelligence), hinting that the wartime head of SIS, General Sir Stewart Menzies, had vetoed the plan for dubious political reasons. He spoke of what he considered his main service to the Russians during the war and which, if true, may well have altered the course of history.

Philby told me about his part in frustrating Western intelligence actions against the Soviet bloc in the early days of the Cold War, though he was careful not to reveal KGB operational methods which might still be valid. Talking about the human side of these covert actions, he was frank about his feelings towards those Western agents he betrayed and sent to their deaths.

He spoke of what his appointment to Washington meant to his KGB career, the friends and enemies he made in the American intelligence world, those officers whose ability he respected and admired and those for whom he had nothing but contempt. He then described in detail an error of judgement he made in Washington which caused his KGB career to begin to unravel, and the desperation with which Moscow tried to correct matters as it saw its star officer losing control because of a friend he had mistakenly trusted.

Philby, with both his SIS and KGB careers in ruins, appeared finished, and he described how he spent several years trying to adjust to this failure. Then a covert operation by the director of the FBI, J. Edgar Hoover, who felt personally betrayed by Philby, went awry and instead of exposing Philby gave him a new lease of life as a spy. The British government rehabilitated him and Philby told me how his old friends in SIS got him back into the service – as an agent in Beirut – without even letting the Americans know. He then made the astonishing claim that when SIS finally received proof that he had been working for the Russians all along, it decided to drive him to defect, rather than face the scandal his arrest would provoke in London and Washington. He admitted that this SIS tactic had worked and recalled how he had decided to flee from Beirut. He described his getaway and what had happened to him when he first set foot on Soviet soil.

But it was when our conversations got on to his time in the Soviet Union that Philby appeared to bare his soul. He said that at first everything had gone well but that then a period of doubt and disillusionment had set in, a time when the KGB appeared to have dumped him, when there was no woman in his life, whisky was his only solace and lost weekends the norm. After some years of this, Philby said, he had found late but true romance with a marvellous woman who was now the centrepiece of his life; the KGB had rehabilitated him and now, aged seventy-six, he was once again active in the intelligence war.

We talked about more than Philby's career. I did my best to get to the core of the man, no easy task with a master spy for whom deception is a professional skill. We discussed the ethics of espionage, politics, motivation, the influence of his father, women, marriage, current affairs, friendship, patriotism, honour, loyalty, treachery, betrayal, and the human condition. Philby gave me his views on Western and Soviet leaders, Afghanistan, China, Vietnam and Europe. He talked about his favourite spy thriller writers, today's youth, modern music, and the difficulties of life in the Soviet Union – but also its rewards. He discussed his health, Soviet medicine, his finances, a trip he made to Cuba, and his travels within the Eastern bloc. He reminisced about his CIA colleagues and those he would like to see again.

Did he know then that he did not have much longer to live?

He told me that he had been in hospital for treatment of a heart condition, but that it was not serious and his doctors had told him that if he took things easy then he had many years ahead of him. But since his death something else he said takes on a new significance. We were discussing how best to publish all that he had told me. The choice seemed to be a book, which would take many months to write, or a series of newspaper articles, which could be published quickly. 'You decide,' Philby said. 'But as far as I'm concerned, the sooner the better.'

There was, of course, a problem about the conversations. How much of what Philby said was the man speaking, and how much the serving KGB officer? How much of it was genuine information and how much disinformation? A lot of what he said was checkable, and in the story which follows I reveal the results of these checks. But a lot of what he said could not be verified without access to the archives of SIS, MI5, the CIA, the FBI, and the KGB.

Basically, Philby replied to my questions in three different ways. He would say that he knew the answer, but that he did not intend to tell me because it involved KGB operational methods. He would say, yes, here is what happened; make of it what you will. And he would say that this was something he honestly did not know and that it would be embarrassing for him to ask his colleagues.

For what it is worth, Philby was at pains to assure me that the idea of meeting and talking with me had not been inspired by the KGB. 'I suggested it to them,' he said. 'They said that if I wanted to talk, why not talk with Graham Greene. He comes to the Soviet Union often these days and they felt he would be more suitable. I told them that Greene is a friend and a former colleague. I wanted to talk to someone who would be objective. In the end they tolerated the idea, but they didn't approve of it.' Here I tend to believe Philby. For one thing, I was given no official red-carpet treatment at any stage of my stay, and there was even some doubt that I would be able to take my notebooks through customs when I left. 'If they take them away,' Philby said, 'then let me know and I'll get them back for you.'

When I published some of the conversations in the London *Sunday Times* there was criticism over the whole venture. Some commentators said that I should not have accepted Philby's invitation, that if Philby wanted to talk about his exploits then he should use *Pravda* or *Izvestia*; Western journalists should not help him by making pilgrimages to Moscow. A former senior FBI officer, Robert Lamphere, was surprised that there was not more outrage. '[Philby] betrayed his country and his generation; he is a rogue of the first order, yet here we have him portrayed as some kind of near-heroic elder statesman of espionage. It really does seem quite disgraceful.'[2]

Others read into the conversations a plea by Philby to be allowed to return to Britain to spend his last years. Ted Allbeury, a former member of SIS who knew Philby personally, said: 'Philby's always wanted to come home. He's a totally sad man, dreaming of a cottage in Sussex with roses around the door. He's the epitome of Britishness – the man who bothers to ring through to the Telecom number to find out the Test match score. I would think that Philby is testing the water – just seeing what the reaction to these interviews will be, what sort of controversy they arouse.

'He's using Phillip Knightley. It's one of those vain hopes where, when you're a young man, you ask your best friend to speak to the beautiful girl with blonde hair on your behalf. Knowingly or not, Knightley's doing that, to the British government and the British people.'

The British thriller writer Frederick Forsyth, author of *The Fourth Protocol*, in which Philby is a character, agreed. '[Philby] is profoundly nostalgic for Old England – he has every magazine and newspaper and cannot wait to do *The Times* crossword. And he's desperate to keep abreast of things going on in Britain – he'll even go into a bar in Moscow just to sit and listen to British businessmen's conversations. And, of course, he's not highly regarded by the KGB. Years ago he was one of their five great stars – Burgess, Maclean, George Blake and Blunt were the others. But it's been a long time. Now he's a fallen star who's been passed over and who is no longer consulted.'[3]

Time magazine decided that whatever Philby's personal reasons for granting the interview may have been, Moscow evidently saw an advantage. Intelligence officials, the magazine said, suggested that the conversations were a public relations gambit to make the Soviet Union appear more open: 'Given the upcoming Reagan-Gorbachev summit, it is not a bad moment from Moscow's point of view to launch this otherwise inexplicable ploy.'[4]

I should say immediately that when the opportunity to talk to Philby came I had no hesitation whatsoever in seizing it. My reason was a simple one. Treachery holds a peculiar fascination for the British – perhaps because they have experienced so much of it – and yet, in this case, despite the millions of words written about him, Philby has remained an enigma. I felt that *anything* Philby said in the course of our conversations would contribute something to our understanding of the man and his motives. And if our claim that a democracy can learn from its mistakes is true, then the more we can learn from the Philby affair the better.

At the end I came away with what I believe to be a full and intimate portrait of an Establishment Englishman who betrayed the West, who decided to go against his class and his upbringing for what he believed to the last were impeccable motives, and who then spent most of his life cultivating two separate sides to his head. I accept that many will be angered by some of the details of Philby's personal life. But not only are they often inextricably interwoven with his professional existence, they are vital to understanding it.

For whatever you may think about Philby the man, one fact remains beyond dispute: professionally, as a spy, he is in a class all by himself.

In 1967, Bruce Page, then editor of Insight, the investigative section of the London *Sunday Times*, took me out of the reporters' room where I had been working for two years, for a secret project. I was to join a team, which eventually grew to eighteen journalists, working to unravel the life of Kim Philby. I cannot say that I was wildly enthusiastic at first because it seemed to me that there was little to unravel.

All I knew of Philby at that time was that he had been a journalist, Middle Eastern correspondent of *The Observer* and *The Economist*, who had vanished from Beirut in January 1963 and turned up in the summer of that year in Moscow, where he was granted Soviet citizenship. Now Page told me that David Leitch, another member of the Insight team, had been in the Soviet Union in 1964 to interview Nikita Khrushchev, and had asked him for permission to talk to Philby. Khrushchev had agreed providing that Philby himself was willing. Leitch went ahead with an official application for the Philby interview but Khrushchev lost power soon afterwards and Leitch heard nothing further.

Page told me that the paper had resumed its interest in Philby in 1965, when the memoirs of the Soviet spy 'Gordon Lonsdale' (Conon Molody) were published in Britain and serialized in the *People*, because Leitch had heard rumours that Philby had ghosted Lonsdale's book. (This later turned out to be true. Philby told Murray Sayle in Moscow in 1967: 'I did polish the stuff up a bit. Gordon is a wonderful fellow but he isn't really a literary man.') But it was not until early in 1967 that *The Sunday Times's* passing interest in Philby turned into an obsession.

The editor, Harold Evans, heard that Patrick Seale, an *Observer* journalist who knew Philby in Beirut, was writing a book with

Philby's third wife, Eleanor. The competition between *The Observer* and *The Sunday Times* had always been fierce and Evans began to think of ways he might match the Eleanor Philby story. A quick look at the cuttings library file on Philby produced little. He had first made the news in 1955, when a government report on the defection to Moscow in 1951 of two diplomats, Guy Burgess and Donald Maclean, threw up his name. Philby had been serving as a first secretary in the Washington embassy at the time of the defection and had shared a house with Burgess. This had apparently led an MP to suggest that he might have been the 'Third Man' who had warned Burgess and Maclean to flee. But soon afterwards the Foreign Secretary, Harold Macmillan, made a statement clearing Philby. He had been asked to resign his diplomatic post but, said Macmillan: 'I have no reason to conclude that Mr Philby has at any time betrayed the interests of this country, or to identify him with the so-called third man, if indeed there was one.'

There were then a few minor news items about Philby's disappearance from Beirut in 1963, with speculation on what had happened to him, and then an announcement from Moscow that he had been granted Soviet citizenship. The last item in the library folder was a parliamentary report. The Lord Privy Seal, Edward Heath, answering questions in the House of Commons, agreed that before his defection Philby had confessed that he had indeed warned Maclean through Burgess. Heath had given the impression that it was all a rather low-key and unimportant affair. And there the clippings file ended.

Evans's first idea was to trace the careers of Philby, Burgess and Maclean in the hope of finding who recruited them at Cambridge in the 1930s, but two incidents soon made him more ambitious. Leitch, hoping for leads, had got in touch with a former colleague, Alun Gwynne Jones, the defence correspondent of *The Times* who had become Lord Chalfont and a minister at the Foreign Office. Chalfont said he wanted to see Leitch and Page immediately. In his office he told them: 'You must stop your enquiries. There is the most monstrous danger here. You will be helping the enemy.'[5]

Then Evans was approached for a job as Africa correspondent by a former Foreign Office official, John Sackur. Evans told Sackur that the only vacancy was in the Middle East. Sackur said later that he accepted the position and moved into *The Sunday Times* to orientate himself. One day Evans told Sackur of the Philby project. Sackur said that the paper was wasting its time – it would never be able to print the story: 'It'll get stopped. D notices, the Queen. It goes to the highest in the land. Philby was a copper-bottomed bastard.'*6

His thirst for a good story aroused, Evans's journalistic instinct was to press ahead as fast as possible, but if there was to be official pressure not to print he needed the Editor-in-Chief, Sir Denis Hamilton, behind him. He consulted Hamilton, who went in great secrecy to the Prime Minister, Harold Wilson, and the Director General of SIS, Sir Dick White, for advice. Eventually an agreement was reached. The Foreign Office would not help, but it would not stand in the way of the investigation. For its part, *The Sunday Times* would not make Philby into a hero and it would show the authorities a draft of the final article so as not to risk anyone's life by some unwitting reference.

The investigation now went ahead very rapidly, with Evans throwing in extra manpower from the newsroom whenever needed. I had two extraordinary pieces of luck. Trying to find any former colleagues of Philby's, I managed to track down Leslie Nicholson, an old-time SIS officer who had fallen out with the service over his pension and who had written a book about his career, *British Agent*, under the name of John Whitwell. Nicholson was broke, dying of cancer, and living in reduced circumstances in a room over a café in the East End of London. I gave him a taste of his earlier high life as an SIS officer by taking him to lunch in a fine restaurant of his choice. Nicholson, an amiable and unassuming man, clearly enjoyed recalling his days with 'the Old Firm', as he insisted on calling it, and my questions, at first deliberately oblique so as not to reveal my own ignorance, became over the third and fourth brandy progressively more direct.

Finally it became clear to Nicholson that although *The Sunday Times* knew that Philby had been in SIS while working for the Russians, it had no idea what Philby's SIS job actually was, and the delightful irony of it. Nicholson now took great pleasure in revealing it: 'The reason for the flap, old man, was that Kim was head of our anti-Soviet section.'

I can remember trying to clear my head of brandy fumes. 'Let me get this straight,' I said. 'The man running our secret operations against the Russians was a Russian agent himself?' Nicholson savoured my amazement. 'Precisely,' he said.

And then, a few days after *The Sunday Times* had rushed into

---

*Sackur did not last at the paper. The Foreign Editor, Frank Giles, who had once worked in the Foreign Office himself, discovered that Sackur had been an SIS officer and warned against his employment. Sackur said later he resigned because he came under increasing pressure to talk about Philby.

print on 1 October 1967 – because *The Observer* had decided to do the Seale-Eleanor Philby story that Sunday – Page handed me a letter from the Sheriff of Shropshire, John Reed.

It gave us the information that enabled us to crack the one aspect of the Philby story which had eluded us, his involvement with the failed defection of the NKVD officer Konstantin Volkov in Turkey in 1945 (see pp. 135ff). It was the first setback in Philby's career as a KGB penetration agent. We published Reed's information the following Sunday, adding to the furore the articles had already caused. For not only did the Foreign Secretary, George Brown, denounce the owner of *The Sunday Times*, Roy Thomson, at a public dinner – 'Your papers are doing a very great disservice to this country' – but Kim Philby himself was sufficiently provoked to get in touch with Evans. He sent a telegram offering his memoirs for publication in Britain and asking that someone be sent to Moscow with powers to negotiate with him. Murray Sayle had a Russian visa to do a story about the Russian space shots, so Evans asked him to try to contact Philby, who, curiously, had given no indication in his telegram how to go about doing this. Sayle staked out the Moscow post office where foreigners collect their mail, and after a two-day wait was rewarded by spotting Philby leaving with his copy of *The Times*. Sayle's interviews with Philby, during which Philby floated a remarkable offer – to forgo publication of his book in exchange for the release from prison in Britain of the KGB husband and wife spy team, the Krogers* – was published on the front page of the paper on 17 December 1967 (see Appendix).

The *Sunday Times* articles brought an immediate offer from André Deutsch who then sold the book to publishers around the world and the Insight team began writing what became *Philby, the Spy who Betrayed a Generation* (entitled *The Philby Conspiracy* in the USA) almost without a break. Although a major success, it was a frustrating exercise to reconstruct a man's life without being able to speak to him. Although Philby said that the book was 'a true bill', I shared with the other authors a feeling that our portrait of him lacked a dimension; we had captured some of Philby but not enough.

Talking to Sayle increased my dissatisfaction. He had formed his own assessment of Philby and found him a charming, entertaining man with a great sense of humour, 'quite kind-hearted and by no means just a mouthpiece of Soviet propaganda'. Sayle had asked him

*Peter and Helen Kroger (really Morris and Lona Cohen) were Americans jailed for twenty years in Britain in 1961 for spying for the Soviet Union. Released in 1969 as part of a spy swap, they went to live in Warsaw.

on several occasions whether he had felt any remorse about being a traitor and Philby had replied, 'I betrayed no one. I have always had exactly the same employer and the same opinions. I was a straight penetration agent. If the other side was silly enough to believe my cover, then that's their lookout.'

But Sayle came away with the impression that Philby had enjoyed his double life. 'There is something about his psychology that gives him great satisfaction to have a secret that the people he's with every day don't know about. And, of course, espionage is a strange kind of adventure, of being a semi-criminal but with official backing. It's a mixture of the courageous and the deceitful, or whatever the exact mixture comes down to – you have to be a spy to sense it. I doubt that Kim is a committed Marxist. He doesn't use Marxist language, doesn't think like a Marxist. In fact whenever I talked to him he sounded for all the world like a transplanted British civil servant.'

This was the beginning of my interest in the business of espionage and the people who practise it, eventually to culminate in an examination of the historical role of intelligence agencies, *The Second Oldest Profession*.[7] But in the meantime I wrote to Philby at his Moscow post box address, and sent him an inscribed copy of the *Sunday Times* book.

He replied thanking me and making a few observations on the introduction, written by John le Carré. I wrote back, and this was the beginning of a correspondence that stretched over the next twenty years. Philby's letters were chatty, informed, and often amusing. In 1979 he complained that the shutdown for a year of Times Newspapers Limited (over an industrial dispute) cut him off from life in Britain.

I confess to feeling a gap. I miss the *Times* obits, the funny letters, the court circular and the crossword (15–20 minutes with my morning tea to crank up cerebration); also *The Sunday Times* Insights and reviews, and the less pretentious parts of *The Times Literary Supplement*. Above all, I miss milor Chalfont on the flight of his rich chum [the Shah of Persia] and the poor generals he left behind to face the death squads. As I recall, he (the milor) was last heard of in Mexico. No wonder that Lopez Portillo [the then Mexican president] bit Jimmy Carter on the ankle.

He was still going on about Lord Chalfont, who often wrote on defence for *The Times*, when the paper resumed publication. 'What is happening at PHS [Printing House Square, the address of *The Times*]? But for the crossword and the cuckoo Chalfont, who is doing our hawks a power of good, I would give the paper up.' Philby seemed hungry for political gossip from Britain and particularly keen for news of Mrs Thatcher. 'I wonder how you are getting on under the regiment of that noisy girl from Grantham [Mrs Thatcher's birth place]? *Pace* the BBC and other media, the Russians do not call her the "Iron Lady" That is a long-forgotten lapse by an obscure writer on the staff of *Red Star*. As the Russians have difficulty with English vowels and the "th", she usually comes out as something like "Meesees Tetchy". Perhaps the bonnet fits.'

Occasionally Philby would make tantalizing references to his activities in the Soviet Union. 'Just back from a few weeks abroad, I have in front of me a dauntingly-large heap of papers in my in-tray.' The 'abroad' was puzzling. Did Philby mean that he had been to one of the Soviet bloc countries. Or had he been overseas? And if so, where and why? When his next letter referred to 'my weeks in the sun' and 'sipping stengahs' it did seem as if he had been to some tropical country.

By coincidence I dined soon afterwards with the former director general of SIS, the late Sir Maurice Oldfield, and I told him about Philby's remarks and the questions they raised. 'He hasn't been anywhere,' Oldfield said. 'He knows we will be reading his letters to you.' (Early in our correspondence Philby had indeed warned me that our letters would be opened 'at each end'.) 'So he just wants to make mischief, to have us rushing around wasting our resources trying to find out what he has been up to. Kim was always very good at making mischief.'[8]

We discussed the latest books and television drama. 'I heard about the Granada production [*Philby, Burgess and Maclean*] from several sources, including my eldest daughter who thought well of it "except that the women were too bitchy". We [the KGB] took a video-whatsit of it, so I shall probably see it soon. No doubt there will be moments of embarrassment.' He seemed to prefer factual spy books to spy fiction but read the latest in each genre.

I read the *Bodyguard* [*Bodyguard of Lies*, by Anthony Cave Brown] with enjoyment: a tricky book, 70% true and much of that 70% important, 15% dead wrong, and the rest distracting decoration which is becoming so regrettably fashionable these days (what-Monty's-batman-had-for-breakfast-on-D-day sort of thing). The snag is that the non-specialist can't know which of the pages fall into the dead wrong category.

I have ordered *The Honourable Schoolboy*. From le Carré's

introduction to your book, I get the vague impression, perhaps wrongly, that he didn't like me. But we are generous, and have no objection to contributing to his vast affluence.

This correspondence was interrupted only once, when I quoted from one of his letters in an article I wrote for *The Sunday Times*. I used a line or two of Philby's opinion of *The Climate of Treason*, by Andrew Boyle, the book which exposed Anthony Blunt as a former Russian agent. Philby himself did not greatly mind being quoted – 'although if I had known you were going to publish my views I would have given a little more attention to my prose style,' he told me in Moscow. But Philby's KGB superiors objected to the use of a personal letter in this manner and our correspondence ceased for more than a year.

During this period, after rumours that he had been ill, I wrote to him saying that there seemed to be an improvement in the international political climate and that it might be the right moment for him to make a contribution to this change. 'You have been around long enough for a new wave of interest in your life, career and beliefs,' I wrote.

There is a generation out there which knows little about you but is fascinated by what it does know. For evidence of this see the enclosed *Observer* clipping about Julie Burchill, prophet of the younger Brits, who acknowledges only two people as her heroes, Graham Greene and you.

I think you and I should have a wide-ranging discussion about you and your motives. This could be recorded in Moscow for showing all over the world via the BBC. The BBC is keen on the idea as an encore to its highly successful series *Comrades* which told the West more about life in the Soviet Union than anything ever shown before.

Philby did not reply directly, but in a letter to one of his children, in which he said he had received my proposal but had to say no. He repeated his opinion of television from an earlier letter to me: 'I have a snobbish block about visual journalism, TV and stills. The clicks and the trip wires, with little men bent double running backwards, seem to ruin all solemn and moving occasions.' Then he added that 'just Knightley and a notebook' might be a different matter.

When I heard this I wrote again saying that I could understand how he felt about television, that I was going to the United States and then to Australia and India, but perhaps on my return we could get together at last. Philby did not reply so I wrote again from India to say that my wife and I would be in Moscow anyway on a package tour for the seventieth anniversary of the Revolution. I enclosed our schedule and a list of our hotels and said that if he had the time and felt well enough perhaps we could meet for a drink.

I heard nothing from Philby during the November tour but back in London, a letter arrived from Moscow dated 13 November 1987. It read:

Dear Knightley,

Your letter from India took six weeks to reach me, so the chance of a casual drink presented itself too late.

However, if you are still interested, I think there is a fair possibility of us getting together for a real talk in the not too distant future.

This would take the form of a telegram from us to you and your wife inviting you to come to Moscow for a few days.

I note that you have agreed to come without TV paraphernalia or tape-recorders. Just your wife, yourself and your notebook – in that order . . .

There are still a few details to be worked out. I put a high value on my privacy, and do not want you to ring my doorbell trailing the whole Moscow press corps behind you. Furthermore, a leakage at your end of the real purpose of your Moscow trip would put the whole enterprise in question . . .

Finally, may I thank you for the patience and courtesy with which you have conducted what must have been a frustrating correspondence?

My regards to Mrs Knightley and best wishes from myself.

H.A.R. Philby

On 2 December I received a telegram: WOULD MOSCOW VISIT SECOND HALF JANUARY SUIT QUERY PLEASE TELEGRAPH – PHILBY. I replied saying that it would. But it was not until 8 January that the actual invitation arrived: LOOK-ING FORWARD ARRIVAL YOURSELF AND WIFE PLEASE TELEGRAPH DATE AND FLIGHT NUMBER REGARDS – PHILBY.

I presented this telegram and our visa applications at the Soviet Consulate in Bayswater Road, London, where there was a worrying moment. Mindful of Philby's warnings that 'any leakage at your end of the real purpose of your Moscow trip would put the whole enter-prise in question' I had told no one and had studiously avoided journalist colleagues.

But when I walked into the consulate there were two men from the London *Daily Mirror* deep in argument with a consular official about their visas for a press trip to the Soviet Union. Fortunately they did not know me and I deliberately chose a visa window as far as possible from them. But everything nearly went badly wrong when the official dealing with me, after examining the application forms and closely scrutinizing the Moscow telegram said loudly: 'Who is this Mr Philby and who does he work for?' I raised my index finger to my lips, made a loud 'shushing' sound, nodded my head in the direction of the *Daily Mirror* reporters, gestured for a pen and a piece of paper, wrote 'Mr Philby is a general in the KGB' and pushed it under the grille to the official. He read it, looked startled, and disappeared into a back room, emerging a few minutes later to tell me in a whisper that the visa would be ready first thing next morning.

We arrived in Moscow on the evening of Monday, 18 January. The Russians were failing to enjoy a mild winter. Temperatures had hovered around zero centigrade for several weeks so instead of the city being covered in snow and ice it was half covered in muddy slush. We went through the usual thorough examination by immigration officials, queued with everyone else to be examined by customs, and then were directed by an Intourist woman to a taxi which took us to the Belgrade Hotel. We had been in the room only twenty minutes when the telephone rang. Since it was my first conversation with Philby, I remember it well. After a pause a voice said: 'Is that you, Knightley?'

Me:	Yes.
Philby:	Kim Philby here.
Me:	Hello Mr Philby.
Philby:	How good to speak to you and hear you've arrived safely. Now look here; are you exhausted, or would you like to spend the evening with us?
Me:	We'd like to spend the evening with you.
Philby:	Can you be ready in twenty minutes or so?
Me:	Yes.
Philby:	Good. If you can be in the lobby of the hotel in, say, twenty-five minutes, then a neighbour of mine will be there to pick you up.

The neighbour turned out to be Vladimir, a large, cheerful young man in a black leather coat. He may have been a neighbour but he was, as Philby later agreed, a KGB officer from the administrative section. He led us to a small black sedan driven by another KGB officer, Boris, who was to take us to all our meetings with the Philbys. Since Philby had warned me how careful he was to conceal his address, we were quite prepared for the car to have drawn curtains, but it did not, and we drove directly to Philby's apartment, pausing only occasionally for Vladimir to give directions. But since it was at night, and a traffic rule in Moscow about left-hand turns leads to lots of detours, I have no idea where Philby lived, except that it is in the centre of the city.

The last part of the journey was down a narrow lane from which there appeared to be only one exit. On one side of the lane was a small park with several trees, on the other a substantial prewar apartment block with entry through a basement. Vladimir escorted us to a rather rickety lift. ('A couple of generals I had been entertaining were stuck in there for hours one night,' Philby joked later.) At the fifth or sixth floor – it was difficult to be exact because the lift opened at each half landing, there were no markings, and Vladimir always pressed the button – we found ourselves in front of the usual Russian padded door with a bell push and a peep-hole but no name plate. Vladimir rang, there was a moment's pause while we were surveyed from inside, and then, suddenly, there was Philby himself, holding out his hand, smiling, introducing his wife, Rufa, taking coats and fur hats, every inch the charming English host. 'Come on through, dear chap,' he said, leading the way to his reception room. 'Please make yourself comfortable. Now what'll you have to drink?'

Over our first whisky, I remarked how well I thought Philby looked. I had seen photographs taken by his family some two or three years earlier in which he had appeared very ill indeed – overweight, puffy in the face, and older than his years. But this was a different man: slim, alert, and bubbling with youthful good humour. 'I *am* well,' he said, 'and that's one of the reasons you're here, one of the reasons I agreed to see you. There has been a rumour which apparently started in Canada of all places that I was on my uppers, ill, abandoned by the KGB and anxious to return to Britain. I wanted you to see for yourself that none of this was true. Now shall we start work straight away?' I said I would rather relax, savour the evening, and start work tomorrow. This was apparently the right answer. 'Good,' Philby said. 'Pass your glass. I like a man who can enjoy himself.'

Kim Philby lived in some style and his apartment was said to be one of the best in Moscow. It had belonged to an official of the Soviet Foreign Ministry. When the official moved to a modern block, the KGB offered it to their star spy who had been living in a smaller apartment in the suburbs. 'I snapped it up,' Philby told me. 'It's in the middle of Moscow, yet it's so quiet you might be miles out in the country. It has east, west, and south-west aspects so I get every ray of sun.' The apartment, for which he paid 80 roubles* a month, including heating and electricity, was actually two knocked into one.

Leading off a large entrance hall there was a master bedroom, guest bedroom, bathroom, toilet, laundry, kitchen, and large reception/dining room which ran almost the width of the apartment. From the hallway you entered Philby's spacious study. This contained a desk, a filing cabinet, a couple of chairs and an enormous old refrigerator. A Turkish kelim and a fur rug covered the floor. Bookshelves on three of the four walls accommodated part of Philby's library of some 12,000 books.

There was a special section of the library set aside for books on espionage, both fact and fiction. These included Peter Wright's *Spycatcher* ('Graham Greene gave it to me'); *The Man Who Kept the Secrets: Richard Helms and the CIA*; *A History of the British Secret Service*; *Top Secret Ultra*; *Bodyguard of Lies*; *The Climate of Treason*; and *An Anthology of Spy Stories*. For spy fiction, Philby read Alan Williams (Philby is a character in one of his books); Len Deighton, John le Carré and Graham Greene – he had all the Greene books. He also read Dick Francis's racing thrillers.

Philby's desk was illuminated by an Anglepoise-type lamp. There were IN and OUT trays, a pile of back issues of *The Times*, and a recent issue of *The Independent*. An old mug held pencil and pens, and there was a pencil sharpener and a calendar. On the wall facing the desk there was a large photograph of Philby's father, Harry St John Bridger Philby (known as 'St John'), the famous Arabist, wearing full Arab clothing. Neatly framed below the photograph were two pages from one of St John Philby's handwritten manuscripts, showing his incredibly neat, tiny writing. 'Look at that,' Philby said. 'What clarity of thought – only two corrections on the whole page.'

There were also two large framed photographs of Che Guevara, a figure never much in favour with the Soviet leadership. One photograph of a revolutionary whose flamboyant career was so much in contrast to Philby's secret one might be understandable; but two? 'I brought them back from Cuba,' Philby said in answer to my question. Did Castro give them to him? 'No,' Philby said. 'I didn't meet Castro. Only my colleagues in the Cuban service.' For some reason or other he did not want to talk further about Guevara, and our conversation moved on.

*About £80 ($144) at the official exchange rate and about £20 ($36) at the real rate.

I asked Philby if his study, where we held most of our conversations, was bugged. He replied: 'I haven't the slightest idea and nor do I care. However, it seems to me unlikely. It's no good bugging someone unless you are going to listen to the tapes or read the transcripts. The manpower required for such an enterprise would be enormous.'

We ate our first meal at a small table in Philby's dining room. The room also contained a larger table, a fine Spanish antique given to him by a friend, Tommy Harris, an art and antiques dealer who served in the war as an interrogator in MI5, but since there were only four of us the smaller table was more intimate. At one end of the room a china cabinet housed a set of fine bone English china, a gift from the KGB on the occasion of Philby's wedding. The walls were decorated with several prints, one of them a farewell gift from a lifelong friend, the Keeper of the Queen's Pictures, Sir Anthony Blunt, who also worked for Russian intelligence. And there were some animal skins and a pair of antique Spanish duelling pistols.

Dinner was prepared by Mrs Philby, who is half-Polish and half-Russian and likes to combine the two cuisines. There was black and red caviar, smoked sturgeon, smoked salmon, smoked pork and smoked sprats, pickled herring and pickled cucumbers, black and white bread, cold fillet of beef, sauté potatoes and a bowl of fresh Egyptian oranges. The food was set out on table mats showing typical London scenes – including, ironically, one of the Tower of London, traditional execution place for traitors. To drink, there was Johnnie Walker Red Label, red and white Georgian wine and Russian champagne.

Philby produced two crystal champagne glasses and offered the first of many toasts. 'This is a double occasion for celebration,' he said. 'One: you're the only Western journalist I've ever invited to my home here. And two: in a few days it will be twenty-five years since I first arrived in the Soviet Union.'

And so the conversations began. They were always held in the evening, usually before and after dinner. Sometimes we proceeded chronologically through Philby's life. On other occasions I would ask him a list of questions I had prepared during the day. Sometimes I would leave him books and papers to read before our next meeting and he would then comment on them. Back in the hotel, no matter how late, I would write up a full account of that evening's conversation so that the next day I could raise with Philby any point of which I was unsure. And each night, as I sat writing, there would be the regular telephone call, always a Russian, always a man, and always,

I gathered, a wrong number. I took this to be the KGB officer responsible for Philby's security, checking that I was not out in the dark streets of Moscow up to some mischief.

At the end of six days both Philby and I were exhausted and I suspect that he was glad to see the back of me and the ghosts from his past that I had raised. I had three notebooks, all crammed, some of Philby's own writings, and three rolls of film. (There should have been four, but all the photographs I took of our evening in the Georgian restaurant – including a marvellous one of Philby in his English trouser braces – were missing. Perhaps because of an early start on the 600 grammes of vodka that Philby had ordered, I had forgotten to put the film in the camera.)

On the plane to London I pondered on how best to present the conversations with Philby to the West. I could simply set them down, divided either by subject or as they had occurred. But this would exclude a whole generation of readers who had grown up in the post-Philby era and who would not understand the background. In the end I decided that the best way was to tell the story of Philby's life, as *The Sunday Times* had done back in 1968, but using all the new information that has come to light since that pioneering effort. And I would weave into this story the comments and revelations about himself and his career that Philby had made in Moscow.

This means that spy buffs will have to go over material they may feel they already know well. (However, even they should be prepared for surprises.) But the convenience of the initiated is unimportant compared with the opportunity to introduce a new generation to the life of a remarkable man, the political and personal passions that motivated him, and to the dark world of espionage that has such undue influence on all our lives.

IN THE SHADOW OF THE GREAT EXPLORER

1

Kim Philby believed that his ancestors came from Denmark and that the name was originally Filby. 'Who first substituted the Greek "Ph" for the "F", heaven knows,' he said. There is certainly a Filby Broad in East Norfolk and a Filby Society which visits there, but in Essex there are Philbys going back to the eighteenth century and Kim Philby was directly descended from them. One, Kim's grandfather, Montie, a dashing but irresponsible coffee planter, married a Queenie Duncan in Ceylon in 1883. Queenie, or May as she was known, came from a long line of military people – no fewer than 141 of her relatives served in the First World War. The tradition continued: one soldier from this family became Field Marshal Lord Montgomery of Alamein, and Kim Philby was thus distantly related to one of the great British military heroes.

May and Montie Philby had four sons – Ralph, Harry, Harold and Dennis. Then, with one of those English family peculiarities that seem to run through generations, the boys were all immediately given nicknames and became Tom, Jack, Tim and Paddy, which caused no end of confusion to outsiders. Jack (really Harry St John Bridger Philby) was to become the father of Kim (really Harold Adrian Russell Philby).

Kim's mother was Dora Johnston, the dashing red-headed daughter of a senior railway engineer in the Punjab Provincial Engineering Service. There is disagreement over whether she had some Indian blood. One account says flatly: 'Although Eurasians, Dora's parents were fully accepted in the British community . . .'[1] But another recounts May Philby's misgivings after she received letters from relations in India raising questions about her future daughter-in-law's social standing. She passed these on to her son and he replied at length about Dora's good Scottish connections on her father's side. However, 'Philby said nothing of Dora's mother, born an O'Connor, except that she had been brought up in India and that Dora brought him some Irish blood.'[2] It seems quite likely that there was some

Indian ancestry on Dora's mother's side but that no one knows for certain.

St John used to explain his own dark exotic looks by telling an apocryphal story about a family journey in Ceylon when he was still a baby. After an overnight stop at a government rest house the servants accidentally left him behind. When they returned to get him they found a gypsy woman nursing two babies – St John and her own child. The babies looked alike and since the woman had helped herself to some of St John's clothes for her own baby, positive identification was impossible. The servants did their best, St John would say with a grin, but did they bring back the right baby?

Not that any of this would have worried St John Philby. He was one of those Englishmen who had a lifelong attraction for the East and a quick affinity for all its races. He got on so well with Indians that one of his superiors in the Indian Civil Service wrote in St John's file: 'He mixes a bit too much with the native element.' He became a Muslim and took a Saudi slave girl as his second wife. He lived in Mecca, dressed as an Arab, could hold his own in a desert ride with any tribesman, ate camel meat and kept Abyssinian baboons. He spoke French, German, Urdu, Persian, Arabic, Pushtu and Punjabi. But he never gave up being an Englishman. He stood twice for Parliament, contributed to *The Times*, won international honour as an explorer, tried never to miss a Test match, and was a member of the Athenaeum. (London clubs then, and to a lesser extent even today, were power centres where men of similar interests met, socialized and helped each other. Those who understood clubland's subtle class distinctions could tell a man's background and aspirations by the club to which he belonged. Membership of the 'right' club could be a reference and a passport to success.)

St John was a man who should have had the world at his feet, a polymath in every sense of the word. He could speak and write with authority on history and the classics, archaeology and the sciences, politics and economics, the rise of Islam, finance and the law, the literature of France and Germany, ornithology and geology, map-making and exploration. He crossed parts of Arabia unknown to Burton or Doughty, mapping them with such precision that oil prospectors still use his maps today. He received the Founder's Medal of the Royal Geographical Society and was awarded the first Burton Memorial Medal of the Royal Asiatic Society. He made large additions to British collections of geological and zoological specimens from Arabia. He took up the collection and study of early Semitic inscriptions in Arabia and increased from some two thousand to over thirteen thousand the number of known Thamudic inscriptions.

He was a fine administrator with many ideas ahead of his time. He should have shot to the upper rungs of the Indian Civil Service; some say that even a post on the Viceroy's staff was not beyond his grasp. But something did not quite click. He seemed to ruin his main chances by falling out with his superiors, usually because of his sheer cussedness. He ended by spending most of his life at loggerheads with the British government, railing at his country for what he saw as its perfidy, deceit and moral decline.

From his boyhood St John remembered his mother's struggle to provide for her children after she had left Montie behind in Ceylon in 1901 and returned to England, and her embarrassment in shops when tradesmen pressed for payment of bills. He vowed that not only would he take May away from all that, but that nothing similar would ever happen to him. Yet he spent most of his life short of money, fending off creditors, worrying how he would be able to support his wife and find the school fees for his children, humiliating himself by borrowing from lesser men. The rare occasions his writings show elation – as distinct from happiness – were when things were going well for him financially: 'The shekels are pouring in now.'

Yet St John Philby was rarely depressed or discouraged. Showing immense energy, he led a rich and varied life. His outspokenness caused many to dislike him, and his utter conviction that he was right and everyone else wrong made him powerful enemies. (The fact that he *was* frequently right did not ease matters.) His married life was strange, to say the least – he always discussed his new mistresses with his wife yet she remained loyal to him. His children and grandchildren adored him. He once wrote: 'My ambition is fame, whatever that may mean, and for what it is worth. I have fought for it hard.' This he achieved. When he died in Beirut in 1960, Kim put a tombstone on the grave with an inscription reading: 'Greatest of Arabian explorers.' The cemetery, in the Basta quarter of the city, was the scene of heavy fighting in the late 1980s, and the headstone has probably been destroyed, but the sentiments remain.

The departure of St John Philby's father, Montie, and his obvious unwillingness to support his brood meant that if the boys wanted a decent education then they would have to work for it. St John was entered for the Westminster Challenge (the examination for a scholarship) at Westminster school and in 1898, aged thirteen, he was elected a Queen's Scholar. The school was founded by Queen Elizabeth I and its very position – close to the Houses of Parliament, within earshot of Big Ben, and in the shadow of Westminster Abbey –

gives it a place in the English establishment enjoyed by few other public schools. Yet it has always produced the odd rebel or two. A recent issue of the school magazine, in a column headed 'Past Comments' has this quotation: 'It will never be well with the nation until Westminster School is suppressed.'[3]

The Queen's Scholars were the elite of the school and were expected to behave as such. St John Philby did not disappoint. Determined to shine, he won school colours for cricket and football, got high marks in all his subjects, took part in the Coronation of Edward VII, and in his last year, to his great delight, was made captain of the school. Trinity College, Cambridge, and Christ Church, Oxford, traditionally offer scholarships for Westminster students and in March 1904, St John won an exhibition to Trinity in classics.

He slipped neatly into university life. He kept up his sport, played chess, took part in plays, and enjoyed the social life of his college to the full. But, conscious that he was at university to learn, he flung himself into work – the reading, thinking, discussion and criticism that lie at the basis of a British university education. In his first term he joined the Trinity society called 'Magpie and Stump', formed to improve its members' debating ability by obliging them to speak on topics, usually light-hearted ones, for which they held little or no conviction.

Philby proposed Jawaharlal Nehru, the future Prime Minister of India, for membership, something Kim Philby mentioned in Moscow some eighty years later. We were talking about India and I suggested that he should consider going there for a visit. 'After all, relations between India and the Soviet Union are good,' I said. 'There wouldn't be any problem about a visa.' Kim Philby replied: 'I should hope not. After all my father and Rajiv Gandhi's grandfather were friends at Cambridge.'

In 1906, after learning that he had got only a second in the first part of the Classical Tripos, St John switched to modern languages and began to spend his vacations working in France and Germany. His industry paid off. He not only got a first in the Modern Languages Tripos but he was awarded a Trinity scholarship which would enable him to stay at college another year if he passed the examination for the Indian Civil Service. He did, coming 47th, and after his graduate year studying Oriental languages and Indian law and history he sailed for Bombay in November 1908.

If St John Philby had thought that a secure job in the ICS, with every likelihood of regular promotion and increments in salary, would be the end of the family's financial problems, then he must have been disappointed. Although living in India was cheap for a young bachelor, married life with its added financial and social obligations was another matter. In fact the ICS discouraged marriage until a young officer had been in India for at least three years, preferably five. But St John could not wait. He defied his superiors and married Dora in September 1910, when he had been in India for less than two years.

His letters home reveal how desperate his financial situation became. Trying to set up house with Dora and, at the same time, keep paying an allowance to his mother, was difficult enough. But St John, already under a small cloud for his defiance over his marriage, had committed a much more serious blunder. Investigating the death of a Hindu beggar who had been ejected from a Muslim wedding, he was presented with a post-mortem report carried out by a Muslim assistant surgeon who had been assisted by a Hindu sweeper, a member of one of the lower Hindu castes. The surgeon had found that the Hindu beggar had a diseased spleen and that even a light blow would have been sufficient to have killed him. St John Philby considered the whole affair too neat, and he suspected that there had been a conspiracy to conceal the truth. He committed the man who had struck the beggar for trial on a charge of murder and arranged to have the surgeon suspended from duty pending further investigation.

A new post-mortem was carried out by an English doctor who found that the dead beggar had a perfectly normal spleen. Philby, pleased to have been proved right, charged the surgeon and the sweeper with perjury, ordered their arrest and then refused them bail. Philby should have realized that the affair now had the potential for serious communal confrontation – a Hindu had been killed, a Muslim charged with his murder, and a Muslim and an untouchable Hindu charged with perjury over their evidence. But he could not have foreseen what happened next. The police taking the surgeon and his assistant to jail had only one pair of handcuffs so the two men were handcuffed together – a high-born Muslim professional to an untouchable Hindu sweeper – and taken to jail by open cart in full view of the public. By the time the district commissioner heard a renewed application for bail and granted it – perjury was a bailable offence – the local press was describing it as 'the Sargodha sensation'.

Eventually calm was restored. The murder charge was dropped because the main evidence, the condition of the spleen, was inconclusive – the second forensic examination had virtually destroyed it. The Muslim assistant surgeon and his Hindu assistant were tried for perjury and acquitted for much the same reason. But blame had to be apportioned and Philby had clearly been wrong in failing to allow bail. He was reprimanded and his personal ICS file was marked with a restriction banning him from being promoted to head of a sub-division until he was considered competent to handle such a post.

This check to his career cut him off from salary increments, and he was forced to turn to his language abilities to make up the loss of income. The ICS encouraged its officers to become proficient at Indian languages by rewarding those who passed the examinations with one-time cash payments as well as salary bonuses. The cash payments were not inconsiderable and between 1911 and 1915 St John Philby earned in this manner Re 10,000 (in today's values, more than £20,000 or $36,000). The money helped, but May was still a drain, so St John invited her to sell up in London and come to India.

She arrived in time for the birth on 1 January 1912 of St John and Dora's first child, a boy they called Harold Adrian Russell. By now the Philbys were stationed at Ambala in the Punjab, a pleasant posting with a varied social life that Dora was determined to enjoy to the full. No mean tennis player, she entered the major tournaments, leaving her baby with her mother-in-law or in the charge of the ayah, the Indian nursemaid. When she and St John had a chance to go camping, she often took the baby with them. It was not long before Harold Adrian Russell, in common with his father, his uncles and his grandmother, had a nickname – Kim, after the main character in Rudyard Kipling's novel of that name. In Moscow, Harold Adrian Russell Philby explained how it happened: 'I spent more time with the servants and other Indians than I did with my own parents so I soon picked up some words in Punjabi. One day my father came into the kitchen and heard me chattering away. "Good heavens," he said. "He's a real little Kim." Everyone began calling me Kim and the name stuck.'

When Kim was only three St John had already started to talk of grooming him for a scholarship at Westminster. He wondered if someone in India could teach him German. He began to spend more time with the boy and when he was transferred to Calcutta as secretary to the Board of Examiners of Bengal he arranged for Dora and Kim to join him before they went to Darjeeling to avoid the hot season.

They were pleasant times – Jack was temporarily in funds – but overlaid with sadness. His brother Paddy had been killed in France soon after the outbreak of war and St John bombarded his mother, now back in Britain, with letters urging her to do something to get him on to active service. His chance came in November 1915 when he was appointed to the British forces in Mesopotamia fighting the Turks. Philby's job was as a civilian administrator in occupied territory, but he seems to have done some intelligence work as well and there are accounts of him wandering the byways of Baghdad disguised as an Arab beggar.

He did not stay long in Baghdad, and was soon deeply involved in implementing Britain's policy of persuading the Arabs to revolt against Turkish rule. As usual, St John had his own ideas about the best way of doing this and fell out with the deputy chief political officer, Arnold Wilson, an army man well remembered in later years in the House of Commons for threatening to horsewhip journalists who wrote anything critical of him. A damaging confrontation was averted when Philby was offered a place on a political mission to Ibn Saud, little realizing how his decision to accept would change the course of his life. For the two men, the English administrator and the bedouin chieftain, formed a lasting relationship. Ibn Saud was fascinated with the tough, argumentative Englishman who was not afraid to speak his mind and who seemed to love the desert as much, if not more, as the Arabs. ('It was possible to distinguish Philby from the thirty-five Bedouin in his group,' wrote an Arab agent in Taif, 'only by the fact that his feet were not quite dirty enough.')

St John Philby liked the austerity, the strict moral code of the Arabs. Their social system, based on a benevolent if autocratic monarchy, appealed to the puritanical side of his personality. And like many other British Arabists, St John Philby felt that his country behaved with unforgivable duplicity towards the Arabs in the First World War. The British promised them self-determination in exchange for help against the German-Turkish alliance. But these public promises were cynically ignored in the Sykes-Picot agreement (1916), by which Britain and France agreed to divide the Middle East to their own advantage. This duplicity was then compounded by the Balfour Declaration (1917), promising the Jews a national home in Palestine. St John Philby's reaction was that the rulers of Britain simply could not be trusted, and he took upon himself the task of trying to advise the Saudis in their relations with perfidious Albion.

This involved spending long periods in Arabia, away from Dora and Kim, who, when St John had been posted to Baghdad, had gone to live in Camberley, an army town in Surrey, with Kim's grandmother, May. May was to be the most stable influence in Kim's young life because Dora was often away following St John. Perhaps the most important result of this relationship with his grandmother was that Kim imbibed May's admiration for St John. 'He learned to blow his nose much earlier than his sisters – three daughters were born to Dora after Kim – because he wanted to make the same noise as his admired father.'[4] On his brief visits to London St John sensed the admiration, noted his son's intelligence, and determined to mould him in his own image. He arrived in London in January 1919, gathered the family together in a rented house in St Petersburgh Place, Bayswater, and took the first step towards getting Kim into Westminster by choosing for him a suitable preparatory school, Aldro, in Eastbourne.

Kim had a remarkable record there. Although he was almost a year younger than other boys of his form he excelled both as a scholar and a sportsman. He was head boy, house prefect, and winner of numerous prizes. He was a member of the cricket first eleven, one of its most reliable bats and the best fielder. He played inside right for the soccer first eleven and inside three-quarter for the rugby first fifteen. He was commander of the drill squad which won the school competition; he won the school welter-weight boxing championships and the school under-ten draughts competition.

In the school's record of its rugby team we can find an early indication of Kim's determination to succeed at anything he attempted. He was dropped from the three-quarter line early in the rugby season because of his size – 'a lack of inches' as the school magazine put it. Kim decided he would become a full-back, where his size was not so important. He quickly learnt the skills of a full back, challenged for the position and was again accepted for the team.

Needless to say, his father was delighted with him and did his best to help. He came to the school to give a lecture to the pupils, called, not surprisingly, 'Across Arabia'. He took Kim in the summer of 1923 on a grand tour of the Middle East, visiting Damascus, Baalbek, Sidon, Tyre, Tiberias, Nazareth, Acre, Haifa and Jerusalem.

This provided Kim with unbeatable material for the school magazine essay competition on the subject of 'My Most Interesting Day in the Holidays'. While the other boys wrote of a visit to the zoo, Kim's essay began: 'The day before, the Sheik of Adwan had sent a defiant answer to Emir Abdullah's order to surrender, so Abdullah had had a council with Group Captain McEwan, and my father, Mr H. St J. Philby, as to what should be done.' The essay went on to describe a punitive raid on the Sheik's encampment in which, according to Kim, seventy or eighty Arabs were killed, and Kim's ride in an RAF bomber. 'We flew around for some time, at a safe distance, and after about half-an-hour we landed and had lunch with Abdullah, and just after lunch a man came in with two long carpets and told us that they were our share of the spoil.' Apart from some understandable exaggeration about the number of casualties, this was a fair description of a real event, and did wonders for Kim's reputation in the school. 'Kim was a golden boy,' Richard Feacham, one of his fellow Aldro pupils, recalls. 'I was lower down in the school and admired him dreadfully.'[5]

In the late spring of the following year, St John Philby arrived in Britain on leave from the ICS. He was retiring from public service for good and cashed in half his pension of £700 a year to buy a London house for his family. (He later settled on a Victorian mansion in Acol Road, West Hampstead, which was to prove large enough to accommodate not only his children, but later their spouses as well.) St John had another reason for returning to London – to encourage Kim in his bid to follow his lead and become a King's Scholar at Westminster.

Kim did not let him down. On 4 July Aldro was given a holiday in honour of Kim's success. In the morning Kim and his friends went to watch Oxford playing H. D. Leveson Gower's XI. In the afternoon they walked over the Downs to Wannock, where Harry and Dora entertained the whole school, pupils and masters, to a strawberries and cream afternoon tea. Then, abandoning Dora who was about to give birth to her youngest child, Helena, the only one born in Britain, Harry and Kim set out for a holiday in France. In Moscow, talking at length about his father, Kim told me: 'One of the few criticisms about my father that I have to agree with, is that he was a terribly insensitive man, especially in his relationship with my mother. He often treated her abominably.'

On 18 September 1924, St John took Kim to Westminster for the first day of school, one of the proudest moments of St John's life. Kim, not yet thirteen, dressed in gown and white tie, joined the elite King's Scholars of the school. He lived in a dormitory and did his studying in a small room containing only a chair, a table and a bookshelf. There was no central heating and the only warmth came from coal fires lit when winter was well advanced. At Westminster, Kim seems to have lost his interest in sports, except gymnastics, replacing it with a passion for classical music. Academically, he was not thought to be brilliant, achieving good results more by hard work and determination than any natural flair. In the fifth form he started off seventeenth in the class and finished second; in the sixth form he began at the bottom and ended up at the top, winning the Marshall Memorial Prize for history. Then, still doggedly following his father's footsteps, when he was just seventeen he was the first of three Westminster boys elected to Trinity. The quiet lad with the slight stammer seemed to his masters as if he might also follow his father into the Indian Civil Service. True, he lacked his father's compelling personality, but this might be no bad thing.

At Westminster Kim had passed through his adolescence, and later there were allegations that, like Burgess and Blunt, he too had homosexual inclinations. It is true that Kim did suffer what appears to have been some form of minor nervous breakdown there. Could the cause have been a homosexual experience, not uncommon in British public schools? One source says bluntly: 'Like many boys growing up in a boarding school he first learned about sex in a homosexual context. Later, in a moment of adult vulgarity, he claimed that at Westminster he had "buggered and been buggered", an experience which appears to have been emotionally disturbing at the time but which left no permanent mark on him.'[6]

But his family remember him being terribly upset over religion, first at the twice daily religious periods which were compulsory at Westminster, and then at the school's insistence that he be confirmed. His father had taught him the value of free-thinking and Kim had developed an agnosticism which urged him to reject the confirmation ceremony as a nonsense. But, against his principles, he obeyed the school, and suffered for what he saw as his moral cowardice. It could have been this, rather than any homosexual experience he underwent, which caused his temporary emotional problems. In fact he emerged from adolescence with what would be regarded today as a most enlightened attitude to sex. He considered a person's sexual preferences a private matter, had close homosexual and lesbian friends, and never passed judgement on either. As for himself, all the evidence is that he was aggressively heterosexual.

Kim spent the summer of 1929 on an extended holiday in Spain, where he learned to ride a motorcycle, handling it with a recklessness that seemed out of character, boasting that he got his machine up to eighty miles an hour. In Moscow he told me that this, and other spells in Spain, had been among the happiest of his life and that the country held a special appeal for him. (It was certainly to figure heavily in his career as a Soviet intelligence officer.)

Then, in October, dressed in flannel bags and a tweed jacket, looking his usual untidy self, he went up to Cambridge to read history at a college which was soon to abandon poetry as its principal pursuit and embrace politics, especially politics of the intellectual Left. The experience was to mould him for the rest of his life.

THE NEVER–ENDING
FIRST OF MAY
2

The Cambridge which welcomed Philby in the last months of the 1920s was a bastion of ruling-class privilege, a place of physical beauty in which the future leaders of the nation amused themselves and grew up. It was a Cambridge of punts and parties, late-night conversations and strawberry teas. Trinity, which sheltered Philby, Guy Burgess and Anthony Blunt, was the biggest and richest college, but it was probably also the most conservative. V.G. Kiernan, an emeritus professor of history at Edinburgh University, went to Trinity to read history two years after Philby. He remembers: 'There was in general a stifling atmosphere of closed windows, drawn blinds, expiring candles, sleep-walking; outside, a mounting tumult of history in the making, instead of history laid to rest in neat, graveyard rows of dusty tomes.'[1]

At first Philby failed to notice this. He moved into a room at 8 Jesus Lane and settled down to work. He could be found most days in the Wren library at Trinity, keeping very much to himself. He joined no club, did not play sport and spent his leisure hours listening to his records and reading Russian classics. One contemporary described him as earnest, modest, and, in view of his later record, surprisingly abstemious.

He found his first real friends among a group of ex-coalminers who were at Cambridge on scholarships provided by the Workers' Educational Association. Two of them, Harry Dawes and Jim Lees, took Kim up and tried to politicize him. It would provide a neat solution to Kim's motivation for later choosing the Soviet Union as his spiritual home if they had succeeded. But the miners found that he had no sense of his middle-class, privileged upbringing and equally no feeling of common cause with the working class; he was indifferent to both, treating everyone he met on his merits.

The change came slowly. Philby himself says: 'It was the Labour disaster of 1931 which first set me seriously to thinking about possible alternatives to the Labour Party.'[2] He was referring to the collapse of Labour which began in 1929 with the failure of its prime minister, Ramsay MacDonald, to tackle the slide of the nation into economic depression. Far from acting on socialist principles, MacDonald's government sought an accommodation with its Tory opposition, gave up trying to ameliorate the lot of the nation's one and a half million unemployed, and broke up. On 24 August 1931, MacDonald, one of the founders of the Labour Party, abandoned it and joined the Conservatives and the Liberals in forming a National Government.

Barely had Labour supporters absorbed this act of treachery when they were assailed by a new wave of disasters. The business world moved its funds out of sterling, forcing the country off the gold standard. There was a mutiny in the British Atlantic Fleet at Invergordon when naval ratings refused to prepare the ships for sea following the government's cuts in their pay. And in the East, Japan invaded Manchuria, one of the first steps towards the Second World War.

At Cambridge the atmosphere altered almost overnight. One term the university was still a self-regarding and escapist society; the next it was a hotbed of political controversy. At its centre was the Cambridge University Socialist Society (CUSS), founded by Harry Dawes and other leftists to replace the university Labour Club which had collapsed under the failures of the MacDonald government. Philby was the CUSS treasurer in 1932–3. 'This brought me into contact with streams of Left-wing opinion critical of the Labour Party, notably with the Communists,' he wrote later. 'Extensive reading and growing appreciation of the classics of European Socialism alternated with vigorous and sometimes heated discussions within the Society. It was a slow and brain-racking process; my transition from a Socialist viewpoint to a Communist one took two years.'[3]

Some idea of the range of the political discussion in the university can be gleaned from the titles of debates in the Union and elsewhere and the articles in undergraduate publications. In 1931, *Varsity* was reporting on 'Soviet Propaganda in Cambridge', 'No Sovietism for India' and, on its front page on 17 October, 'Rowdy Socialist Club Meeting'. *Trinity Magazine* was writing about 'The Fascist Threat' and 'Empire and Anti-war'. And in May 1932, Kim listened in the audience as one of the dons, Maurice Dobb, proposed in the Union 'That this house sees more hope in Moscow than in Detroit'.

Dobb was a lecturer in economics and probably the first academic in Britain to carry a Communist Party membership card (1920). Without Dobb, communism would never have gained the prominence in Cambridge that it did. He was the man who, in June 1931, handpicked a little group of people to meet the Indian communist, Clemens Palme Dutt, sent by party headquarters in King Street, London, to start a communist cell at the university. Dobb came from a landowning family in Gloucestershire and was educated at Charterhouse and Pembroke College, Cambridge, where he got a double first in economics. His commitment to the Soviet Union was deep, and it is said that when his train crossed the frontier on the way to Moscow in 1921, Dobb exclaimed: 'How thrilling to be moving across this sacred soil at last.'[4] He lived at 'St Andrews' in Chesterton Lane, such a frequent meeting place for Cambridge communists that it was known locally as 'The Red Household'. Dobb made no secret of his Marxist views and was several times thrown fully dressed into the River Cam by outraged 'hearties'. But V.G. Kiernan recalls what a breath of fresh air Dobb's Marxism brought to the university:

> We had no time then to assimilate Marxist theory more than very roughly; it was only beginning to take root in England, although it had one remarkable expounder at Cambridge in Maurice Dobb . . . We felt, all the same, that it could lift us to a plane far above the Cambridge academic level. We were quite right, as the rapid advance of Marxist ideas and influence since then has demonstrated. Our main concerns, however, were practical ones, popularising socialism and the USSR, fraternising with hunger marchers, denouncing Fascism and the National Government, warning of the approach of war. We belonged to the era of the Third International, genuinely international at least in spirit, when the Cause stood high above any national or parochial claims.[5]

But what Marxism and Dobb's cell in Cambridge needed to give it impact on the university at large was a communist hero. He arrived in the form of David Haden Guest, who had gone up to Trinity in the same term as Kim to read philosophy and mathematical logic under Ludwig Wittgenstein. In the summer of 1930 he went to the university of Göttingen to study under the great mathematician David Hilbert. In Cambridge signs of an impending war were few but in Nazi-dominated Göttingen they were as real as the armed police in the streets and the drunken Nazi meetings which went on in the beer cellars. He saw enough on that trip to convince him that only communism could stand up to the political violence of the Nazis. He was arrested at a communist youth demonstration and released after a fortnight's solitary confinement only after he had gone on a hunger strike.

When Guest got back to Cambridge he took over Dobb's cell, and was soon recognized as a glamorous figure who flaunted his communism with pride – he would stride into hall at Trinity wearing a hammer and sickle pin in his lapel. Largely because of Guest, communism, which had been only a fringe political activity at the university, moved into the limelight. He gave a talk on his experiences in Germany, ending with an account of his arrest and imprisonment. 'I shall never get myself into danger again so long as I live; or at least only on very urgent matters of principle.'*

The communist cell grew quickly. Two new recruits were Donald Maclean and James Klugman, who came up in 1931 to read modern languages and spent much of their time working for the party, organizing study groups, and trying to get Marxism accepted as a philosophy in the university curriculum. They argued that Marxism led to good degrees – 'Every Communist is a good student.' They kept lists of fellow-travellers and sympathizers and devoted a lot of effort to recruiting. They attacked the CUSS for being weak-kneed, screaming and shouting at political debates in a manner Cambridge had never seen before but which the students tolerated because of their obvious conviction.

At this stage of their respective careers, Maclean and Guy Burgess were far to the left of Kim Philby. While Kim still hesitated about taking the step from socialism to communism, Maclean and Burgess had jumped. Maclean had no doubt whatsoever that he knew what was wrong with contemporary Britain: 'The economic situation, the unemployed, vulgarity in the cinema, rubbish on the bookstalls, the public school, snobbery in the suburbs, more battleships, lower wages . . .'[6] He spoke openly against capitalism and the rising tide of opinion which was going to sweep away 'the whole crack-brained, criminal mess', expressing in succinct terms the disgust that the Cambridge Left felt at the picture of decay and confusion which Western society presented in the early 1930s, and, at the same time, their belief in a quick and absolute cure.

Burgess held similar views. He had come up from Eton to Trinity in 1930, set the university buzzing with his homosexual exhibitionism, and had been elected an Apostle, a mark of outstanding and all-round distinction. (The Apostles was a mixture of a dining club and a secret society which divided itself between King's, its spiritual home, and Trinity, where it had many members.) At his first meeting in November 1932, Burgess who had been recruited to the Party by Dobb made it absolutely clear to all present that he was a communist and over the next two years he managed to inject into the society's

*Guest went off to fight in the Spanish Civil War on principle and was killed in 1937.

debates a note of passionate left-wing political content to replace the usual literary, artistic and philosophical subjects. On these occasions he was often supported by Anthony Blunt, the present Queen's third cousin once removed, an art historian who had been elected to a Trinity Fellowship in 1932, and who will figure later in this story.

But while his friend Burgess was making his commitment, and Maclean, whom he knew, but not well, was planning to go to Russia as a teacher, Philby still clung to his CUSS convictions. In the 1931 General Election he had campaigned for Labour, speaking on the hustings. 'My friends,' his set speech began, 'the heart of England does not beat in the stately homes and castles. It beats in the factories and on the farms.' He was still a socialist in October 1932 when he watched in sympathy as the north-east contingent of the hunger marchers trudged into Cambridge. David Guest led a group of students out to meet them and marched into town with them, the students carrying the workers' knapsacks.

Kim was part of a group of students which organized meals for the marchers and negotiated the loan of the Corn Exchange for them to sleep in – 'I remain proud to this day that I helped feed them,' he told me in Moscow. The marchers were tough trade unionists, determined to maintain their solidarity in the face of a ruthless government. But, impressed though Kim was, he still did not commit himself. He was feeling his way slowly. In the vacation at Christmas 1932 he rented a flat in Nottingham and then found lodgings with a coalminer at Huthwaite, his first real experience of working-class life.

'One of the problems,' Philby told me in Moscow, 'was that I wanted to be absolutely certain. I had already decided at nineteen, after a good look around me, that the rich had had it too damned good for damned long and that the poor had had it too damned bad and that it was time that it was changed. In England at that time the poor really were a different people. It wasn't just a question of some of us being better off. With many of the poor it was a question of getting enough to eat. People like my grandmother thought that was the natural way of things. I can remember her making remarks like, "Don't play with those children, Kim. They're dirty and you'll catch something."

'The question I kept asking myself was what I could do to change matters. All the Ramsay MacDonald business left me very disillusioned. But while others moved quickly to communism, I had to consider the possibility that what had happened represented perhaps a peculiarly British failure of the Left rather than a wider one, so I made up my mind to travel to see how it was in other countries.'

He went to Germany, Hungary and France, once on his motor-bike, sometimes accompanied by Tim Milne, a friend from West-minster, who had gone up to Christ Church, Oxford, where he lived on the same staircase as Hugh Trevor-Roper, later the his-torian, Lord Dacre. (Both became colleagues of Philby's in SIS.) Trevor-Roper recalls Milne talking of these trips and referring to his travelling companion as 'the communist, Kim Philby'. John Midgley, a Trinity contemporary, later foreign editor for *The Economist*, remembered meeting Kim in Berlin in March 1933, not long after the Reichstag fire. On their wanderings around the city they came across an anti-Jewish demonstration, and when they remonstrated with the Germans taking part they were threatened with violence.

In Moscow Philby recalled these days and the impression they made on him: 'It was clear to me that other countries were just as bad as Britain and that what I was witnessing was a failure of the capitalist system. In Germany unemployment was rife, fascism was on the rise, and the working class fared equally badly. The democratic socialists were unimpressive. They seemed to fold at critical moments. But all the time there was this solid base of the Left, the Soviet Union. I felt that it should be kept there at all costs.'

By mid-1933, just before Kim went down, many other under-graduates felt the same. The small communist cell started by Maurice Dobb had expanded to take over CUSS, the Heretics (an anticlerical society founded in the Twenties) and *The Outpost* (an independent radical journal started by Midgley), and had seriously weakened the Apostles. Of course, not all students chose communism. Others pre-ferred religion and some even made it through university untouched by all the tumult around them. George Orwell has suggested that the collapse of all that an earlier generation had believed in created a void which communism or religion then filled. This could be one explanation for Kim's commitment.

Another theory is the example set by his father. G. Kitson Clark, who taught both Burgess and Philby at Trinity, said he had noticed in Kim the enormous power of St John Philby's influence. 'We all felt a bit sorry for Kim just because of his father.'[7] By now St John Philby had abandoned government service and was living in Jidda as an Arab, seizing any opportunity to attack the British government. Was Kim simply following his father's example of dissent?

All this sounds too facile. Professor Kiernan, who like Philby remained faithful to his Marxist principles, presents a more con-vincing description of the pressures that moved Kim and his gen-eration:

Some of us have lived to see multi-national capitalism, instead of international socialism, in control of most of the world; but at that time we had not the shadow of a doubt that capitalism was nearing its end. It was both too abominable, and too inept and suicidally divided, to last much longer. Socialism would take its place, and mankind be transformed not much less quickly.

At such a time, punctilios of 'loyalty' to things of the dying past seemed as archaic as the minutiae of drawing room manners. And it was about the defenders of the old order that a strong smell of treason hung. We saw pillars of British society trooping to Nuremberg to hobnob with Nazi gangsters; we saw the 'National' government sabotaging the Spanish Republic's struggle, from class prejudice, and to benefit investors like Rio Tinto, blind to the obvious prospect of the Mediterranean being turned into a Fascist lake and the lifelines of Empire cut.

From Spain the vibrations of civil war spread over Europe. The frenzied enthusiasm of the French Right for Franco was the overture to its eager surrender to Hitler in 1940. Amid that tumult the sense of an absolute divide between 'whatsoever things are good' and everything Tory was easy to acquire, and with some of us has remained unshakable. Our watchword was Voltaire's: *Ecrasez l'infame*.

Feelings like these were to carry a small number of our generation, from Cambridge and elsewhere, into acts of 'treason', in the lawyer's meaning, not the only or best one. These acts, amounting in sum to very little, have been sedulously embroidered and exaggerated, and the public has been continually reminded of them. For good measure, politics and sex have been mixed up, as if radicalism went hand in hand with homosexuality . . . The aim of all this pseudo-patriotic hubbub is to distract attention from the distempers of our ancien régime, keep people from thinking about the nuclear war they may well be drifting towards, and make them fancy that without zealous leaders to fend off a legion of spies and subversives, all would be lost. It also helps nourish the illusion of Britain as a great power, with priceless secrets to be stolen.[8]

And a former Apostle of the period has suggested that the emotions of the young at that time were intensified by a deep disgust:

We were all of obvious military age, and the war we saw coming was clearly not going to be one that we wanted to fight. It was already clear to anyone with any sense that the main aim of British policy was to send a re-armed Germany eastwards. We didn't think that it would work, or that it ought to work, and we were damned well right. And it gave us, our consciousness of what was going on, a special kind of disgust for our elders, the politicians and so forth.

It left me, for example, permanently an anarchist, at any rate in the sense that I never expected to find much decency or honesty in any government. And I can very easily imagine that for men like Philby, Burgess and Maclean, the same disgust could lead on to more active 'treachery' as you evidently want to call it. It may deserve the name but a good part of the blame lies with 'the Establishment' of which they were so much a part that their disgust was intensely personal . . . so much under their own skins. Any government or state of society which fails to win for itself some measure of the generosity and loyalty natural to youth is in for grave trouble.[9]

We have learnt why Kim would have been attracted to communism. Several of his contemporaries thought that he was already a communist. The most dogmatic of these was one of his colleagues, Richard ('Otto') Clarke, later Sir Richard, a senior Whitehall administrator. Kim and Clarke had argued on Kim's return from Berlin over the unexpected collapse of the German Communist Party. Why had Stalin done nothing to support the Germans, asked Clarke. Maybe Stalin was not as left as he made out. Kim was angry. 'What Stalin does *is* left,' he said. Clarke was convinced by his answer that Kim had definitely taken the final step and was now a devout communist. How is it then, that Philby never actually joined the Party?

In Moscow, Philby explained. 'On my very last day at Cambridge I decided that I would become a communist. I asked a don I admired, Maurice Dobb, how I should go about it. He gave me an introduction to a communist group in Paris, a perfectly legal and open group. They in turn passed me on to a communist underground organization in Vienna. Matters were at crisis point in Austria and this underground organization needed volunteers. I helped smuggle wanted socialists and communists out of the country.'

This explains why Philby never became a member of the Party, which was a great advantage when he came to join the British Intelligence Service – no security check would ever turn up his name on a list of members and he could swear with a convincingly clear conscience that he was not and never had been a member of the Communist Party. But Philby's account of Dobb's role is puzzling.

Philby stressed that Dobb had done nothing illegal in introducing him to the communist organization in Paris. (The most likely organization would have been the World Committee for the Relief of Victims of German Fascism, run by the German communist

Willi Muenzenberg and his aide Otto Katz.)* The illegality began only when Philby began to work for the underground group in Vienna. But, again according to Philby, all he had asked Dobb was how to go about becoming a communist. Dobb could have told him that the simplest way of doing this would be to go to the Communist Party headquarters in King Street, Covent Garden, and apply for membership.

Instead Dobb sent him to Paris. Dobb may have decided that a recruit of Philby's calibre would be of greater service in Europe than in Britain. Philby, because of his recent experiences in Germany, may himself have expressed a wish to work outside Britain. (He was not forthcoming on this point in our talks.) Or, and this is only speculation, Dobb was a talent-spotter and steered Philby towards the man who recruited him for the Russian intelligence service.

For there is no doubt that the Russian service was very interested in British undergraduates at that period. In the first years after the Revolution it had concentrated on internal subversion. Stalin used it to help suppress the peasants, to purge the army, and to gather evidence for the great show trials of the period. Its overseas interest was concentrated on émigré organizations, such as the Trust, which received help from Britain and the United States. Most of these organizations were successfully penetrated by Russian intelligence, which allowed them to function as long as they proved useful. It then eliminated them by luring their most important officers onto Soviet soil and arresting them.

When the service's founder, Felix Dzerzhinsky, died in 1926, his officers had had no success in penetrating the British intelligence establishment – a priority since the Revolution, when British intelligence agents nearly succeeded in toppling the Bolsheviks. The means appeared impossible to find – young Englishmen who would be prepared to make a lifetime allegiance to the Soviet Union and who would agree to 'remain in place', to serve Soviet interests wherever their careers in Britain took them. The qualities needed were rare: a political commitment at odds with their upbringing, a willingness to betray their country and their class – it would be no use recruiting sympathetic working-class lads because it would be unlikely they would ever have access to worthwhile secrets. And the recruits would need a natural talent for duplicity, because they would have to deceive not only their colleagues but their family and

---

*Muenzenberg became too independent for Moscow's liking and broke with the party in 1937. Interned by the French in 1940, he escaped and was later found hanging from a tree. The mystery of his death was never solved. Katz was a victim of the Prague trials in 1952 and was executed.

friends. By the early 1930s, Moscow was well aware that conditions for finding such young men were never more favourable. The obvious first move was to find sympathizers at the universities who would keep their eyes open for possible recruits. Was Dobb one such sympathizer?

Dobb died in 1976, but nine years earlier Bruce Page interviewed him as part of the *Sunday Times* inquiry about Philby. It was not a revealing interview. Dobb was frank but rather vague, although Page formed the impression that this was due to difficulty of recall and not deliberate. Dobb said that Philby was under his supervision for economics instruction because one of the Trinity dons was farming out some of his students to Dobb, who was then at Pembroke. He thought that Philby was politically left Labour, although Philby would have attended a certain number of communist study groups and meetings. Dobb said he did not see Philby again after Philby went down from Cambridge. We shall return to Dobb later.

In June 1933 Philby took his finals in economics, emerging with a two-one (a good second-class honours) and a Trinity College prize of £14 with which he bought the collected works of Karl Marx. St John Philby was on one of his increasingly rare visits to London and got Kim to read the proofs of his book, *The Empty Quarter*, paying him £50 for the job. A Cambridge colleague, Joe Grigg, who had known Kim since their days together at Westminster, recalled: 'He went out and bought a motor-bike. He seemed to be in no hurry to start looking around for a job, and the next thing I knew, he announced that he was riding off to Austria for a few months.'[10] We know now that Philby went to Vienna under orders from the French Comintern, but of course he could not tell that to his friends or family. Instead he said that he wanted to improve his chances of getting into the Foreign Service and was going to Austria to brush up his German.

It was Philby's second visit. On the first, he had been captivated by Vienna, by its beauty, leisurely elegance and polished manners. This time he found a vastly different city, one which was to give him some practical experience of the bloody side of European politics.

A BLOODY INITIATION

3

Kim Philby arrived in Vienna in the midst of a fierce clash of ideologies which was to shake the country until the Anschluss, the union with Germany enforced by Hitler in 1938. To a Marxist involved in this turmoil it would have seemed as if the master's texts were springing to life before his eyes. Austria was still suffering from the effects of losing her empire after the First World War. The country the Hapsburgs had ruled stretched from the Carpathian mountains to the Adriatic, but victory for the Allies in 1918 reduced this to Vienna and its hinterland. The population, cut to six million, split into two bitterly divided groups – the poor and backward peasants, who were devoutly Roman Catholic, and the socialist city dwellers, who were strongly anticlerical.

The country, ruled by a succession of conservative coalition governments, soon became crippled by inflation. The *Daily Telegraph* correspondent in Vienna during this period, Eric Gedye, has described the strange sensation of visiting someone for dinner, and walking across costly Oriental rugs under the eyes of Old Masters to dine off a little cold sausage and black bread. At first, no one seemed to care: as far as the rest of Europe was concerned, Austria could rot. But a prominent churchman, Monsignor Seipel, the Austrian Chancellor, knew how to play on the Allies' secret fears. A depressed Austria, he said, would be ripe for communism: 'Let the masses continue to starve and they will bring Moscow to Central Europe.' The Allies began a grudging programme of relief and reconstruction, but Seipel, a bitter anti-communist, set about sowing the belief that the foreign money flowing into Austria would never be safe until the Austrian Left was crushed.

So while the Austrian socialists laboured to turn Vienna into an early model welfare state, with blocks of well-designed workers' flats, free clinics, baths and schools, the conservatives and monarchists did their best to sabotage these plans, hoping to 'drive the Reds out of Austria' and restore the monarchy. Both sides raised private armies to impose their political aims, if necessary, by force. The socialists had the Schutzbund, or Republican Defence Corps; the conservatives the Heimwehr, led by Prince Starhemberg, who had taken part in Hitler's abortive beerhall putsch in Munich in 1923, and Major Emil Fey, a professional soldier.

The two armies clashed on 15 July 1927. Two weeks earlier the Heimwehr had opened fire on a socialist demonstration, killing a cripple and a child. Several members of the Heimwehr were put on trial but promptly acquitted, so the socialists called for another demonstration to protest. When the demonstrators reached Parliament House they found their way barred by armed police. They tried to break through, and the police drew their sabres and charged. Fighting spread throughout the city and by nightfall four policemen and eighty-five civilians were dead.

This was a crucial moment for the socialists. Faced with the choice of throwing open their hidden arsenals and fighting, or relying on the workers' traditional weapon of the general strike, they chose to strike. The government brought in blackleg labour and in three days the strike had collapsed. The Heimwehr celebrated its triumph; it now knew that when the socialists were faced with violence and terrorism they would collapse.

In May 1932, Dr Dollfuss, the leader of the extreme right wing of the Christian Social Party, became Chancellor. Within a year he had suspended the constitution, adjourned Parliament for an indefinite period, prohibited political meetings, strikes and demonstrations and imposed censorship on the press. The situation steadily worsened. Dollfuss and the Heimwehr feared that the socialists would proclaim a general strike and use the Schutzbund to try to seize power and restore parliamentary government. The socialists feared that growing agitation within the Heimwehr and in Dollfuss's own party for union with Germany would lead to a nazi rebellion and a fascist dictatorship. It became a matter of who would strike first. This is what Philby meant when, describing how he committed himself to communism, he said that in Vienna at that time 'matters were at crisis point'.

On arriving in Vienna he went straight to the contact address given to him in Paris. This was Latschkagasse 9, in the ninth district, the house of Israel Kohlman, a Pole who had arrived in Austria before the First World War. Kohlman had a job as a minor civil servant and he and his wife Gisella spent most of their spare time in Jewish welfare work. But it was not this self-effacing couple who were to induct Philby into the communist underground. It was their daughter, a dark, attractive divorcee called Alice Friedmann.

Alice, then twenty-three and usually known by the diminutive Litzi, had been married to Karl Friedmann when she was eighteen but she divorced him fourteen months later. Friedmann had founded a Zionist organization called the Blau Weiss to provide recreation for young Viennese Jews, and had tried to enthuse Litzi in its work and in the principles of socialism and Zionism. But she found all three rather stultifying compared with the demands and excitement of the Communist Party and left both Friedmann and the Blau Weiss for underground work against the Austrian government. Her recruiter was a Hungarian, Gabor Peter, a refugee from the dictatorship of the Hungarian fascist leader Admiral Horthy. Physically, he was a most unattractive man: he limped, he had a slight hunchback and a thin, ugly face. But he had a powerful personality and was absolutely dedicated to the Party. Friedmann described him as 'a real Stalinist, a tough, ruthless and professional operator'.*

Philby's original assignment was to work as a courier, using his British passport and posing as a freelance journalist, to maintain links between the outlawed Austrian communists and sympathizers in Hungary, Prague and Paris. But in February 1934 his work changed dramatically. Dollfuss decided to disarm the outlawed Schutzbund, occupy the offices of socialist organizations, dismiss socialist mayors and prefects, put the trade unions under State control and establish a one-party corporate State on the lines of Mussolini's Italy.

On 12 February he was given the excuse he needed to move. In Linz, Upper Austria, police and army units, claiming later that they were planning to search for hidden arms, had surrounded the People's House which contained the offices of the Social Democratic Party. Soon after dawn someone fired a shot at the police from one of the upper windows of the building. This shot triggered off a nationwide attack by government forces on trade union headquarters, newspapers, socialist offices and welfare centres, and eventually on the huge council housing estates in Vienna's outer suburbs.

The socialists were caught unprepared, their leaders arrested before they could organize proper resistance. The rank-and-file blundered around in confusion. The militants rushed to their hidden armouries to take up arms but found them either locked or already

---

*In 1945 Peter became head of the secret police in Hungary. He was purged in 1953, served six years in prison, and when last heard of was working as a tailor.

in police control. The Heimwehr, professionally led, stormed over those workers who did manage to arm themselves. Two of the biggest housing estates, the Karl Marx Hof and the Goethe Hof, were destroyed by artillery fire and more than a thousand civilians killed, including many women and children. In the courtyard of the Supreme Court, the Heimwehr tried to hang nine socialist leaders but botched the job – the men were strung up and allowed to strangle to death. One of them, Karl Munichreiter, had been wounded in the fighting but was hanged anyway, carried to the gallows on a stretcher.

Philby heard on the radio at the Kohlman house that a state of emergency and martial law had been declared. He and Litzi hurried to do battle, working with an underground organization called Revolutionary Socialists, a hasty and uneasy alliance of communists and socialists. Their job was to try to smuggle people on the police 'wanted' list out of the country. They were heady days for the young Englishman, barely twenty-two – days of police charges, broken heads and sabre wounds; nights of conspiracy and fierce debate.

Philby soon showed his physical courage. He was there when the Heimwehr artillery opened fire on the housing estates and helped a group of workers who had escaped from the flats to hide in a nearby sewer. The men, mostly communists, were in the ragged uniform of their underground group, easily identifiable by the police, so Philby set out to find them some clothing. He went to the apartment of the *Daily Telegraph* correspondent, Eric Gedye. 'I opened my wardrobe to select something,' Gedye recalled. 'When Kim saw several suits there, he cried, "Good God, you have seven; I must have them. I've got six wounded friends in the sewers in danger of the gallows." ' Gedye stuffed the suits in a case and was later happy to learn from Philby that he had moved the men to a safer hiding place and finally on to the underground line out of Austria and into Czechoslovakia.[1]

Everywhere the Left was on the run. Philby felt that this reinforced his earlier conclusion that only the communists could resist the rise of fascism. The collapse of the Austrian socialist movement – until then considered one of the strongest in Europe – the sordid end of its leaders, the growth of the nazis and their revival of beheading for political offences made a powerful impression on him and strengthened his commitment. He became more open in his communism. E.H. Cookridge, an Austrian journalist who worked for socialist publications and who later developed British secret service contacts, wrote:

I greatly admired Kim Philby. Here was a young Englishman, determined to risk much to help the underground freedom movement in a small country which must have been of very limited interest to him. He had shown his courage when joining the defenders of the shelled council estates during the February fighting; he had shared their ordeal in the sewers, had rescued several of them, and he continued to do a good job as a courier.

But doubts began to dawn on me when Philby appeared as a communist go-between and when he declared that he could provide all the money we needed for our work. He mentioned that he had close contacts with the Soviet consul, Ivan Vorobyev, and Vladimir Alexeievich Antonov-Ovseyenko, a mysterious emissary from Moscow, who had arrived in Vienna after the putsch and was obviously a GB [intelligence] agent. The money which Philby offered could only have come from the Russians and the last thing my friends and I wanted was to accept financial help from Moscow.[2]

The British writer Naomi Mitchison, who had come to Austria to do relief work, and whose *Vienna Diary*, published that year, helped rouse British sympathy for the plight of the Austrian workers, recorded on 2 March 1934: 'I came back to the hotel, to find several telephone messages, and an urgent note from an unknown man. After lunch the unknown turned up, a nice young Cambridge Communist, all "het up" about some of the Reichstag prisoners, and wanting to know if I or anyone I knew could fly at once to Berlin and see about it.'[3] In 1967, *The Sunday Times* asked Lady Mitchison if she could recall the meeting, if she could confirm that the young man was indeed Kim Philby, and how she knew that he was a communist. Lady Mitchison said that she could indeed recall the meeting, that the young man was definitely Kim Philby, and that she knew he was a communist because 'he told me so'.

Others also knew that Philby was a communist, or that he moved in communist circles. Teddy Kollek, later an Israeli diplomat and then Mayor of Jerusalem, remembers meeting Philby about this time. 'Kim moved in communist intellectual circles and people I knew to be convinced communists were among his closest associates.' (Kollek later became the only person with knowledge of Philby's communist connections to tell Western intelligence authorities.) Lilly Jerusalem, the daughter of a former Austrian government official, was nearly drawn into Philby's work. She recalled: 'Kim telephoned me and asked me to meet him urgently. I suggested that he come to our house but he said it wasn't safe, so finally we met in some little café. Then he told me in a whisper that he wanted me to hide in our house his girlfriend Litzi Friedmann, who was underground since the Dollfuss revolt. I knew Litzi was an extreme left-winger but I couldn't help because of my father's position.'

The police were obviously closing in on Litzi, so Philby took a dramatic step to save her. They were already lovers, and on 24 February 1934, in the Vienna Town Hall, he married her. It was a quiet, hurried ceremony. She later recalled:

When I first met Kim he had just come down from Cambridge and had come to Vienna to learn German. He stayed with my parents as a paying guest and we went out together sometimes. He had very leftish views and was very progressive. I was a member of the Communist Party, which was then illegal and worked underground. We had an affair and I was fond of Kim. The police were hunting down active communists, and I found out that they were after me. One way I could avoid arrest was to marry Kim and get a British passport and leave the country. And this is what I did.

I wouldn't call it exactly a marriage of convenience. I suppose it was partly that and partly love. Anyway, we didn't stay married very long. We both left Austria together and went to stay in England. As far as I know, apart from marrying me, a communist, Kim took no part in communist underground activities while he was in Vienna. He knew some communists, of course, through me. I was one myself – and, as I say, he was very progressive with decided leftish leanings. I feel fairly certain that he never travelled to Budapest or any other place as a courier for the party. If he did, I knew nothing about it.[4]

In Moscow I showed Philby this statement because it sounded almost legalistic, something to have in case the security services of one of the Western countries in which Philby was later to work ever got around to checking his early days. Philby said: 'Yes, we foresaw that sooner or later Litzi would be asked about my time in Vienna and we prepared for it. This is exactly what we agreed she would say and I'm moved that she kept our bargain.'

In May 1934 Philby and his new bride left Vienna for London, travelling via Paris. They were short of cash so moved in with Philby's mother, Dora, at her home in Acol Road, West Hampstead. It was a tense household. Philby had written to his mother from Vienna telling her about the marriage and explaining the reasons for it, but Dora considered that her son had been caught. She passed on to St

John Philby in Jidda her views on Kim and Litzi. Kim had ruined his chances; Litzi was attractive enough but hard and domineering. 'You wait till you see her . . . I do hope [Kim] gets a job to get him off this bloody communism. He's not quite extreme yet but may become so if he's not got something to occupy his mind.' That did not look like happening immediately because Kim's political activities were already prejudicing his career. In his application to the Civil Service Commissioners he had named two referees at Trinity, one his tutor in economics, Dennis Robertson, and the other his father's old friend, Donald Robertson (no relation). The two men consulted about what to say and then Dennis Robertson wrote to Kim about their problem. They were both prepared to praise his energy and intelligence but felt duty-bound to add that his 'sense of political injustice might well unfit him for administrative work'. This judgement was the last thing Kim wanted on record anywhere, so he withdrew his application.

When St John Philby got the news in Jidda he was furious. He wrote home saying that no one should be victimized for views honestly held and that Kim was perfectly entitled to his leanings towards communism. Then he got off a letter to Donald Robertson saying that the only serious question was whether Kim intended to be disloyal to the government while in its service. 'Some people may think . . . that I was disloyal to the government but that was never the case. I was in opposition to its policy and always made this clear, and I resigned in order to have freedom to express my views more publicly.'[5]

Kim Philby made one last trip to Cambridge to address the CUSS and to collect money to continue the fight against fascism in Vienna. There he met Guy Burgess, doing a fourth year at Trinity on a research scholarship, and persuaded him to organize the Vienna fund-raising. One would have thought that he would call on Maurice Dobb, if only to tell him what adventures had been sparked off by the introduction to the Paris Comintern. But Dobb's statement in 1967 that he never saw Philby again after Philby went down from Cambridge seems confirmed by a remark Dobb made at a luncheon in mid-1934 – 'Pity Kim never joined the Party.'

In short, what evidence there is suggests that Dobb was a talent-spotter, on the lookout for undergraduates who could be steered to various communist organizations, and not a recruiter for the Russian intelligence service. Philby's account of his own recruitment to this service, as given to me in Moscow, bears this out: 'My work in Vienna must have caught the attention of the people who are now my colleagues in Moscow because almost immediately on my return to Britain I was approached by a man who asked me if I would like to join the Russian intelligence service. For operational reasons I don't propose to name this man, but I can say that he was not a Russian although he was working for the Russians.

'He told me he appreciated my commitment; the question was how best to use me. I should not go off and die on some foreign battlefield or become a war correspondent for the *Daily Worker*. There were more important battles for me to fight but I would have to be patient. For the next two years he gave me virtually nothing to do. He was testing my commitment. I would turn up for our meetings with nothing to offer and would receive in return patient encouragement.'

From what we know of other recruitments we can suggest the nature of the approach that Philby so quickly accepted. The recruiter would have painted for Philby a grim picture of the coming struggle between fascism and the Left. He would have dwelt on the growing might of Germany and on the danger this posed to the Soviet Union. He would have recalled the days of the Allied intervention when half the world had joined forces to crush the communist Revolution at birth. He would have pointed to the military, financial and trade deals going on between Britain and Germany and the admiration Hitler was attracting from many members of Britain's ruling class. He would then have voiced the Soviet Union's major fear: an alliance between Germany and Britain to try, once again, to overthrow the Soviet State.

The recruiter would have said that the Soviet Union could protect itself against this danger only by having someone at the centre of the British decision-making process, someone who could warn Moscow of any conspiracy against the USSR and its peoples. The details, initially, would have been left vague; the aim would have been to arouse Philby's interest in a secret assignment of international importance, an appeal to his ego and his sense of adventure. Philby would have been given the impression that he was being offered a chance not only to take part in momentous events but to have a hand in shaping their course. This would have been heady stuff for a twenty-two-year-old, and a chance to show his father that he too had a part to play in history, even if, for the moment, that part had to be a secret one. Small wonder that Philby quickly accepted this approach. As he has written: 'It is a sobering thought that, but for the power of the Soviet Union and the Communist idea, the old world, if not the whole world, would now be ruled by Hitler and Hirohito. It is a matter of great pride to me that I was invited, at so early an age, to play my infinitesimal part in building up that power . . . When the proposition was made to me, I did not hesitate. One does not look twice at an offer of enrolment in an elite force.'[6]

I pressed Philby to name this recruiter, this man of such intelligence and patience, arguing that he must now be dead and surely there could be no harm in revealing his identity, but Philby declined to say anything more about him. One explanation for this reticence has been offered by Dr Christopher Andrew, Fellow and Senior Tutor of Corpus Christi College, Cambridge, who is working on a history of the Russian intelligence service:

> At the root of Philby's evasions is the knowledge that his seventeen most active years as a mole (from 1934 to 1951) coincided with the most brutal period of the bloodstained history of Soviet intelligence . . . The Soviet intelligence officers Philby admired most in his early years with the KGB perished in the Stalinist Terror . . . Philby [cannot] bring himself to mention the name of his first Soviet control, Teodor Maly, a Hungarian priest who became an idealistic convert to Communism and entered the KGB. But like Muenzenberg, his idealism made him suspect in the Stalinist era. In 1937 he too was ordered back to Moscow. Maly knew the fate which awaited him but went all the same. 'If they don't kill me there, they will kill me here,' he told his friends. 'Better to die there.'[7]

There are other candidates. E.H. Cookridge says that the recruiter was Simon Kremer, a Russian who was nominally a clerk at the embassy but was in fact the main Soviet intelligence service officer in London. Andrew Boyle says it was Samuel Borisovich Cahan, the resident director of the Soviet service in Britain. Others suggest it was Leonid Tolokonsky, who worked with Cahan. None of these fits Philby's description of a man who was 'not a Russian'. Of course, Philby would have every reason not to name his recruiter and to muddy his identity. He would not want this man's descendants and friends exposed to a public grilling, and by maintaining the mystery, the paranoia of the security services is kept simmering away.

Philby was, however, forthcoming with explanations for other puzzles about Soviet recruitment in Britain at that time. Philby, Burgess, Maclean and Blunt were all from Cambridge. Why did nothing similar happen at Oxford? 'You are looking for a complex answer instead of seeing what is right ahead of you,' Philby told me in Moscow. 'It needed only one to start it all off. The first move was made by me, then I recommended others, people I knew, and they in turn recommended others. The answer is as simple as that.'

This clears up the often-asked question why, if a Soviet recruiter was active at Cambridge, has no one ever come forward to say: 'The Russians tried to recruit me but I turned them down'? The answer now would be: no one would be able to say that they had been approached by the Russian intelligence service, only that they had been obliquely sounded out by a friend. And, if they had resisted the approach, loyalty to that friend would inhibit them from reporting what had happened to the authorities.

Philby's answer led to an exchange over whether or not there was a Cambridge spy ring, or a Comintern cell, a question that has long intrigued the security authorities. Cells of the Comintern usually consisted of five people so as to limit the damage if one of them was caught or turned traitor – he could name only four others. Philby, Burgess, Maclean and Blunt made four. If they were in the one cell, then who was the fifth man? The hunt for him has been going on for more than thirty years.

Philby vehemently denied that there had been such a cell. 'I was the first to be recruited and that was after I came down. I know that Burgess was recruited after me. I know that Blunt was recruited after me. I didn't know about Maclean until after the war started, but I doubt that he was recruited at university. So the whole idea of a Cambridge ring or a Cambridge cell just doesn't stand up.'

I told Philby that I knew it was the view of at least one retired director general of SIS that the Russian intelligence service inherited all four from the Comintern, where they had operated as a cell of 'highly motivated amateurs'. Philby said: 'There was certainly no Comintern cell and we were amateurs only in the sense that we were not paid for our work.' He then repeated his earlier statement that he knew of Burgess's recruitment but not the others'. 'We were recruited individually and we operated individually. I only knew about Burgess's recruitment at the time because he wrote to me and told me and I replied congratulating him. Later it was Burgess who insisted on maintaining the links with all of us.' Burgess's compulsion, with its origins in the pleasure and comradeship of a shared yet secret commitment, was to bring them all down.

GOD SAVE THE FÜHRER
4

Britain in the mid-1930s was undergoing a crisis. After the shock of the depression years, the country's continuing economic decline alerted the sharper members of the ruling class to the fact that the wonderful underpinning of Englishness, the great bluff and bravado of empire that had sustained people's confidence so absolutely, was steadily ebbing. What was to be done? Some followed the nineteenth-century pioneers, those aristocratic families who saw that the Americans had reached the stage where they could pile up fortunes so vast they were worth marrying, and signed up with Uncle Sam. Others thought salvation lay with the new leader in Germany, Adolf Hitler: the Duke of Windsor, no less, thought the Nazis so deserving of support that even after the outbreak of war, when he was attached to the Anglo-French Supreme War Council at Versailles, he passed military secrets to Germany.[1] As British historian Dr Scott Newton has said, 'If glib accusations of treachery are to be made, they should not be restricted to Philby and Stalin's Englishmen.'[2] Kim Philby and his friends thought the best hope lay with communism.

But, at twenty-three, recently blooded in battle in Vienna, it must have occurred to Philby that the road leading to the 'never-ending first of May' was going to be a long one. Already he faced problems which could well have disturbed a man twice his age. He had a foreign wife who met with the approval of neither his father nor his mother; he had no job and little prospect of one; he had no place to live except with his parents; he was short of money; and his Soviet control had just given him his lifetime assignment – '[I was] given the job of penetrating British intelligence and told it did not matter how long it took to do the job.'[3] Philby was a realist and must, if he were honest with himself, have considered this just about impossible.

Recruitment to SIS was traditionally limited to a chosen few, usually relatives and friends of officers already in the service. It was not the sort of organization one could apply to join because not only would this be considered terribly bad form, it would also arouse suspicion. As with the Masonic Lodge, one waited for an invitation. Of course, some places were better to wait than others. The armed services, the Foreign Office, Fleet Street (the work of a spy and a journalist are uncomfortably similar) and London clubland were prime recruiting grounds for SIS.

Philby was in none of these fields and his political past seemed to rule them out. But after consultation with his control, he developed a plan. He would begin to erase his left-wing background, and, at the same time, cast around for a job in journalism. On this front, St John Philby did what he could to help by writing to friends among the Fabians and in journalism. One to receive such a letter was Sir Roger Chance, who had been at Trinity with St John and, like him, was a member of the Athenaeum. Chance was the editor of the *Review of Reviews*, a Liberal monthly with offices in King William Street, in the City. The magazine was slowly dying and Chance would probably not have done anything about Kim Philby had not another journalist, Wilfred Hindle, brought him to the office. After some discussion, Chance engaged Philby as a sub-editor and feature writer at four guineas a week.

After the excitement of Vienna, Philby must have found the work boring and unrewarding. He cut out articles from other magazines, did excerpts of them, and occasionally wrote an article of his own. The few that survive – 'Lawrence of Arabia, the Work behind the Legend', 'Japan's Pacific Islands', 'The Balkan Tragedy' – are competent if dull. Alison Outhwaite, another journalist who shared the small office with Philby, remembers wondering why he stayed. When she asked him once he replied in a rare moment of candour: 'What's the point in leaving? I'll be in the trenches in a few years anyway.'[4]

The real reason was that the job gave him the time and the emotional energy for the much more important task of erasing his communist background and constructing his new right-wing front. First, his Marxist friends from his Cambridge days had to go. One, Anthony McLean, was visiting London and telephoned to suggest that they meet. 'I'm very busy,' Kim said, and when McLean then proposed that they get together in a month or two, Kim said he would still be busy then. McLean got the message. So did Maurice Dobb. He had written to Kim asking him to contribute a chapter to a book he was editing to be called 'Britain Without Capitalists'. Philby ignored the letter. Dobb recalled: 'I decided to call a meeting of all the possible contributors to put the project into final form. I phoned Philby to ask if he were coming. He was distinctly negative. "I don't want anything to do with it," he said. It was as if he had given up all his left-wing associations. I thought it a little shabby.'⁵ And Dobb told Page in the 1967 interview that he had been surprised to hear that Kim had moved so far to the right.

Jim Lees, Philby's coalminer friend from Cambridge who had helped politicize him, was stunned to hear Philby tell him when they met in London late in 1935 that he thought communism was finished and that, in the present state of the world, the sensible choice was fascism. Philby's boss, Chance, who had dinner with the Philbys once or twice, thought Philby was 'a liberal democrat, middle of the Labour Party, but definitely anti-communist'. He was less certain about Litzi: 'She was rather bizarre, with hair like rats' tails, that kind of thing.'⁶

We can see in these manoeuvres Philby developing his skills as an intelligence officer. He was cutting himself adrift from his communist past with some subtlety, letting the word of his new political beliefs percolate through his old circle. This was much more convincing in his case than the sudden, almost overnight conversion which Burgess affected to have undergone. Presumably under similar instructions from his own Soviet control, Burgess announced after a visit to Moscow that his enthusiasm for the communist system had evaporated. He now favoured a system like the one Mussolini had created through the corporate state.

Both Philby and Burgess now became involved with the Anglo-German Fellowship, a strongly pro-German organization which kept up a staunch anti-communist line until its dissolution on the outbreak of war. The Fellowship was a mixture of English fascists, appeasers, anti-semites, hard-headed businessmen, fanatical anti-bolsheviks, eccentric aristocrats and neurotic Mayfair society women. They included Nancy Mitford's father, Lord Redesdale, who described Hitler as the greatest man of the twentieth century; Wilfred Ashley, Minister of Transport in the Baldwin government, who had a violent hatred of anything that smacked of socialism; and General J.F.C. Fuller, a military historian, who had a grudge against the British authorities for not honouring his work with a knighthood.

The lavish dinners and receptions the Fellowship gave attracted prominent politicians who, although not necessarily advocating fascism for Britain, nevertheless felt that Hitler's Germany was a stabilizing force in Europe and a barrier against communism. Among these politicians were the Marquess of Londonderry, lately Secretary of State for Air; Rab Butler then Under-Secretary at the India Office but soon to move to the Foreign Office; the Marquess of Lothian, British Ambassador in Washington; and Sir Horace Wilson, the man behind Britain's appeasement policy.

At a swastika-decked dinner the Fellowship gave on 14 July 1936 to honour the Kaiser's daughter, the Duchess of Brunswick, and her husband, the guests included Admiral Sir Barry Domvile, former director of British Naval Intelligence, who was the founder of a more sinister pro-German organization called 'The Link' (he was imprisoned in 1939 as a security risk), Prince and Princess von Bismarck, Dr Fritz Hesse, Baron von Bieberstein, Count Albrecht Montgelas, Dr Gottfried Rosel – and Mr H.A.R. Philby.

In short, the Fellowship was so pro-German that some of the more liberal elements in the Foreign Office saw it as a danger. Government files for the period contain a memorandum written by a foreign diplomat for his colleagues in the Foreign Office:

> The propaganda department of the Anglo-German Fellowship is in constant contact with the German Ministry of Propaganda and Enlightenment in Berlin . . . The Ministry in Berlin sends the Fellowship in London lots of literature printed in England – for distribution in this country. Some of the stuff is in pamphlet form. It includes also a sort of journal giving press opinions. The aim of the last named is to suggest to the British public that it is being misled by the British press about both British and German policies.

To this a Foreign Office official added his comment: 'The Germans are spending more money and energy in this country than the Soviets.'[7]

The Soviets had Kim Philby, so they too knew exactly what the Fellowship was up to. Philby had worked so enthusiastically part-time for the Fellowship that in 1936 it offered him a full-time job. He was to start a trade journal, which would be financed by the German Propaganda Ministry, and which would have the aim of fostering good relations between Germany and Britain. Philby flew to Berlin several times for talks with the Ministry and with the Ambassador in London, von Ribbentrop.

Philby's magazine was never published because the Fellowship switched its backing to a rival, the *Anglo-German Review*, which started in November 1936, edited by C.E. Carroll. It did not matter to Philby because, as he has made clear, he was already reporting to his Soviet control from his privileged position within the Fellowship – 'Overt and covert links between Britain and Germany at that time were of serious concern to the Soviet Government.'[8]

Philby's control must have been pleased with him. He was doing useful work for the Soviet intelligence service and his communist past had been successfully blurred. But it could not be made to disappear entirely until one major problem was solved – the presence of Litzi. Litzi was a constant reminder to Philby's friends and colleagues that he had spent time in Vienna, that he had rescued this Austrian girl because she was in danger of arrest as a communist, and that he married her to get her a British passport. If, as the Russians wanted, Philby was to establish an impeccable right-wing persona, Litzi, a Jewish communist, was going to be a continuing handicap. There is evidence that Philby's Russian control told him – and perhaps Litzi too – that from now on Philby would operate better alone.

In July 1936 the ex-miner Jim Lees, who had come down from Nottingham to see Guy Burgess, went to the Philbys' for Saturday lunch. It was not a happy occasion. The food was bad because Litzi had never really learnt to cook, and then Philby and Lees got into a heated argument, first over what was going to happen in Spain, already on the brink of civil war, and then over Germany. 'I remember Kim saying that Franco's rebels were romantics who could not possibly threaten the Spanish Republic . . . Then Kim and I quarrelled violently about what was happening in Central Europe, with him defending the Germans and maintaining that the left was finished. That was why he had taken his job with the Fellowship, he said, and (in an aside to me) that was why he would have to get rid of Litzi.'[9] Lees stormed out of the house.

The outbreak of the Spanish Civil War in July 1936 offered Philby a quick solution. Moscow had been following developments in Spain for some time and had sent Philby there twice – in the summer of 1934 and again the following year. He had gone with Litzi as if on holiday – although the source of the money for these trips was later to give him an anxious moment or two with his interrogators from MI5, as we shall see. The Spanish immigration records show that Philby travelled on British passport 383531 and Litzi on a British passport issued in Vienna on 26 February 1934, number 2516. Now the Russians wanted him to return 'to get first-hand information on all aspects of the Fascist war effort'.

First Philby needed a cover. He could hardly move around the front as a tourist, so he managed to persuade the London General Press, a news and syndication agency, to give him a letter of accreditation. It was quite understandable that a freelance journalist covering a war would not take his wife with him, so Litzi was left behind, the beginning of their split. All this took some time to arrange, so it was not until February 1937 that Philby arrived in Spain. He immediately began to bombard *The Times* with unsolicited articles, all written from the fascist side. One was published and this encouraged St John Philby, in London on a visit, to take to lunch the assistant editor of *The Times*, Robin Barrington-Ward, another old Westminster boy.

It worked. On 24 May 1937, when Philby was only twenty-five, *The Times* appointed him as its second correspondent with the Nationalist forces in Spain – the other was James Holburn – an important job by any reckoning. He came back to London for a couple of days to agree his salary and be introduced to the rigorous attitude of *The Times* towards journalists' expenses. Philby recalled in Moscow: 'I was warned that they were incredibly strict about even the tiniest details. I did my best but when I sent in my first expense account I couldn't itemize it all. It had been a very active period with lots of fighting and I just couldn't remember where every peseta had gone. But it only came to about forty pounds for more than two months, so I wasn't too worried. Well, the accounts department was very reluctant to accept it and memos flew back and forth. Finally they said that just this one time my expenses would be approved but in future I would have to itemize everything. I wrote back and said that if the war hotted up this might be impossible so would they consider instead a fixed expenses allowance. Expecting that whatever I suggested they would cut, I took a chance and asked for forty pounds a month. The accounts department came back and said they would accept the idea of a fixed allowance – but only two guineas a day!'

Everything arranged, Philby then returned to Spain, now protected by all the prestige accorded to *The Times*, on his first major mission as a Soviet intelligence officer.

WORKING ON THE
FASCIST FRONT
═══ 5 ═══

On one side in Spain were ranged the representatives of the old order: bankers, landlords, clergy and army. Against them stood the peasants, the workers, the best of Spanish writers and poets, and a democratically elected government. Both sides saw the war as a crusade. The old order, the Nationalists, led by General Franco, fought to purge their country of the Reds, to resurrect their ideal of a pure, Christian Spain. The Republicans fought for a new age, the New Jerusalem, or, in the case of the communists, a Marxist Utopia. Most saw it as something far wider than a civil conflict. 'In essence it was a class war,' wrote George Orwell. 'If it had been won, the cause of the common people everywhere would have been strengthened. It was lost, and the dividend-drawers all over the world rubbed their hands.'[1]

The intervention of Hitler and Mussolini on the side of Franco and of the Soviet Union on the side of the Republicans turned the war into an apocalyptic moment in history, a point in time at which to choose and make a stand. From all over the world thousands of young men made their way to Spain to fight in the International Brigades, the sort of personal commitment to the fight against fascism described by Ernest Hemingway in his famous Spanish Civil War novel, *For Whom the Bell Tolls*. Many of the correspondents, too, committed themselves with passion. One of them, Martha Gellhorn, says: 'We knew, we just *knew*, that Spain was the place to stop Fascism. This was it. It was one of those moments in history when there was no doubt.' Another, Herbert Matthews of the *New York Times*, wrote: 'Today, wherever in this world I meet a man or woman who fought for Spanish liberty, I meet a kindred soul. In those years we lived our best and what has come after and what there is to come can never carry us to those heights again.'[2]

Emotionally, this must have been the stand that Philby, too, wanted to take. But he had chosen the secret path; not for him the open declaration, the brotherhood of those who fought for Spanish liberty. He had signed up for a longer war and the first objective was to conceal from all his true allegiances. He was eminently successful. To almost everyone who met him, Kim Philby appeared a serious, slightly stodgy, young English journalist, rather taken with his own importance, who wrote reports about the Franco side in which his objectivity did not quite conceal his fascist sympathies.

One of the Nationalist press officers, Enrique Marsans, remembered that Philby could always be relied on not to make difficulties, or to object to censorship. Once at the front when the Nationalists were particularly sensitive about the number of Italians who might be fighting alongside them, Philby wrote a small news item about a football match between Spanish and Italian soldiers. Marsans challenged him about it, demanding to know if he had actually witnessed the match itself. 'Philby admitted that he had not; he said he had heard about it second hand. He told me, "The news was a bit thin today and I thought I'd better send something to London." He cut out the item without any argument.'[3] Another Franco officer, Luis Bolín, said that Philby was a 'decent chap who inspired confidence in his reports because he was so objective'.

As if to confirm these Spaniards' impression of Philby as an English gentleman sharing the normal conservative reflexes of the ruling class, Philby found himself a mistress – Frances ('Bunny') Doble, the divorced Canadian wife of Sir Anthony Lindsay-Hogg, an English baronet. Lady Lindsay-Hogg, a former star of the London stage, was ten years older than Philby. An ardent royalist, she had fallen in love with Spain when she had visited it as a tourist nine years earlier and had now returned to do what she could to support the Franco side. She had used her influence with a Spanish diplomat to get into Spain and to persuade the Spanish press officers to allow her to stay. She too thought Philby was 'attractive, very sincere, and a perfect gentleman'. (On one occasion when a press officer looking for Lady Lindsay-Hogg telephoned Philby, Philby angrily demanded to know why the Spaniard thought she would be in his room.) Of course, Philby concealed his real political views from her. 'We often talked about his father's exploits in Arabia, or about Vienna and the Austrian girl he had married there, but he never breathed a word about socialism, communism, or anything like that.' He resisted her attempts to jolt him out of his cool, detached stance. 'I'm passionately for this side,' she would say. And, '*We've* won another battle.' But Philby would only smile and refuse to be drawn.[4]

While Philby was establishing his long-term cover, there was plenty for him to do. But his career both as a journalist and a spy nearly came to an abrupt end on three occasions. One Philby was blissfully ignorant of – the defection to the West in 1937 of Walter Krivitsky, a

Soviet military intelligence officer stationed in the Netherlands. During his debriefing Krivitsky told a British interrogator, Jane Archer, that the Russian intelligence service had a young Englishman working for it in Spain under cover as a journalist. This was obviously Philby, but Krivitsky could add nothing to his bare statement and the British security service had more pressing things to do than to work on this slender, and at that time, unimportant lead. (Its failure to do so later, when it was important, is another matter and we shall return to it.)

Philby's second escape was one he knew about only too well. One weekend in Seville he decided to go to Cordoba to see a bullfight. Assured by the local authorities that he did not need a pass for the trip, he caught a train to Cordoba, checked into a hotel, ate a solitary meal and went to bed. He was awakened by two Civil Guards hammering on his door. They told him to pack his bag and accompany them to headquarters. It turned out that he *did* need a pass to visit Cordoba. Philby was confident he could talk his way out of this trouble, but in the ticket pocket of his trousers he had concealed a slip of paper containing instructions for the use of a Russian intelligence service code. If this was found on him he could well end up in front of a firing squad before the British consul could intervene.

While the Civil Guards searched his luggage, Philby worked out a plan. When the officer in charge of the search asked Philby to turn out his pockets, he acted. 'Taking first my wallet, I threw it down on that fine table, giving it at the last moment a flick of the wrist which sent it spinning towards the far end. As I had hoped, all three men made a dive for it, spreadeagling themselves across the table. Confronted by three pairs of buttocks, I scooped the scrap of paper out of my trousers, a crunch and a swallow and it was gone.'[5]

On another occasion Philby had a narrow escape from being killed by a Republican gun, ironically, a Russian 12.40 cm, known in the war as a 'quarter to one'. On 31 December 1937, a group of journalists were driving from Saragossa to witness a battle in progress at Teruel, a grim walled town on the high inland plateau. When they stopped for a break in the main square of a village called Caude, the Spanish conducting officers got out to stretch their legs and have a smoke, but Philby, Dick Sheepshanks of Reuters, and two Americans, Ed Neil of the Associated Press and Bradish Johnson of *Newsweek*, remained in their car because of the bitter cold – it was eighteen degrees below zero. When a shell fell about half a mile away no one paid much attention. Then suddenly there was an enormous explosion and the Spaniards were knocked to the ground.

When they staggered to their feet they saw that the journalists' car had caught the full impact of the shell. They forced the door open and found a scene of shocking carnage. Johnson was dead, a huge hole in his back.* Sheepshanks was unconscious, badly wounded in the head and face, an eye missing. He died that evening. Neil's leg was broken and riddled with shrapnel. He died two days later. But Philby, who had been sitting in the front passenger seat, escaped with a cut to his head and another to his wrist. He was treated in a field hospital and was driven back to Saragossa. There he went straight to a bar where he created something of a sensation. The blast had destroyed most of his clothes, so he was wearing a pair of old sandals and a woman's pale blue coat with a moth-eaten fur collar. The customers stared at him but a waiter, who had heard of the incident, came rushing up with a large drink. Philby was treated as something of a hero.

Two days later he filed a modest dispatch for *The Times* describing the death of his colleagues and playing down his own injuries: 'Your correspondent was able to leave the car and cross the square to a wall where a group of soldiers were sheltering. Thence he was taken to a first aid station where light head injuries were speedily treated. Meanwhile Spanish officers worked gallantly in an attempt to rescue the occupants of the car regardless of falling shells.'

Philby had a good reason for minimizing his injuries. It emerged in a letter written on 14 January by E.G. de Caux, the *Times* correspondent in Biarritz and Philby's contact in France, to the *Times* foreign news editor, Ralph Deakin:

The *New York Times* correspondent, Bill Carney, told me yesterday that he arrived on the scene of the accident in Teruel just after it occurred. Philby showed great pluck. Though he had received a bad scalp cut that bled profusely and many minor scratches on his face, and was also suffering from shock, he was quite cool and collected. Back at Saragossa he begged his colleagues not to exaggerate their stories with regard to his injuries as he feared he might be called back to London.[6]

---

*Johnson had the worst luck imaginable. He had been travelling in another car but when the Spanish conducting officer got out of Philby's car to smoke with his fellow officers, Johnson came over and slipped into the empty driver's seat. Seconds later he was dead. An American cigarette company later offered the Spanish officer an enormous sum of money to say that his life had been saved by its brand of cigarette. He turned the offer down.

Obviously, the last thing Philby wanted, as he settled into his secret role for the Russian intelligence service, was for *The Times* to take him away from Spain, even for a short period.

Instead, on 2 March Philby was received by Franco, who personally pinned to his breast the Red Cross of Military Merit. (There were posthumous decorations for the correspondents who had been killed.) This caused the only communist member of the House of Commons, Willie Gallacher, to ask if the British government was aware that 'Mr H.A.R. Philpot' was authorized to accept the decoration. Rab Butler replied: 'I assume that the Hon. Member is referring to Mr H.A.R. Philby, a newspaper correspondent serving with General Franco's forces. I have seen in the press a report of the award of a medal by the Spanish nationalist authorities to this gentleman. Mr Philby has not sought and has not been given any official authority to accept the distinction in question.'[7]

The award turned out to be important. Philby told me in Moscow: 'My wounding in Spain helped my work – both journalism and intelligence work – no end. Before then there had been a lot of criticism of British journalists from Franco officers who seemed to think that the British in general must be a lot of communists because so many were fighting with the International Brigade. After I had been wounded, and then decorated by Franco himself, I became known as "the-English-decorated-by-Franco" and all sorts of doors opened for me.'

His cover established, Philby was now getting on with his real work in Spain, espionage. For a brief period he thought that he had struck it lucky. A German intelligence officer befriended him and Philby thought he was about to be offered work as a German agent, which would have given him access to information valuable to his Soviet employers. But it turned out that the German only wanted an introduction to Lady Lindsay-Hogg, and when she rejected his advances the German's attitude to Philby cooled.

There was still plenty to see and hear. At press briefings when other correspondents were interested only in the overall military situation, Philby developed a reputation as something of a bore because he pressed for details – number of aircraft, type, calibre of artillery, number of rounds fired, composition of attacking infantry force and so on. The correspondents – and presumably the Franco press officers – put this down to the traditional interest *The Times* seemed to have in military matters. When he had enough material to justify a meeting with his Soviet control, Philby would make an excuse to *The Times* for a visit across the border, to Hendaye, the town astride the frontier, or to St Jean de Luz, where most of the correspondents took their leave periods. These places seethed with gossip and intrigue, and were thus not only convenient for passing on information but for gathering more. The British government's representative in St Jean de Luz, Sir Geoffrey Thompson, remembered Philby in the middle of it all, perhaps the best-informed among the correspondents – 'There was little that Philby did not know about the extent of the German and Italian military participation on the Franco side.'[8]

There were periods when he did not have time for much espionage, his journalistic duties keeping him fully occupied. This was the case in the spring of 1937 when Philby was busy with the crucial fighting in the north. The industrial cities there, though cut off for many months from the rest of the country, were still in Republican hands and were playing a vital role in the government's war effort. To win the war, Franco had to get control of the steel industry which was established there. General Emilio Mola, leading the Franco forces, began a campaign to do this by issuing the following threat on 31 March 1937: 'If submission is not immediate I will raze all Vizcaya [a Basque province] to the ground, beginning with the industries of war. I have the means to do so.'

The means were squadrons of German planes with German pilots which helped Mola roll back the ill-organized Basque troops until by Monday, 26 April, Mola's forces were only ten miles from a small town outside the Basque capital of Bilbao. The name of this small town was Guernica. During the next twenty-four hours, Guernica was destroyed, levelled by Franco's bombers. The death roll has never been established, estimates ranging from 100 to 1,600.

One of the first journalists to enter Guernica was Philby's opposite number, George Steer, the *Times* special correspondent with the Republican forces. His story ran prominently in *The Times* and the *New York Times* on 28 April. It began:

Guernica, the most ancient town of the Basques and the centre of their cultural tradition, was *completely destroyed* yesterday by insurgent air raiders. The bombardment of this open town far behind the lines occupied precisely three hours and a quarter, during which a powerful fleet of aeroplanes consisting of three German types – Junkers and Heinkel bombers and Heinkel fighters – did not cease unloading on the town bombs weighing from 1,000lb downwards, and, it is calculated, more than 3,000 two pounder aluminium incendiary projectiles. [emphasis added]

The most important paragraph in his account read:

In the form of its execution and the scale of the destruction it wrought, no less than in the selection of its objective, *the raid on Guernica is unparalleled in military history. Guernica was not a military objective.* A factory producing war material lay outside the town and was untouched . . . *The object of the bombardment was seemingly the demoralisation of the civilian population and the destruction of the cradle of the Basque race.* Every fact bears out this appreciation . . . [emphases added]*

Steer's report, backed by those of other journalists who had been to Guernica, sparked off a wave of outrage that has never really subsided. (Herbert Matthews of the *New York Times* said later that Guernica aroused more indignation worldwide than did Hiroshima.) It became the point in time at which total war was said to have begun – the indiscriminate bombing of a civilian target as a deliberate experiment in terror – and it passed into the traditions of the Left as a symbol of everything hateful about fascism.

Two days later Guernica fell to the Franco forces, which immediately issued press releases claiming that the Basques themselves had caused most of the damage so as to win over world opinion. It is unlikely that this would have been believed anywhere had it not been for *The Times* and the *New York Times*, which carried a story from their common correspondent, Holburn, datelined Vitoria 4 May. It began: 'It is feared that the conflagration destroyed much of the evidence of its origin, but it is felt here that enough remains to support the Nationalist contention that incendiaries on the Basque side had more to do with the razing of Guernica than General Franco's aircraft.' The report continued: 'It has been asserted that Guernica was subject to bombing of exceptional intensity, but the distinctive marks of an aerial bombardment are not numerous . . . Few fragments of bombs have been recovered, the façades of buildings still standing are unmarked, and the few craters inspected were larger than anything hitherto made by a bomb in Spain. From their positions it is a fair inference that these craters were caused by exploding mines which were unscientifically laid to cut roads.'

Then the report concluded with this damning paragraph: 'In view

---

*Steer said later that the *Times* editor, Geoffrey Dawson, already deep into his appeasement stance, was unhappy with the story but felt obliged to run it.

of these circumstances it is difficult to believe that Guernica was the target of bombardment of exceptional intensity by the Nationalists for an experiment with incendiary bombs, as is alleged by the Basques. In the investigators' opinion, it will be difficult to establish exactly how the fires started.'⁹ This story was widely quoted and met with warm approval from Franco and his international supporters. One noted that *The Times* 'became a very different paper about a month after the exposure of the Guernica swindle'.¹⁰

I have quoted the *Times* report at length because, after Philby's defection to Moscow in 1963, it was linked to him, and many commentators found particular significance in it. Authors Patrick Seale and Maureen McConville noted: 'Kim had seen his opportunity and seized it . . . This pharisaical piece of writing was Kim's passport into the confidence of both the Spanish Nationalists and of Geoffrey Dawson, the editor of *The Times*.'¹¹ One Spanish writer drew a fundamental historical parallel from the fact that George Steer took one side over Guernica and Philby took the other.¹² It was seen as typical of Philby's duplicity that he was prepared to sacrifice the truth about Guernica in order to ingratiate himself with fascists and thus please his Moscow masters.

There is one major flaw in this analysis – Philby did not write the article about Guernica. He had nothing to do with it. It was written by the other *Times* correspondent with Franco, James Holburn. I discovered this by first writing to ask Philby if he had indeed written it. He replied:

I should start with two words of warning about *The Times* correspondents from Franco Spain during the Civil War. First, until a few days after the fall of Bilbao, James Holburn and I worked in tandem. We covered different parts of the front and sent our dispatches at the first opportunity, sometimes together and sometimes separately. Then the sub-editors' room at PHS jumbled our reports together in such a way that it is impossible to distinguish our respective contributions. I mention this because I have no recollection of the passage which you attribute to me. I may have written it but I suspect that Holburn did.

Second, you will already have realized that my overriding interest in Spain was to get as close as possible to the Franco authorities and to the Germans. I never filed anything that I knew to be untrue (swelp me), but the truth can be looked at through many pairs of spectacles, and the pairs I used, for ulterior purposes, were supplied by Franco and the Legion Kondor.

This was interesting but inconclusive, so I went through *The*

Times archives. Details of the actual dispatch had been preserved, and it is clear from these that it had been sent by Holburn alone. For confirmation I went to Holburn himself. He remembered the story well and said that he had written it. He then gave an interesting explanation as to why he had done so. There was rigorous censorship, and correspondents who did not toe the line could find themselves in trouble – at the time of Guernica there was a correspondent of the French news agency Havas in a Franco prison and another under house arrest.

Holburn wanted to let *The Times* know that the Nationalists *had* bombed Guernica, a fact that until then they had strenuously denied. So almost buried in the propaganda necessary to get the point past the censors, Holburn told London that some fragments of *bombs* had been found, that *not all* the buildings were still standing, that there were some distinctive marks of an *aerial bombardment*. But, unfortunately, the sub-editors at *The Times* must have missed Holburn's signals and printed his dispatch as he sent it.

So what *was* Philby's view on Guernica? 'I was never impressed by the Franco claim that Guernica had been destroyed by the Basques to provide material for propaganda or for any other reason,' he wrote in his letter to me.

Three objections, among many, stand out. One, nowhere else did the Basques resort to a scorched earth policy (the destruction of bridges is something else). It seems most unlikely that they should have chosen as their only target for such an experiment the town of Guernica, with its deeply felt associations for the Basque people. To have done so would have implied a degree of ruthlessness in Aguirre and Co [the Basque leaders] which, unfortunately, was quite lacking in them.

Two, at the time of the destruction, Basque units were holding lines east and south of the town. If they were to hold these positions, Guernica was a vital point on their supply lines; or, alternatively, if they were to lose them, a vital bottleneck on their line of retreat. So why destroy it before the troops had extricated themselves? And three, the Franco authorities made no attempt, beyond repeated assertion, to substantiate their claim, while the Germans, privately, made no attempt to deny the fact of the air-raid.

Does this leave George Steer in possession of the field? Not quite, I think. Look at the statements you quote. *Completely destroyed by insurgent air raiders*. Not true. I did not make a detailed survey at the time – the war was moving on, and I think that Franco's people might have looked askance at too much research into the question. But my impression was that perhaps a third of the town was destroyed, another third damaged, and the rest, including the famous tree, unscathed. Of course, these too symmetrical proportions are of suspect accuracy, but I think that they are of the right order of magnitude. In any case, they imply a damned heavy raid in relation to the size of the target.

Guernica was not a military objective. Well wasn't it? A fair-sized town, a few miles behind the front, without a doubt sheltering Basque command posts, combat and L of C [line of communication] troops; also a centre of communications. It was certainly a military target in the sense that Caen was; more so than central Cologne which got it just five years later. A raid *completely unparalleled in military history*. I do not know what the Italians had done in Abyssinia or the Japanese in China, but Steer may well have been right. But we know much more now. Guernica came in the opening bars of a new symphony of frightfulness which *may* just have ended in Cambodia – of all unoffending places! *The object was seemingly the demoralisation of the civil population*. I have no doubt that that was one of the purposes of the raid. It was soon to become a legitimate military objective in the eyes of most people; in recent years, the Americans have defended it as a legitimate political weapon as well.

So I think we may fairly say that Steer, with understandable professional, political and personal ardour, over-reacted to the news from Guernica. He was an able journalist who knew a story when he saw one; he was deeply committed to the Basques; he felt deep and genuine indignation at the frightfulness which was soon to become pretty run-of-the-mill. Herbert Matthews was probably right when he said that Guernica aroused more worldwide indignation than Hiroshima. But that means only that, by the time the dust had settled over Hiroshima, pretty well all the world's media were under anti-Japanese control. Besides, the Japanese were only Asiatics.

In that connection, I have a curious story to tell you, which bears on the subject under discussion. In the autumn of 1945, I attended a function at the Spanish Embassy in London, where, in conversation with a Franco Spaniard unknown to me, I dropped the name of Hiroshima. The Spaniard commented, 'La ultima barbaridad', and turned away. He was quite obviously sincere, and I immediately thought of the distance we had come since Guernica.[13]

Philby came back to Guernica in a later letter, in case I had misconstrued his views:

Reverting to our previous correspondence, mostly about Guernica,

I saw in a recent *TLS* that Brian Crozier is maintaining his view that the town was never bombed by the Germans. He bases his conviction on two items of evidence: (a) the opinion of Wing-Commander James, an airman who examined the ground shortly after the event, and (b) a visit to Guernica made by Crozier himself 'three years ago' when he found that the ancient centre of the town was unscathed, and all the new buildings were on the outskirts. Ergo, the Basques burnt Guernica.

Both arguments are puerile. James was wholly committed to Franco, unfailingly regurgitated the official Franco line and, in addition, was a very silly fellow by any standards. (I saw a lot of him in Spain.) The second line of argument is open to even more objection, and could lead to startling results if applied elsewhere. For example, using almost the same words, I could 'prove' that the siege of Leningrad never took place. I visited Leningrad 'three years ago' and can assure you that the centre of the town is quite 'unscathed'. 'All the new building is on the outskirts.' Ergo, the story of the siege is just a piece of propaganda. The same could be said of the Warsaw uprising, the battle of Budapest, etc. (It occurs to me that the *ST* Insight team might find a story in investigating the origins of Crozier's Institute for the Study of Conflict – a front organisation if ever there was one.)*

So although Philby rejected the right-wing view that Guernica was never bombed, he did not accept the Left's account either. He believed that Guernica was a legitimate military target and that it was bombed for sound tactical reasons. Then Steer, for understandable reasons, over-reacted to the event and turned it into the symbol of barbarity helped by Picasso's *Guernica*[14] that it remains today. The story of Guernica is important in helping us understand Philby, not only because, free to give his real views on it, he did not automatically adopt the Left position as one would have expected, but also because, not for the last time, he was blamed for something he did not do.

As the war ground on, Philby continued to write his undistinguished dispatches, neatly tailored to suit the prejudices of his newspaper and all cleverly calculated to enhance his reputation as a serious

*Crozier left the Institute in 1979, but in June 1987 the *Guardian* revealed that the Institute had close links with Western intelligence agencies and had channelled covert American funds to right-wing groups backing the deployment of Cruise missiles in Holland.

young Englishman of impeccable right-wing political views. Some of the things he had to do, and some of what he wrote, must have nearly made him sick. On one occasion he was with a Franco press party taken to see members of the International Brigades who were being held in à monastery near Burgos as prisoners of war. Among them were two Englishmen, Isidore Konigsberg and Donald Eggar. As they stood there, filthy, louse-ridden, and feeling thoroughly humiliated, Philby came over and introduced himself. He spent twenty minutes talking to them, appeared sympathetic with their plight, and readily agreed to write to their relatives in Britain. He never did, presumably because he thought it could endanger the image he was so carefully constructing.

Then when the Franco forces entered Madrid in March 1939 Philby filed a dispatch, part of which read:

> Uppent emotions burst fullstop Huge crowds collected all main thoroughfares cheering wildly every passing car fullstop shouts Franco Falange mingled with sounds patriotic hymns broadcast by lorries propaganda of the front fullstop Carloads young girls dressed dash who knows how undash Falange uniform blue shirts red berets tore through streets yelling quote they have passed unquote dash parody former Republican slogan quote they shall not pass unquote fullstop.

St John Philby, who had been so delighted that Kim had finally found a job that, on his way to Cairo by car, he had stopped off to see him, now expressed some bewilderment at his son's attitude. 'He's not only reporting for the Franco side,' St John wrote to a friend in the Foreign Office, 'but he seems to think that they're right.'[15] Others had also noticed Kim's articles, and occasionally word of their contempt for their former left-wing friend must have reached him. Eric Gedye, the journalist Kim had met and worked with in Vienna, passed a message to Kim via a colleague, a Communist Party member: 'Tell him I was sorry to find him in such bad company.' Perhaps because the messenger was a communist, Philby trusted her with his reply: 'Tell Eric not to be misled by appearances. I'm exactly what I've always been.'[16]

Not everyone was misled. One of Philby's Cambridge colleagues, A. Tudor Hart, said he knew from discussions with Philby at university that such a convinced Marxist would never have swapped his allegiance. 'When Kim went to Spain on the Franco side, I automatically assumed that this was a cover; that he had been approached by the Soviets, had accepted, and was working for them. I knew Kim too well to be taken in by the Franco business.'[17]

Some of Philby's journalist colleagues were also not entirely misled, even if they were wrong in the detail. They scented a hint of the intelligence officer about him, but thought that it was the British Secret Service he was working for rather than the Russian. Marsans, the Spanish press officer, considered it odd that Philby was strangely uncompetitive. 'He never fought for his own way or resorted to ruses to obtain good copy like the others.'[18] This made Marsans wonder whether Philby was primarily not a journalist, but a British military intelligence officer.

And Pedro Giro, another press officer, recalled an odd incident in a café. While talking to some friends, a man Giro knew to be working for German intelligence slipped him a note warning him that two men nearby were British agents. Later Giro was surprised to see these two men in deep conversation with Philby. Samuel Pope Brewer (later to lose his wife to Philby) had no doubt: 'I was sure that Philby was working for British intelligence.'

The effort Philby would have had to put into his dissembling changed his character. He came back from Spain a tougher, more disciplined person, with an ability to call on a reserve of ruthlessness when the moment needed it. Spain had made him. It would turn out to be one of the main reasons that British intelligence did eventually recruit him, and it would be because of his work on Spain that he would rise through its ranks. He acknowledged the debt in his conversations with me in Moscow, adding: 'It occupies a special place in my memory. If my travelling days were not over, then, along with France, it would be the country I would most like to see again.'

Philby left Spain in August 1939 for a short holiday in London, intending to return to write about reconstruction. But when he called at *The Times* office he was told to stand by to go to France. On 3 September, the Prime Minister, Neville Chamberlain, announced a state of war with Germany. That morning, a family friend of the Philbys', Flora Solomon, an executive of Marks and Spencer, the department store, had introduced him to her young assistant, Aileen Furse, who was to become Philby's second wife. 'So it was a date well remembered,' Philby told me later, 'because it was disastrous for the world and to myself.'

INVITED TO PLAY
6

Britain went to war reluctantly. The massive slaughter of the First World War was still fresh in memory; many Conservatives in high places still admired Hitler, there were pessimistic predictions of the effects of bombing on large cities – mass panic was predicted – and a substantial section of the wealthier classes made clear their plans to escape from any unpleasantness. A lack of clear understanding of what the fight was about brought many demands for peace – twenty-two Labour MPs signed a manifesto calling for an early armistice, an event that was scarcely reported. Nobody knew what was coming, or what they were going to do.

The Times was optimistic in telling Philby to stand by to travel to France as its top war correspondent, for, as yet unknown to newspaper editors, the Allied general staffs, alarmed by the development of short-wave radio, had decreed their intention to make the war a newsless one. The system for controlling war correspondents would be exactly the same as in 1914–18: a limited number of correspondents, escorted by conducting officers, would be tolerated at headquarters and allowed to send back carefully censored dispatches. All major newspapers were urged to put forward the names of men to accompany the British Expeditionary Force (BEF) to France, so that they could be vetted for suitability, get their commissions, have their uniforms tailored, and vote on whether their insignia should be a 'C', or – more appropriately, said some army officers – a 'WC'.

But after the Germans had pulled off several publicity coups by allowing neutral correspondents a free run of the front, and after complaints that news from Germany dominated the American press and newsreels to Britain's disadvantage, Major-General J.H. Beith, the War Office's director of public relations, promised improvements: 'A large body of correspondents, including a fully representative American contingent, [is] now with our forces in France.'[1] This group had arrived on 10 October 1939, and consisted of fifteen British and Commonwealth correspondents (one of whom was Philby), nine Americans, and eight press and newsreel photographers. They were to be based at the British HQ in Arras, northern France, where they would be under the control of army conducting officers.

The antipathy between the journalists and the conducting officers was immediate. The officers, all First World War veterans, were relics of a vanished England – one, a former cavalry officer, boasted of his failure to become trained in tanks. Another, Captain Charles Tremayne, one-time captain of the English polo team, drank neat gin for breakfast and was known to have finished six bottles in two days. One correspondent, O.D. Gallagher, says: '[The conducting officers] were either drunk half the time or half drunk all the time. Whenever you were out driving with them it was always, "Let's pull up and have a snifter at that café, old chap", or if there were no cafés, out came a flask from some pocket of their expensively cut uniforms.'[2]

While outwardly polite to the correspondents, the conducting officers actually hated them. 'Although Charles Tremayne's brain had been pickled by drink,' one officer wrote, 'he still had five times more brain than the journalists he conducted.'[3] Curiously, the one correspondent the conducting officers would tolerate was Philby. When I asked him about this, he replied:

> Of course, they were pure Evelyn Waugh characters, but they were on Christian-name terms with a large number of senior officers and therefore got us entrées to places where less authentically military types could never have ventured. If the second part of the sentence [about Tremayne's brain] had read, 'We knew twice as much about getting places, in a military context, than all the correspondents we were conducting', I would happily countersign it. Their chief trouble was that they believed in horses and 'cold steel' as the surest way of winning wars.[4]

At this stage there appeared to be no war in France to fight, much less win. But what was happening elsewhere must have convinced Philby and his friends that their analysis of the international situation had been absolutely correct. After the Russians invaded Finland on 30 November 1939, to prevent the country's becoming an anti-Soviet base, the old delusion of 1918–20 – that one combined push, one last intervention, could topple the Bolsheviks from power – again started to affect Allied leaders. A campaign was begun to switch the war away from Germany and against Russia. Major Kermit Roosevelt, of the famous American family, who had offered his services to the British army on the outbreak of war, was relieved of his duties and promoted to colonel in command of a British volunteer brigade to fight against the Russians. Britain sent off arms to Finland and *The Sunday Times* suggested that the Baku oilfields on the Caspian Sea should be bombed. A British officer told Drew Middleton of the Associated Press: 'We'll all be marching against the Russians in the spring.'[5]

But in France, after rushing 158,000 men, 25,000 vehicles and 140,000 tons of stores to the Belgian border, the British did not so much as see the enemy for the next nine months. This was the time of the Phony War, the Great Bore War, the *drôle de guerre* or, as the Germans called it, the *Sitzkrieg*. The troops built pillboxes as a back-up for the famous Maginot Line – a series of underground fortresses, linked by tunnels, the whole said to be impregnable. (Philby referred to it in one piece of purple prose for *The Times* as 'The Mistress of the Great Divide'.) The correspondents, housed in the gloomy Hotel du Commerce at Arras, broke their hearts trying to find stories that were interesting and yet which would get past the censor – one dispatch from Philby which survives in the *Times* archives is so scored with blue pencil as to be almost unreadable. Poor Bernard ('Potato') Gray of the *Daily Mirror*, desperate for a story, wrote one day: 'An occasional shell removes the washing from the line.' The conducting officers pointed out that not a single gun had been fired, accused him of writing a mischievous lie, and 'sent him to Coventry'.

Another dispatch from Philby captures the picture perfectly:

> Only a narrow vista meets the eye from the turf-banked block-houses that form the British front. A damp heavy atmosphere, foreboding copious rain, obscures the further horizons. Towns and villages, built of brick and set closely together amid the endless fields, are stained by persistent smoke to a monotonous reddish-grey. 'La Belle France' seems far away. Comfortless skies follow one another in dreary procession . . . Many express disappointment at the slow tempo of the overture to Armageddon. They expected danger and they have found damp.[6]

The correspondents became increasingly desperate. Philby, Douglas Williams of the *Daily Telegraph* and Alan Moorehead of the *News Chronicle* set up a mess in a house owned by a French wine merchant and invited a group of high-ranking army officers to dinner. The idea was to ply them with the wine merchant's cellar until they broke down under the influence of fine claret and told all. The generals dined well, drank heartily, and said nothing.

Years later, looking back on it all from Moscow, Philby admitted that the correspondents had allowed the military to fool them into believing that the Germans had not attacked because they knew that the Maginot Line was impregnable.

> Only one of us, the late Webb Miller [of the United Press], far gone in drink, vouchsafed a hint of things to come. 'The Germans', he said, 'will go through that line like shit through a little tin horn' – prolix Americanese, no doubt, for a dose of salts. The rest of us were hugely surprised by the collapse of the front; perhaps Webb was too, when he sobered up.
>
> Of course, we were systematically misled by the military; but anyone who allows himself to be misled for eight solid months must take on himself a heavy slab of blame. During the bore war, I heard only two remarks which subsequent events were to bear out: one from the egregious Anthony Eden, then Secretary of State for War, the other from the Duke of Windsor. During an off-the-record press briefing at Arras, Eden remarked that 'it would be madness to risk an encounter battle with the Germans in Belgium'; which was exactly what we did.
>
> On the second occasion, I was having a lonely night-cap at the bar in Metz, round about Christmas, 1939, when the DOW [Duke of Windsor], presumably on the strength of my correspondent's shoulder straps, opened a conversation in which he said, *ipsissima verba*, 'if the Germans do attack, there'll be the very devil of a mess.'
>
> I doubt whether the military wittingly misled us on basic issues. At the time (after the fall of France) I thought that they must have, since no experts could have been so hopelessly wrong. But later I saw what were undoubtedly genuine and 'expert' British assessments of the Red Army's capacity to resist, which proved to be wholly ludicrous. So perhaps they really did believe in Arras that they were 'winning the war comfortably'.
>
> Luckily, apart from my censored despatches to *The Times*, I was able to transmit news to another quarter which was not in the least interested in the optimistic lucubrations of GHQ, only in the hard facts of military life: unit strengths and locations, gun calibres, tank performance, etc. But for that, my time at Arras would have been completely wasted.[7]

The Phony War ended on 10 May 1940. The Germans struck through Belgium, Holland and Luxembourg and events moved so fast that the correspondents could not keep up. Philby and a few others got briefly to Brussels, where they ordered a round of beer in a café opposite the main station. The waiter protested at their choice of brand – German. 'It's still good beer,' Philby said. Back in Arras, they were told to pack for the retreat to Amiens – the Germans were already in Brussels. 'Good job we drank some of that Munich beer in Brussels,' Philby said. 'Or the Germans would have got it all.'

In Amiens the correspondents had managed to get only an hour's sleep when they were awakened with the news that German tanks were on the outskirts of the town. They left in a hurry and by 18 May they were in Boulogne. At last they had a story to tell, but now they could not send it – all communication with London had broken down. Nor could they get to the front; GHQ had commandeered their cars. Philby suggested a game of golf at Le Touquet but that, too, turned out to be in German hands. On Tuesday, 21 May, they sailed for home.

It was typical of the complacency that reigned in Britain at that time that Philby had to spend hours on his return arguing with the accounts department at *The Times* over his luggage, which the army had left behind in the frenzied retreat from Amiens. As he rightly pointed out: 'I fear certain misapprehensions exist in London about the conditions of life [in France].' He attached a list of nineteen lost items with their values: 'Camel-hair overcoat (two years' wear), fifteen guineas; Dunhill pipe (two years old and all the better for it), one pound ten shillings; hat, one pound.' The total came to one hundred pounds sixteen shillings. Philby could not resist adding that he had judged the prices by consulting the Army and Navy stores catalogue. *The Times* paid up.

Three weeks later he was back in France. The humiliating evacuation of the BEF from Dunkirk had taken place but more British troops were being sent to help the French try to hold Paris. Philby was to represent *The Times* and the *Daily Telegraph*; Gray the *Daily Mirror*, the *Daily Herald*, the *People* and the *Sunday Pictorial*; and Evelyn Montague the *Manchester Guardian* and the *Daily Express*. They lasted four farcical days. The first they spent getting drunk in the NAAFI canteen at Cherbourg, the second driving to Le Mans, the third digesting the news that they had been ordered to return, and the fourth being bombed in Brest while they waited for the last boats to Britain. Back in London next day, Philby heard over the radio that France had surrendered.

Philby's Cambridge contemporary, Donald Maclean, had also been on the run from the Germans. While Philby had been in Spain, Maclean had been pursuing a very successful career in the Foreign Office. He came down in the summer of 1934 with a First in French and German, and in October started at Turquet's, a fashionable crammer's near the British Museum, known for its ability to get well-born young men through the Foreign Office examinations. Maclean did just well enough in the written papers to qualify for the interviews, where the examiners were impressed with his pleasant if staid personality and conventional views.

For Maclean, too, had by now cast off his Marxist shell. (When taxed about this by a communist friend, Maclean said: 'I've decided that my future lies with the oppressors rather than the oppressed.') Since we know that the volte-face of both Philby and Burgess came immediately after their recruitment to the Russian intelligence service, Maclean's conventional views as expressed to the Foreign Office examiners suggest that he had been recruited by the Russians late in 1934.

Of course, the examiners could easily have found out about Maclean's Marxist past; all they needed to do was to make a few inquiries at Cambridge. But it is unlikely that even if they had known it would have made any difference. Maclean would have denied his commitment, and the examiners would have believed him. They would have considered his communism a youthful aberration; Maclean was obviously of such malleable material that a few years in the service would produce the perfect diplomat.

And so it appeared to be. He served his probationary period in London to everyone's satisfaction and in 1938 received his first posting – to Paris, a 'Grade A' embassy. There he impressed the Ambassador and the Minister with his capacity for hard work and his regular, if reluctant, attendance at diplomatic corps parties. He was thought to be a 'high flyer', one of the few Foreign Office people capable of making a mark even in such a lowly position as third secretary. With his grey suit, tasteful tie, his typical 'English good looks' and a Turkish cigarette at his lips, he already gave the impression of Sir Donald Maclean, Ambassador to Washington.

What was 'Sir Donald' doing for the Russian intelligence service during this period? In 1967 The Sunday Times was able to find no evidence that he was doing anything. But since then, new information on what Maclean was able to learn in his job at the embassy, and of the importance this material would have had for Moscow at that time, strongly suggests that he was already 'active'. Robert Cecil, a Foreign Office official who knew Maclean and who met him in Paris in 1938, points out that Maclean saw as part of his duties copies of virtually all the embassy's correspondence.

The ambassador, Sir Eric Phipps, had previously been ambassador in Berlin, where he had been strongly anti-nazi. In Paris, however, he came to believe, correctly, that the French would not fight to the end. Concerned about Britain's ability to stand alone, he turned to appeasement as the answer. Phipps's assessment of the French will to resist Hitler, and the fact that such an important British diplomat favoured appeasement, would have greatly interested the Russian intelligence service. Maclean would also have had access to Anglo-French military plans to support Finland in her winter war against the Soviet Union and to attack the Soviet oil wells at Baku in order to cut supplies to the German forces.[8]

In his private life, Maclean, perhaps because of the pressure of his double role, was already discovering a taste for alcohol that was later to figure in his disintegration. He became an habitué of the Deux Magots and Café de Flore in St Germain, where he spent long evenings drinking and talking. Occasionally the drinking got out of hand and ended in wild disorder, but when two pretty American girls who lived in a small hotel next to the Flore were around, Maclean was on his best behaviour.

The girls were the Marling sisters, Melinda and Harriet, daughters of Francis Marling and Melinda Goodlett, who, after a divorce, married Hal Dunbar, a wealthy American businessman. In 1939, Melinda was spending a year in Paris taking a French literature course at the Sorbonne and Harriet had come to visit her. Maclean and a friend, Mark Culme-Seymour, picked them up one night in the Flore. It was soon obvious to all Maclean's friends that he was smitten with Melinda. They did their best to discourage him, arguing that Melinda was too American for an English diplomat's wife. She was also set on reforming Maclean, delivering long lectures on how to conduct his life. Maclean ignored them and pressed Melinda to marry him. Her letters home showed her ambivalence; on the one hand she was genuinely fond of him and liked the idea of marrying a diplomat from a titled family; on the other she had the feeling that he would be a difficult husband.

As the situation in Europe deteriorated, Mrs Dunbar began sending her daughters cables urging them to return to the United States. Harriet finally did so, but Melinda stayed on, and the Allied collapse in May 1940 catapulted her into marriage. When the British embassy packed up, Maclean got permission to remain in Paris for a few more days and proposed yet again. He told Melinda that if they did not get married there and then, she would have to go home to the United States and they might never see each other again. Still she hesitated, then on 10 June, with the sound of gunfire in the outer Paris suburbs, she said yes. They were married in the *Mairie* of the seventh *arrondissement* in the rue de Grenelle. They spent their

wedding night driving south, aiming for Bordeaux, where they hoped
Melinda might be able to get a boat for America, but the roads were
so choked with refugees that they stopped the car and slept in a field.
Even when they eventually reached Bordeaux, their troubles were
not over. There were no ships going to the United States, and those
going to Britain were full. Maclean's position as a diplomat got them
on a British destroyer, and on the afternoon of 23 June, two days
after France had surrendered, they sailed for England.

Philby soon found that there was not much work for a twenty-
eight-year-old war correspondent in Britain in the summer of 1940.
He wrote a couple of articles for *The Times* about the lessons to be
learnt from the débâcle in France and contemplated the fact that if he
did not quickly find some sort of job that exempted him from military
service then, as he had predicted to Alison Outhwaite, his colleague
on the *Review of Reviews*, he was going to end up in the trenches.

Meanwhile he made an effort to get his domestic affairs sorted
out. His separation from Litzi was now complete. After he went
to Spain she moved to Paris for a while and then had gone back
to Vienna to bring her parents to safety in London. Philby found
that she was living with Georg Honigmann, a German communist
refugee who had a job monitoring German broadcasts for the news
agency Extel. Although Philby thus had good grounds for a divorce
he made no move to obtain one, possibly because it might have
endangered Litzi's right to hold a British passport and her residence
status in Britain.

Although still married, he devoted himself to courting Aileen
Furse, the woman he had met through Flora Solomon. Aileen,
an attractive blonde, then aged twenty-nine, had left home and
taken a job on the advice of her family doctor. She had shown
signs of a self-destructive streak – her family said she sometimes
deliberately injured herself to gain attention when she felt she had
been neglected. But her career under Mrs Solomon appeared to
have helped her. Philby found that she had an open manner, an easy
laugh, and was a good companion. He treated her with sentimental
affection, talking to her about his adventures, listening to her stories
about her work – he often jokingly introduced her as 'Miss Marks
and Spencers'. They were obviously in love and soon they were living
together.

What this rather reserved woman from a sheltered family background thought of Philby's friends is hard to fathom. She met
most of them over the next months at 5 Bentinck Street, near

Harley Street, in a basement flat that hád belonged to Victor (now Lord) Rothschild. The flat housed an ever-changing set of young people whose common ground was that they were somehow connected with intelligence or security work. They included Teresa Mayor, who later married Rothschild and who at that time was his assistant in counter-sabotage work; Guy Liddell, Desmond Vesey and Anthony Blunt, all MI5 officers; two of Guy Burgess's friends, Peter Pollock and Jack Hewit, who did part-time intelligence work, and, of course, Burgess himself.

They weré a remarkable group – all very bright, hard-working, and dedicated to the war against Hitler. They sought relaxation from the tensions of the time in drink and in each other's company, yet they were security-conscious to a surprising degree – it was simply 'not done' to talk about the job once one entered the front door of Bentinck Street. True, they considered themselves a class apart, but then they were. Who else would have tolerated the drunken, aggressive, dirty, drug-taking Guy Burgess, seducer of sailors, lorry drivers and chorus boys, except the Bentinck Street clan who saw beyond his appalling façade into a brilliant and original intellect and the most loyal of hearts?

Burgess had had a chequered time since leaving Cambridge in the spring of 1935. For a while he had no job at all, despite all the strings he pulled to find one. Then his Trinity friend, Victor Rothschild, introduced Burgess to his mother, Mrs Charles Rothschild. She engaged Burgess at £100 a month to give her advice about her investments. This was a sum five times what his contemporaries were earning, and the effort needed to earn it was so slight it left him time for other enterprises.

He had a trial as a sub-editor on *The Times*, but the paper decided he was not quite right. He made three trips to Germany, once for the Berlin Olympics, once as leader of a group of pro-fascist schoolboys who wanted to see a Nuremberg Rally, and the third time as a member of a 'fact-finding group' that included an Archdeacon of the Church of England, a War Office official, and the eccentric Conservative MP, Captain Jack Macnamara. They decided that Hitler was doing wonders for Germany.

Finally, in October 1936, through his Apostle contacts, he managed to get an appointment to the Talks Department of the BBC, producing programmes on current affairs. Later he ran 'The Week in Westminster', which opened for him a wide range of contacts among MPs and gave him considerable status in political circles. He met Churchill, for instance, and Churchill gave him a copy of his speeches, *Arms and the Covenant*.

Slowly Burgess began to create an intelligence network that he used mainly to gather political gossip and tittle-tattle, but one which occasionally gave him a role in more important matters. French and Italian politicians who did not trust the British Foreign Office but who wanted to contact the Prime Minister, Neville Chamberlain, did so through channels to which Burgess had access. Burgess thus had confirmation of Maclean's information about the attitude of the French and was able to paint a depressing picture of the extent and influence of pro-German feeling in Britain. Burgess naturally passed whatever he could pick up in this way to his Soviet control, and, presumably on instructions from this control, Burgess established contact with the British Secret Service. At first he was a paid agent, and then, in January 1939, a short-contract staff officer, working in a new department to handle propaganda and subversion.

Burgess was virtually the founder of the Bentinck Street crowd, and was Philby's closest friend there. But Philby's friendship with Anthony Blunt, previously only a casual relationship, grew rapidly during this period. They had a lot in common. Blunt too, had been forced to flee from the Germans in France. He had offered his services to the army just before the outbreak of war but – such was the confusion at the time – he received two replies, one ordering him to report for duty to the Military Police, and the other rejecting him. Blunt ignored the rejection and went on a course for security intelligence officers. Despite a hiccup – he was hauled before the War Office to explain why he had written articles for left-wing magazines and why he had visited Russia – he finished the course and was posted to France. There he spent most of his spare time writing to friends in London asking them to try to get him a job in MI5 or SIS. Burgess put Blunt's name around the secret world and assured him that something would turn up. In the third week in May, behaving in his usual cool and languid manner, Blunt pushed his officer's car off the end of the jetty, and then got out of Boulogne just before the port fell to the Germans. Back in Britain, he soon found that Burgess was right: in August 1940 he was invited to join MI5.

One reason for Philby's growing friendship with Blunt could have been that he now knew that Blunt was also working for the Russians. In Moscow Philby told me how he learnt about this time that both Maclean and Blunt were Soviet agents. 'I had only met Maclean once in the mid-Thirties,' Philby said. 'I met him next when I got back from France. I'd lost my Paris contact and I needed one in Britain. I knew by then of Maclean's work [presumably his Paris contact was also Maclean's] so I got in touch with him and asked him to help me. I met him twice. The first time he was rightly cautious and merely made arrangements for a second meeting. Then he was able to help me. As for Blunt, he approached me one day early in 1941 and gave me a terrible fright by saying: "I know what you're doing. Well, I'm doing the same." For some reason he had lost touch and needed help to re-establish it. I checked out what he said and I was able to help him.'

We can see in these manoeuvrings that although there may not have been a Cambridge cell of spies as such, once these ex-Cambridge men had learnt of each other's commitment to Moscow, they certainly did their best to help each other. And we can detect, in the way this help was directed, the Russian intelligence service's master plan. It is clear that Philby was not Moscow's only candidate for the penetration of Britain's secret world. Burgess and Blunt had been given the same assignment – the vigour with which they applied themselves to getting into any section of either SIS or MI5, in whatever capacity, is evidence enough. And we can make an informed guess as to why the Russians were pushing three candidates. Once one was in, he could help the others gain entry. And once all were in, they could use their privileged positions to protect each other from exposure. As we have seen, Burgess was first to make the penetration. Once in, his recommendations then helped Blunt and Philby.

Before Burgess came to Philby's rescue, his main hope had been a job with the Government Code and Cypher School at Bletchley Park, centre of the wartime effort to crack Germany's military and diplomatic codes. This had fallen through because his sponsor there felt he could not offer him enough money. Philby was disappointed at the time – as was his Soviet control – but, as he told me in Moscow in 1988, the job would probably not have suited his temperament anyway. 'Those cryptanalysts lived in a world of their own. They were an eccentric, pernickety lot. My work in SIS often brought me in contact with them. One day one of them showed me a German message he had been working on. It was about a meeting to take place at the Brenner Pass between Mussolini and someone else. The cryptanalyst said the original message had the second person's name but he hadn't been able to get all the letters. All he had was "H-TL-R". He asked me if I had any ideas. Straight away I said: "Hitler. It's got to be Hitler." He looked at the message again and after a while he said: "Well, yes. But there's not a shred of cryptological evidence for such a conclusion. Not a shred." '

In July 1940 Philby had actually taken the medical for his call-up when, as Philby describes it, there were sudden developments. Captain Leslie Sheridan of the War Office telephoned *The Times* and asked if Philby was available for 'war work'. 'Soon afterwards I found myself in the forecourt of St Ermin's hotel, near St James's Park Station [and very close to SIS headquarters], talking to Miss Marjorie Maxse. She was an intensely likeable elderly lady (then almost as old as I am now). I had no idea then, as I have no idea now, what her precise position in government was. But she spoke with authority, and was evidently in a position at least to recommend me for "interesting" employment. At an early stage of our talk she turned the subject to the possibilities of political work against the Germans in Europe.

'For ten years I had taken a serious interest in international politics; I had wandered about Europe in a wide arc from Portugal to Greece; I had already formed some less than half-baked ideas on the subversion of the nazi regime. So I was reasonably well equipped to talk to Miss Maxse . . . I passed this first examination. As we parted Miss Maxse asked me to meet her again at the same place a few days later. At our second meeting she turned up accompanied by Guy Burgess, whom I knew well. I was put through my paces once again . . . Before we parted, Miss Maxse informed me that, if I agreed, I should sever my connection with *The Times* and report to Guy Burgess at an address in Caxton Street, in the same block as the St Ermin's hotel.'

Since he could hardly say that he was joining the Secret Service, Philby needed a cover story to tell *The Times* and quickly invented a plausible one – he was going to write up the official records of the BEF campaign in France. The next Monday Philby was in; one Russian intelligence agent had recommended another for employment in SIS and he had been accepted. Philby says that he learnt later that the only inquiry made about his background was the usual reference to MI5, which went through its card indexes and reported 'Nothing known against'. He says that this seemed so easy to him that when he told his Russian control and gave him his first reports of how SIS worked, the control wondered if Philby had perhaps joined the wrong organization.*

It was not quite as sloppy as this. SIS tended to recruit on the basis of recommendation from friends and relatives, believing that

---

*Malcolm Muggeridge thought much the same. 'I went in for an interview with SIS at Broadway headquarters. It seemed to me that the whole place was so absurd that it must be some kind of façade. I reasoned that this was where they tried you out and that when you passed they'd say, "Well, he's all right. Now we'll show him the real Secret Service." Then I found out that it was the real Secret Service.'[9]

the interlocking networks that ran Britain and the Empire knew as much about their members as any prying 'policeman' from MI5. Kim Philby's name had gone around 'the firm' before he was recruited, and it turned out that Colonel Valentine Vivian, deputy chief of the service, had served in India with St John Philby and therefore felt able to vouch for Kim: '[Philby] came to SIS from the "pool" [a list of potential recruits drawn up early in the war]. I was asked about him, and I said I knew his people.'*[10]

Philby must have had an anxious moment when, only a month after he had joined SIS, his father, the man whose reputation had helped ensure his job, was arrested in Karachi under the Defence of the Realm Act, Section 18b, as being a risk to the security of Britain. St John had been behaving in his usual unpredictable manner. In July 1939 he stood for Parliament in a by-election at Hythe, a safe Conservative seat, representing the British People's Party, an anti-war group which had strong overtones of fascism and anti-semitism. Although he attracted support from the Left and the Right he won only 576 votes and lost his deposit.

On the outbreak of war he tried to get into military intelligence as an Arabist attached to Ibn Saud, but someone else got the job. He then launched himself into a scheme to raise money for Ibn Saud from the Zionists; in return for £20 million, the Jews would be allowed to take over most of Western Palestine. There is some confusion over how much Ibn Saud knew of this scheme, because he later angrily described it as an attempt to bribe him, but the principle was certainly considered feasible by the Zionists. While waiting for this and other projects to mature, St John was peripherally involved with the publication of 'Stop the War' pamphlets, put out by the British Council for a Christian Settlement in Europe, an operation which attracted the attention of the police.

He returned to Arabia early in 1940 and told the King that the war was going badly – the Germans were sinking so much shipping that within eighteen months Britain would have to surrender. An outraged Stonehewer Bird, the British Minister, reported to London:

> [Philby's] attitude . . . is briefly as follows: the Allies should not
> have embarked on an unnecessary war, which is ruining Arabia
> and may ruin the world. They will not be defeated but they cannot

*This system failed over Philby, but there are those SIS officers who still say there is no evidence that so-called 'positive vetting' – an exhaustive investigation of a person's background, combined with probing interviews, carried out by an independent investigator, and repeated at intervals during the person's career – or the American use of lie detectors, is any better.

win, and will in time be obliged to conclude with Herr Hitler a patched up peace. The British news service is contemptible and figures for British shipping losses are deliberately falsified . . . It is highly improper, if not dangerous, for him to talk as he does in mixed company of Syrians, Indians, Iraquis, Egyptians and Americans.[11]

But St John was just warming to his theme. He told a French diplomat that Hitler was a great man and a mystic comparable to Christ and Mohammed. He said openly that the sooner the Germans took Paris the better because the war would then stop. At a party at the house of an oil company representative he described BBC broadcasts as 'contemptible rubbish', and, according to Bird, he told the King that he now wanted to go to India and the United States to conduct anti-British propaganda. When word of all this reached London the authorities decided to arrest Philby the moment he landed in India.

This happened, and the former ICS officer found himself being conveyed to a police station in Karachi, formally charged with having carried on activities prejudicial to the safety of the realm, and then shipped back to Liverpool. 'Those who tell the truth are traitors,' he complained in his diary. On arrival in Liverpool, he was held in Walton prison and then, in November, moved to the Mills Circus ground at Ascot. Philby's friends and former colleagues now began to agitate on his behalf, writing to say that although he was the sort of person who liked to be against the government of the day, he was not disloyal or unpatriotic.

Finally, in February 1941, St John appeared before an advisory committee of three: Sir Norman Birkett, a lawyer; Sir George Clerk, a diplomat; and Sir Arthur Hazelrigg, Lord Lieutenant at Leicester, to see whether his detention should continue. He knew all three, and spent most of the hearing giving them a lecture on what was wrong with British foreign policy, especially as regards the Middle East. As his son Kim told me in Moscow when talking of his father's appearance before this Star Chamber, 'He bored them into submission.' St John was released on 18 March, having been detained for seven months, and moved to Wales, where he spent most of the war working on a study of the pre-Islamic history of Arabia.

One view of Kim Philby is that he followed St John's example, like father like son, and turned his back on Britain in a similar manner. But, outspoken though St John was, there was never any evidence that he worked actively against his country. If he had been given a worthwhile job where his talents could have been put to good use, then there is every reason to believe he would have swung whole-heartedly behind the war effort.

The job Burgess had got for Kim Philby was in Section D of SIS (the 'D' standing for 'destruction'). His salary was £600 a year, and no nonsense about income tax. The aim of the section was to stir up resistance to the Germans in Europe by sabotage. The work consisted largely of sitting around at conferences discussing ways of interrupting the supply of Romanian oil to Germany, or considering plans to launch balloons over Central Europe in the hope that the incendiary bombs attached to them would set the grain fields on fire and cripple German food production. Section D was starved of funds, distrusted by other sections of SIS, and viewed with extreme suspicion in Whitehall. It was soon taken over by the newly created Special Operations Executive (SOE), set up in July 1940 to 'set Europe ablaze'. Given the exclusive responsibility for sabotage operations overseas, one of SOE's first moves was to take over Section D.

But by then Philby had already made his mark. At Burgess's suggestion he had written a paper outlining the creation of a school for training agents in the techniques of underground work. Out of this grew a large establishment based at Brickendonbury Hall near Hertford, where a staff that included such famous secret agents as George Hill, who had worked against the Bolsheviks during the Russian Revolution, taught groups of men and women from the countries of Occupied Europe the skills of sabotage and subversion. When SOE took Section D over, Burgess was sent packing. Tommy Harris, the art dealer Philby first met at Brickendonbury and who was to become a close friend, found a job with MI5. But Philby was kept on by SOE and made an instructor at the agents' school at Beaulieu in Hampshire. He did the agents' course himself and performed so well that he was briefly considered for service in France, but his French was not quite good enough. Instead he taught a course in underground propaganda.

Philby was good at it. To prepare himself for the job he consulted Richard Crossman (later a Labour minister) and Sefton Delmer (a well-known newspaper correspondent), who were working in a 'black propaganda' outfit at Woburn Abbey. 'At Beaulieu [Philby] developed the notion of the "subversive rumour" which, he insisted, should be both concrete and plausible. It was his idea, for example, to feed to the enemy the alarming information that French girls suffering from VD were being *encouraged* to go to bed with German soldiers – in contrast with the commonly held view that savage head-shaving was the penalty inflicted for such fraternization.'[12] The alarm and despondency this caused in the German army can well be imagined when we recall that in those days some types of VD took three painful years to cure.

Philby soon showed the ingenuity that was to distinguish his spying career. He argued that it was useless to teach SOE agents merely the methods of disseminating political propaganda; the content of that propaganda was equally important. If the SOE field agent was to inspire people under the nazi heel to risk their lives, then the propaganda he put out would have to offer them some hope for a better future. So Philby got permission to seek political guidance on Britain's views of Europe after victory. He turned to Hugh Gaitskell, later leader of the Labour Party, but at that time principal private secretary to Hugh Dalton, the Minister for Economic Warfare, who was also responsible for SOE. Gaitskell had met Philby in Vienna and, now, anxious to help, he took Philby back to his office to consult Dalton himself.

In this way, Philby, ostensibly a humble SOE instructor, learnt that the British government's view of postwar Europe was a simple return to the pre-Hitler status quo, with a reinstatement of those governments which had shown themselves to be reliable in maintaining the cordon sanitaire against the Soviet Union. This was very important information for the Russian intelligence service because it meant that, although Britain might be willing now to support communist resistance movements in Europe if they were more effective than others in fighting the Germans, it would turn against them if they looked like becoming the postwar rulers. This knowledge coloured relations between communist resistance movements and London throughout the war.

Important though this was, Philby remained impatient. He was on the periphery of the real intelligence world. His elation at joining SIS had faded as he was pushed further away from his goal. For once Burgess had no inside influence and could not help him this time, but his newly found friend Tommy Harris did. Harris, half Spanish and half English, had been a fine artist in his youth but had given up painting for dealing. He and his wife Hilda ran the Spanish Art Galleries, and had a magnificent house called Garden Lodge in Logan Place, just off the Earls Court Road. Both were brilliant cooks, they entertained lavishly and during the war Harris's house became a sort of drinking club for off-duty MI5 and SIS officers. (It differed from Bentinck Street in that it was usually a male enclave.)

As Philby recalled in Moscow, 'Tommy was an amazingly generous fellow. He'd already made a lot of money buying cheap from English country houses and selling dear and he liked to entertain a lot. So we had a little drinking circle at his place . . . You'd drop in to see who was around. Tommy, as the host, was there most of the time. The others came and went. The regulars were me, Burgess, Blunt and perhaps Aneurin Bevan. Victor Rothschild dropped in from time to time but he wasn't one of the regulars.'

Another occasional guest was a thin, retiring man who always looked ill, as indeed he was. This was Dick Brooman-White,* Harris's boss, then head of MI5's Iberian section, which defended Britain against any spies who might come from neutral Spain or Portugal. In July 1941, Harris told Philby that he had heard from Brooman-White that there might be a job going in SIS that would suit him. It was in Section Five, the counter-espionage department. The actual work involved SIS's own Iberian sub-section, which was supposed to provide MI5 with advance information of espionage operations originating in Spain and Portugal. The theory – that SIS would identify spies and their mission before they reached Britain and MI5 would catch them when they arrived – had broken down in accusation and acrimony. SIS had been forced to expand its Iberian sub-section, Harris said, and was on the lookout for someone with knowledge of Franco's Spain. This Philby certainly had, so if he was interested, Harris said, he would mention his name to Brooman-White.

The extent to which recruitment to the secret services in those days went on recommendation can be seen in what happened next. Harris recommended Philby to Brooman-White, who in turn recommended him to Dick White, then a senior officer of MI5 who had close relations with SIS. White then recommended Philby to the head of Section Five, Major (later Colonel) Felix Cowgill, a former officer in the Indian Police. Cowgill approved of Philby but first had to recommend him for the job to Valentine Vivian, because, as well as being deputy chief, Vivian had special responsibilities for counter-espionage.

Vivian, who had already passed Philby as suitable for the defunct Section D, thought he had better have another look at him, so he invited St John, just out of detention, and Kim to lunch. As he later told Patrick Seale of *The Observer*, 'When Kim went out to the lavatory, I asked St John about him. "He was a bit of a communist at Cambridge, wasn't he," I enquired. "Oh, that was all

---

*Not to be confused with Sir Dick White, head of MI5 (1953–6) and SIS (1956–68).

schoolboy nonsense," St John replied. "He's a reformed character now." ' Vivian accepted St John's assessment of Kim's political past and told Cowgill to go ahead and engage him.

So in a remarkably short time – it was just seven years since Philby had been given his assignment to penetrate SIS – he had made it. He was now a fully fledged SIS officer in a department where the very nature of the work – counter-espionage – opened the door to virtually all the service's secrets.

THIS IS THE
SECRET SERVICE?
7

The idea of a permanent secret service as part of the bureaucracy of a country is a comparatively recent one. The CIA came into existence only in 1947; Britain's SIS, from which the others sprang, dates from 1909. Before that, major powers got by with small military intelligence departments that were expanded during a war and starved for funds the rest of the time – in the early years of this century Britain's MO5 (military operations counter-intelligence), the spy-catching organization, was run by one man and two assistants, who were allowed to spend the ludicrously inadequate sum of £200 a year.

Then about 1905 a wave of anti-German hysteria began. Germany was intent on invading Britain, it was said, and she was about to embark on a campaign of sabotage and subversion. So every German in Britain was a potential spy and saboteur. The extent of this xenophobia can be gauged from the fact that a letter sent to the *Morning Post* by a J.M. Heath, warning of this danger, was taken seriously in Whitehall. Heath claimed that there were 90,000 German reservists in Britain, caches of arms and uniforms concealed in warehouses and bank vaults, and plans to sabotage railways and telegraph lines on the first day of any war.

A military intelligence officer clipped this from the newspaper and sent it to his superior officer, Colonel A.E.W. Gleichen, with a note saying: 'There is much truth in some of this, as you know. I heard last night of a German who has been seen constantly about the country between Brentwood and the River Thames at Tilbury, sketching and photographing. No one knows who he is or where he lodges. I can perhaps get more details but what's the use?' Gleichen, in turn, forwarded the note to the counter-intelligence department, asking testily: 'Is there no law under which these objectionable aliens can be got rid of?'

One of the main sources of this irrational fear of German spies can be traced directly to the larger-than-life William Tufnell Le Queux, Queen Alexandra's favourite thriller writer. Le Queux (pronounced Kew), who assumed that his readers had a mean mental age of twelve, had published his first novel in 1890, and then produced an average of five a year until his death in 1927. His most successful, *The Invasion of 1910*, was published in 1906 and given enormous advance publicity by Lord Northcliffe's *Daily Mail*. It expressed in fictional form one of Le Queux's private nightmares – that Britain was riddled with Germans waiting for the day when the Kaiser would invade. Its instant appeal – it sold more than a million copies and was translated into twenty-seven languages – made Le Queux realize that he was on to a winner, and other books on the German spy theme quickly followed.

His triumph was to use the techniques of popular journalism to add spurious authenticity to his books: 'As I write I have before me a file of amazing documents which plainly show the feverish activity with which this advance guard of our enemy is working to secure for their employers the most detailed information.'[1]

Readers of Le Queux's ravings about the German menace began to see spies in every German barber, waiter, hotel keeper and tourist in the country. They reported them to the police, or sent the details to Le Queux himself, who, failing to discern the mirror image of his own fictional plots, passed them in triumph to the British authorities. By now he was so obsessed with his fantasies that he began to drive around the country on spy hunts, trying to track down mysterious lights, following German tourists, and travelling to Europe to meet his contacts who, he said, had penetrated the German High Command.

At first the British authorities tried to ignore him, writing him off as an annoying fanatic. Soon Le Queux believed he had discovered the reason. At a meeting in the Dolder Hotel in Zurich with a renegade German spy he referred to only as Herr N—, Le Queux reported that he was handed a list of British traitors, members of a secret organization called the Hidden Hand, who were working for Germany. 'I was aghast at the sight of this list. I sat staggered. It was appalling that persons whom the nation considered highly patriotic and upright . . . should have fallen into the insidious tentacles of the great German octopus.'

The list, Le Queux said, included members of Parliament, two well-known writers, and officials of the Foreign office, Home Office, India Office, Admiralty and War Office. Le Queux put all these fairy stories into his next book, *Spies of the Kaiser*, published early in 1909. It was an instant bestseller and it soon became clear that its thousands of readers considered it – reasonably enough, in view of Le Queux's ambiguous presentation of the book as fact in fiction form – as being totally true.

Spy fever now swept the country. Amateur spy hunters set out to locate the five thousand German agents who, Le Queux wrote, were 'working in our midst on behalf of the Intelligence Department in Berlin'. Normally level-headed ministers and their civil servants became alarmed and this alarm was a major factor in the government's decision to set up a sub-committee of the Committee of Imperial Defence to consider the question of foreign espionage in Great Britain.

As a result of the sub-committee's recommendations, the government decided to establish a Secret Service Bureau, with a home department to protect British secrets from the Germans, and a foreign department to steal German secrets. These were the forerunners of today's MI5 and SIS, and the models on which many other countries' secret services were based.

Yet the German spy scare was entirely without foundation. On the outbreak of war in 1914, the British authorities arrested twenty-one Germans suspected of being spies: only one was brought to trial. So why was Le Queux believed? His stories – like those of Erskine Childers before him and John Buchan after him – had a basic plot which is almost as ancient as man himself: the overcoming of the monster. The story of how the hero alone recognizes the danger the monster poses to the tribe, how he prepares for the confrontation, how he divines the monster's secret and eventually kills it, has been told for centuries in all civilizations as a harmless allegory for man's struggle against evil.

Le Queux, obviously a disturbed personality, created a real monster, Imperial Germany. The authorities, while rejecting Le Queux himself, soon realized what a powerful and useful nationalistic force he had discovered and used it for their own ends. As the First Sea Lord, 'Jackie' Fisher, one of the few who kept his head over the German menace, put it, the swarm of spies released in 1909 'served the double purpose of supplying false information to subserve expansion of armaments, and of increasing the ill-feeling which had already been worked up between England and Germany'. It was in this atmosphere of fantasy and xenophobia that the British Secret Intelligence Service had its origins.

The first chief, or 'C', of MI-1c, as SIS was called until the 1920s, was Captain Mansfield Smith-Cumming, an eccentric even by the standards of the Royal Navy. He wore a gold-rimmed monocle, wrote only in green ink, and after he lost part of his leg in an accident, used to get around the corridors of power on a child's scooter. He considered intelligence work a game for adults, played for fun, with points awarded for style rather than results. When he was trying to persuade the author Compton Mackenzie to stay on in the service he told him: 'Here, take this swordstick. I always took it with me on spying expeditions before the war. That's when this business was really amusing. After the war is over we'll do some amusing secret service work together. It's capital sport.'

Since the government wanted to deny all knowledge of SIS – it does not officially exist even today – Cumming's offices could not be in the War Office. Instead SIS occupied one part of Whitehall Court where Cumming had a small flat in the east turret. One of his staff has described what it was like. 'To approach Cumming's office it was necessary for a visitor to climb a staircase and wait while the secretary pressed a secret bell, whereupon Cumming would operate a system of levers and pedals which moved a pile of bricks revealing more steps.' In the office itself a row of half a dozen telephones stood at the left of a big desk littered with papers. Another table had maps, and drawings and models of ships and submarines. 'This atmosphere of strangeness and mystery was rather destroyed by the fact that Cumming's secretary kept on coming up through a hole in the floor.'[2]

Cumming's problem – one which still besets the intelligence world – was that the sort of man likely to be attracted to espionage often did not have the character to resist the many temptations it offered. One of these was for the agent to invent intelligence in order to justify his own existence. Another was to misuse the large sums of money an agent could command. One SIS man in Hungary staged a suicide and went off to the United States under another name with all the service's cash he could lay his hands on. Another, asked to explain what he had done with £28,000 sent to him to pay his agents, simply shot himself. An army intelligence officer, Captain Sigismund Payne Best, wrote: 'C always employed scoundrels, and his people were always ready to do the dirty on me.'[3]

The outbreak of war in 1914 was welcomed by the Secret Service Bureau because it gave it the first real chance to prove itself. Cumming set up a large organization in Holland, a country which was neutral. It employed more than 300 people who recruited agents and sent them into Germany, sought out neutral war correspondents passing through Holland and tried to get them to work for Britain, and debriefed German deserters who had fled across the border into Holland. SIS also infiltrated its men into the internment camps in which the Dutch authorities held German deserters. Here they mixed with the Germans and tried to draw military information from them.

Germany was, of course, up to the same sort of tricks and this brought to the fore a series of moral propositions that relate to the State's attitude to spying, propositions that remain relevant today. Some of these were arbitrary and hypocritical. Thus German spies caught during the war were considered to deserve the death penalty, but were admired as patriots, while neutral spies or 'traitor' spies were considered beneath contempt but usually escaped capital punishment. An American convicted of spying for Germany drew attention in one of his petitions for his release to inconsistencies in Britain's attitude: 'Espionage for England is a commendable deed, but espionage for Germany is a crime; an English spy is a man of honour, a German spy is a felon.'[4]

At the end of the war both sides took stock. A former MI5 officer admitted: 'None of the German spies in Britain ever picked up much that could not have been read in our newspapers, most of which went to Holland and so found their way into German hands.'[5] And Brigadier-General W.H.H. Waters, a British military attaché of wide and long experience, wrote: 'My view always was – and experience has only tended to confirm it – that the results of secret service are usually negligible.'[6]

So the end of the war found British intelligence in a crisis: the service chiefs were not impressed with what SIS had brought them and the government had yet to be convinced that the growing expense of maintaining a full-time intelligence organization was justified in peacetime. In the drive for economy, the intelligence service was a natural target. SIS and MI5 had both been under War Office control. SIS was now hived off to the Foreign Office, as were the code-breakers, previously part of the navy, who were deliberately misnamed the Government Code and Cypher School (GC and CS). The navy continued to pay for the code-breakers but the Treasury slashed SIS's budget in 1919 from £240,000 a year to £125,000, and MI5's from £80,000 to £35,000.

Fortunately, rescue was close at hand. The most durable monster the Western intelligence world has ever faced had surfaced in Moscow. Admiral 'Blinker' Hall, head of British naval intelligence, was probably the first to draw attention to it. 'I want to give you a word of warning,' he told his colleagues at the end of the war. 'Hard and bitter as the battle has been, we now have to face a far more ruthless foe. A foe that is hydra-headed and whose evil power will spread over the whole world. That foe is Soviet Russia.'[7] Intelligence agencies should erect a monument to Hall: he identified a weakness in the justification SIS had put forward for its existence and, in one brilliant stroke, eliminated it. SIS had come into being by promising to provide timely warning of a menace to Britain's security. That menace had been Imperial Germany. But it suffered from one major drawback for the part of the out-and-out villain: it was a Christian country that bore too close a likeness to the hero to be portrayed as irremediably evil.

But communist Russia was, on its own admission, godless, a murderer of princesses, and bent on world domination. John Buchan quickly saw the trend. His *Huntingtower*, published in 1922, was the first anti-communist thriller; ever since, fictional KGB agents have continued to meet their match at the hands of Her Majesty's Secret Service or the CIA – except, that is, in Soviet fiction, where it is the other way round. Communism was a godsend to SIS. It was here, there and everywhere. It was as much a threat in peace as in war, and it was capable of corrupting the hero's own kith and kin. Therefore, it was not only necessary to discover the other side's secrets but to protect your own from disciples of communism, one of whom could well be the colleague beside you.

So throughout the 1920s and early 1930s, until the rise of Hitler showed that the threat to Britain could come from the extreme Right as well as the extreme Left, the communists became SIS's main preoccupation. It devoted the largest single part of its budget to Russia – in 1920 it spent £20,000 on agents in Helsinki to cover North Russia alone; this should be compared with the £2,000 it spent in Berlin. It sent its best officers – fluent Russian-speakers with long experience of the country and its people, capable of passing as Soviet citizens – to Moscow and Petrograd with virtually a free hand to establish networks of agents, finance counter-revolutionaries, and to do all in their power to crush the communist menace in its infancy.

They nearly succeeded. Sidney Reilly, George Hill, Paul Dukes and Robert Bruce Lockhart (the British 'agent' in Moscow who became deeply involved in SIS plots) came so close to toppling the communist regime as to instil in its leaders a fear of SIS conspiracies that still exists today. Reilly, a flamboyant Russian-born arms dealer, organized what has become known as the Lettish plot (although the Russians call it 'the Lockhart conspiracy'). This called for an uprising of the troops from the Baltic province of Latvia, the Letts, who acted as bodyguards for the communist leaders. The Letts were to seize Lenin and Trotsky, and then Reilly and his followers were to establish a provisional anti-communist government. There was a sub-plot which required a fanatical socialist, Dora Kaplan, to shoot Lenin if the opportunity arose. It did, but Dora Kaplan shot too soon, and Lenin was not killed, only seriously wounded; the Letts had been penetrated by agents loyal to the communists, and the whole plot fell apart.*

But in assessing how a handful of determined SIS officers had got so far with their subversion, Felix Dzerzhinsky, a Pole who was head of the Cheka, the forerunner of the KGB, must have been impressed with the fact that these British spies had not only been able to lose themselves among the Russian population but that two of them, Reilly and Dukes, had masqueraded at various times as Cheka agents. Foreigners, it seemed, had penetrated the very organization which was supposed to be the guardian of communist purity. How should the Cheka respond? How could it learn of Britain's plans? How could it identify and neutralize British spies before they became a danger to the Soviet Union?

The obvious answer was to penetrate SIS, but here the Russians were under a serious handicap. Reilly had been able to operate in Russia because he was a Russian. Dukes and Hill could pass as Russians, any shortcoming in their accent or mannerisms being easily overlooked in a country of such diverse nationalities. But for a Russian agent, Britain posed a different challenge. No Cheka officer would ever be able to master English mannerisms or acquire the necessary English background to pass as the sort of Englishman who would be approached to join SIS.

However, there was an alternative. Although Reilly was Russian he had committed himself ideologically to Britain and had worked against the country of his birth. Could the Russians find an Englishman who would commit himself ideologically to communism and work for the Russian intelligence service against Britain? The idea was certainly feasible. Three Frenchmen had thrown in their lot with the Russian Revolution and even Robert Bruce Lockhart had considered staying on in Russia, where the Cheka had offered him 'interesting work'. It was at this moment that the long-term plan for the Soviet penetration of Western intelligence began.

---

*Reilly fled to Britain, where he continued to work for SIS on anti-communist operations. He entered the Soviet Union on one such mission in 1925 and was never heard of again.

The plan had to be long-term because of the difficulty in finding the right man. Lockhart had been influenced by the drama of the Revolution and had realized that it was 'a cataclysm which would shake the world to its foundations'. But Lockhart was exceptional in that he had had personal experience of the Revolution. In 1918 there were no likely ideological recruits for the Cheka in Britain or the United States because few people there understood what the Revolution was all about or what communists stood for.

But in five years' time, or ten, would there be a young man in the West so moved by social injustice, or Marxist theory, or both, that he would be prepared to take the enormous step of committing himself to the Russian intelligence service for life, and to working against the country of his birth? The Cheka, with the patience that has since distinguished the Soviet intelligence apparatus, believed that there would be such men, and it was proved right. Philby, Burgess and Blunt were all recruited for the specific purpose of penetrating the British intelligence establishment and Philby, as we shall see, was stunningly successful.

All organizations develop a character of their own and that of SIS in the interwar years was formed largely by 'the Indians'. Britain had always believed that Russia posed a threat to India, and the arrival in power of the communists strengthened this belief – they planned, said SIS, to bring revolution to the sub-continent by exploiting nationalist and religious sentiment. British rule in India was certainly vulnerable. She controlled the country by a feat of political legerdemain; a few thousand sahibs kept in check several hundred million Indians. They did this by quickly identifying and neutralizing subversive elements, the task of the Indian Intelligence Bureau (IB), a highly efficient organization that had a network of spies and informers throughout the country.

The IB suspected the presence of two powerful communist networks in India, one associated with the Indian nationalist trained in Tashkent, M.N. Roy, and run by him from Moscow and Berlin; and the other operated in India itself by one 'Comrade Gamper or Hamper' and controlled from the Far East, probably from Shanghai. There were also Russian agents active on the North-West Frontier, financed from Afghanistan. I have been able to find no evidence that such networks ever actually existed, or, if they did, that they ever posed a real threat, but there is no doubt that the IB considered that Soviet subversion was everywhere and that they passed this attitude on to their colleagues in Britain.

For SIS and MI5 not only received regular reports from the IB, they were also keen to employ IB officers when they returned to Britain, relatively early in life, still active and looking for work – hence the group in the services known as 'the Indians'. The highest-ranking recruit, something of a triumph for 'the Indians', was Sir David Petrie, head of the IB from 1924 to 1931, who began a second career in intelligence by becoming director general of MI5 in 1940.

The Indian faction in the British services produced two reactions. One was to reinforce a belief in the Red menace and the extent of its tentacles. The other was to exacerbate the British tradition of 'closed' government, as typified by the obsession with secrecy that had marked SIS since its founding. For the IB men brought with them the habit of never discussing work in front of the natives or any outsider. And although there were no longer any natives around to listen – if they had ever bothered to do so – Indian habits were not easy to discard and in Britain 'the Indians' continued to distrust anyone they did not know personally.

SIS's concentration on the communist threat warped its recruiting policy and perpetuated its inefficiency. In the 1930s, the national political sentiment was vaguely leftist, and the universities were full of men with radical ideas, so no one could be recruited there. SIS had to be recruited against the trend by seeking out men whose hearts were in the preservation of empire, the maintenance of the ruling class and the protection of privilege and inherited wealth. Their bias against intellectuals and radicals knew no bounds.

A recruit who joined SIS after the outbreak of war tells an anecdote to illustrate the absurd measures still being taken even then to 'keep out the lefties'. He learnt that Edwin Muir, the poet, was working in the Food Office at Dundee, Scotland, so he mentioned to a colleague that Muir might be a good man to recruit. The colleague replied: 'He's been thought of but he's been turned down on political grounds. He's a communist.' When the recruit protested that this could not be true, his colleague replied: 'Oh, well, he may not exactly be a communist, but he's rather suspect, you know. He's the kind of person who's been kind to refugees, so he wouldn't be suitable here.'[8]

The historian Lord Dacre (Hugh Trevor-Roper), who joined SIS in the war, was appalled by the quality of the prewar recruits:

It seemed to me that the professionals were by and large pretty stupid and some of them very stupid. They formed two social classes: the London end which consisted of elegant young men from the upper classes who were recruited on the basis of trust, within a social class. It is said that they were recruited in Boodle's and White's. I believe this to be basically true . . . Then there were the Indian policemen . . . They were of quite extraordinary stupidity in my opinion. They were socially distinct from the club men. They didn't move in the White's Club Boodle's world. They were rather looked down upon.[9]

In Moscow I discussed this with Kim Philby, and something he said confirmed that the club to which an officer belonged played a major role in the divisions within SIS. I had asked Philby what he thought of the wartime head of SIS, General Sir Stewart Menzies. Philby replied: 'I didn't respect him as an intelligence officer. He had primitive ideas about intelligence. But I liked him as a man. Of course, we were in different sets. I was Athenaeum. He was White's and Cavalry.'

Leslie Nicholson, the SIS man in Prague and later in Riga, described to me what it was like working with such people as an officer in the field. He had been recruited in 1930 from the intelligence section of the British Army of Occupation in Wiesbaden, given a three-week course in communications, codes and cyphers, and SIS accounting practices, and sent off to meet the station chief in Vienna before taking up his posting. Talking with this man, 'one of the most experienced operators in the business', Nicholson ventured to ask him: 'Look here. Can you give me a few practical hints?' Our man in Vienna looked nonplussed and then replied: 'I don't think there are any, really. You'll just have to work it out for yourself.'

When he was later transferred to Riga, Nicholson discovered the perils of paying for information.

[The agents] used to take morning coffee together at a café near the stock exchange. They'd discuss the business among themselves, very much like the brokers on the other side of the street. They traded tit-bits of information and would sell their services to the highest bidder and then, later, with no compunction, pass the same information to the opposition, usually at a higher price. But all the intelligence officers used them, even if only to plant false information on each other for our own purposes.[10]

Small wonder that the main weakness of SIS was that it had no system for seriously assessing the reliability of the intelligence gathered by officers like Nicholson. And the reason it had no such system was that to have done so would have involved discussing sources of information, a breach of the service's rules on security. Thus not only did SIS resolutely refuse to tell its consuming departments in Britain anything about its sources, but even the discussion of sources within the organization was discouraged. One cannot escape the conclusion that one of the reasons for this attitude was the suspicion that it would put the entire shaky edifice at risk, that stripped of its secrecy SIS would stand revealed as an enormous bluff which allowed overgrown boys to enjoy some fine sport.

Presiding over this inefficient and incestuous organization as the Second World War approached was Admiral Hugh Sinclair, who had taken over when Cumming died in 1923. Sinclair, a short stocky figure with a single good eye and a friendly if vague smile, left operational matters to three senior officers – Stewart Menzies, Claude Dansey, and Valentine Vivian. The service which Kim Philby penetrated was largely their service. Of the three, Menzies was the most important because he was Sinclair's deputy, and when Sinclair died on 4 November 1939, Menzies succeeded him.

Menzies, then forty-nine, was a regular soldier who had served with distinction in the First World War, winning the DSO and the MC. There was a widespread belief in the services that Menzies was the illegitimate son of Edward VII. He was certainly closely connected with the Court through his mother, Lady Holford, who was lady-in-waiting to Queen Mary. He married three times – once to an earl's daughter, once to a baron's grand-daughter, and once to a baronet's daughter who had been married to the son of a viscount. He was a Grand Officer of the Legion of Honour, a Grand Officer of the Order of Leopold, Crown of Belgium; a member of the Legion of Merit (USA), a Grand Officer of the Order of Orange Nassau (Holland), a member of the Order of Polonia Restituta (Poland) and a Commander of St Olaf (Norway).

A man of such impeccable upper-class British background naturally had considerable influence in important government circles, and, as a 'ruthless intriguer', used it shamelessly. He had no great intellect – one of his political masters described him as 'not quite illiterate' – but he had charm, many friends, and a great natural facility for surviving. Like Sinclair, he left the day-to-day running of SIS to his subordinates and devoted his time to maintaining his service's position in Whitehall. This annoyed ministers who had to deal with him. One said: 'Whenever I ask Stewart about something on the telephone, he invariably says he must check and ring me back.

I have ninety-nine business interests but I have the details of them all at my fingertips.'[11]

But Menzies had two essential qualifications for a British secret service chief – he ran his outfit on pennies and he inspired a feeling in his political masters that he was never likely to do anything really silly. In personal relationships he was polite, but never warm. He loved horses and racing, drank heavily, and was happiest in his clubs among his peers. Philby described him to me in Moscow as 'an officer without any sophisticated ideas about intelligence but very likeable as a man'.

When Menzies became 'C' he appointed Dansey as his vice-chief, in charge of intelligence gathering, and Vivian as his deputy chief in charge of counter-intelligence. Dansey, 'a man who thinks nine ways at once', was a former soldier, country club proprietor and then MI5 officer. Rugged, hefty, blunt in manner and with few scruples, he had joined SIS only to fall out with his then chief, Sinclair, allegedly over some financial mismanagement. Sinclair, unable to stand the sight of Dansey in the office, got rid of him by allowing him to go out and create a new ring of spies in Europe, the 'Z' network, a sort of parallel organization to SIS, run by amateurs, mostly businessmen and journalists, who reported to Dansey in a small office in Bush House, Aldwych. The idea was that if anything happened to the regular SIS network, the 'Z' officers would be in place to take over. Although some of Dansey's agents submitted expenses for running non-existent sub-agents and pocketed the money, Dansey did nothing about it. He preferred a rogue to an intellectual any day, and was fond of saying: 'I would never willingly employ a university man.'

Vivian, known as 'Vee-vee' to his colleagues, was a tall elegant man with crinkled hair and a monocle. His years in the IB scarcely fitted him for the much more complex tasks he faced in SIS. He was handicapped in his office feuds with Dansey – the two hated each other – because of his modest background (he was the son of a portrait painter) and the fact that he depended on his service pay, having no independent means. In fairness, he was among the first in SIS to realize that the war would provide a challenge the service was in no state to meet, and that the first step should be the recruitment of a more sophisticated staff. It seems clear that he was responsible for the influx of academics, journalists and writers that occurred soon after the outbreak of war.

One of the academics, Hugh Trevor-Roper, was horrified at what he had joined:

When I looked coolly at the world in which I found myself, I sometimes thought that, if this was our intelligence system, we were doomed to defeat. Sometimes I encouraged myself by saying that such an organisation could not possibly survive, unchanged, the strain of war; it would have to be reformed. In fact, I was wrong both times. We won the war; and SIS, at the end of it, remained totally unreformed.[12]

The series of setbacks that shook SIS in the first months of the war certainly made Trevor-Roper's fear of defeat seem entirely justified. It was a period of almost unrelieved disaster. The German blitzkrieg of May 1940 virtually closed down SIS's European network. It had already lost Czechoslovakia, Austria and Poland; now Norway, Denmark, Holland, Belgium and France followed. To rub in the humiliation, Himmler, the head of the Gestapo, made a public speech, the text of which was kept secret even within SIS, naming all the senior officers of SIS from 'C' downwards.

This loss of its European network was regarded as a terrible blow at the time, but Trevor-Roper thinks it was all for the good. 'We would have [been] drawing information from a lot of rotten spies on the continent who would have then been controlled by the Germans . . . The leaders of SIS, being of remarkable stupidity, would have accepted it . . . and would have presented it as hard information and it would have got mixed up with real information and I think it would have done nothing but harm.'[13]

Then the collapse of France highlighted SIS's grossly inaccurate assessment of French fighting strength and French morale. SIS had accepted a French Deuxième Bureau argument that the answer to blitzkrieg tactics was the Maginot Line, which would present a major obstacle to the German motorized forces. The view was circulated to consumers in London as an SIS assessment, and not attributed to the French, so when it proved badly wrong, SIS had to accept the blame.

As for French morale, the question is whether SIS did not know, or whether it knew but failed to tell its consumers. At least one SIS officer told Menzies that France would make a quick, separate peace with Germany, either before a major military clash or immediately after it. 'I suspect that [Menzies] did not tell Churchill because he knew it was not what Churchill wanted to hear and Menzies needed to keep Churchill's favour.'[14]

So in summer of 1940 SIS found itself in deep trouble. It was scorned by the services, which were busy expanding their own intelligence departments, and attacked by the Joint Intelligence Committee, which had been set up in 1936 to coordinate intelligence gathering operations and to assess and distribute the results. The committee even discussed in June a proposal to split SIS among the three services, and it required all Menzies's skill at Whitehall in-fighting to prevent this from happening. Again, in November that year, SIS came under threat, this time from Churchill himself. He asked the Chiefs of Staff to report to him on the feasibility of shutting down SIS and replacing it with a new inter-services intelligence group which would come under the Chiefs of Staff themselves.

SIS was saved by GC and CS, at Bletchley Park, fifty miles from London, where a hastily recruited team of academics, intellectuals, mathematicians, linguists, technicians and support staff produced 'Ultra', the code name given to information gathered through deciphering German signal traffic produced by the radio encyphering machine known as Enigma. Polish intelligence had presented the British with a version of this machine in 1939, and the existence of Ultra was one of the best-kept secrets (at any rate from the Germans and the British themselves) of the Second World War. Briefly, Ultra originated in the following manner. Wireless operators would tune in to the frequencies used by the German services and take down all they overheard. This raw material, which the Germans had put into a supposedly unbreakable code with their Enigma machines, would be relayed to Bletchley, where the cryptographers would do their best to break the code. The results would be translated, and intelligence officers would then take over and try to interpret the messages and assess their importance. They would then pass on the final product, Ultra, to the services. Bletchley Park glowed white-hot with talent and Ultra, at its best, really was 'like reading the enemy's mind'.

The first Ultra, from Abwehr (German military intelligence) communications, came on stream in 1940 and saved SIS. Menzies was smart enough to realize that if SIS could control the distribution of Ultra it would receive at least some of the glory. The SIS representative at GC and CS, Wing Commander Frederick Winterbotham, was told to provide a continuous supply of the best Bletchley Park material, and each day Menzies or his personal assistant, David Boyle, took a packet of intelligence material direct to Churchill. Menzies, who brought the material in a special case, and Boyle, who carried it in his bowler hat, would give it to Churchill with a short commentary on GC and CS's current progress, all in the manner of a leader reporting on his staff. Churchill loved it – 'he ran the war on it,' says Winterbotham – and his confidence in Menzies and SIS soared.

Of course this did not endear Menzies and SIS to GC and CS, which considered its subordination to Menzies to be a purely administrative arrangement. They knew what was happening and they despised 'the miserable SIS which lived on our credit', a feeling so deeply rooted that it persisted long after the war was over. Sir Harry Hinsley, recruited to Bletchley Park while still an undergraduate, later to become vice-chancellor of Cambridge University and official historian of British intelligence during the war, has said of SIS: 'The espionage men were sort of lounge lizard types, you know. You had to be to do that kind of stuff. Whereas the Bletchley types were dour, upright, very charming-but-professional Englishmen and women. They were in a different kind of world. There was this quality difference between what their work was, and the old-fashioned spy stuff.'[15]

Saved by Ultra and now admired by Churchill, Menzies continued to preside over a decrepit and incompetent service, riddled with nepotism and run by a chain of command remarkable for its feebleness. SIS was ripe for Philby's penetration. It deserved him, and he devastated it.

CRUSHING THE
COMMON ENEMY
8

Kim Philby had been recruited to SIS on the basis of his knowledge of Franco's Spain, an important battleground in the intelligence war. Officially Spain was neutral, but Franco's sympathies were with Hitler and he allowed German intelligence an almost free hand in his country. However, unwilling to compromise his neutrality, he also tolerated a British intelligence presence there. Much the same situation existed in Portugal. So in these two countries British and German intelligence officers actually met face to face, with all the opportunities for intrigue, conspiracy, cross and double-cross that this proximity presented.

One story, no doubt apocryphal, sums up the espionage atmosphere on the Iberian peninsula at the time Philby took over that desk in SIS. There was a small-time agent, a Portuguese code-named 'Blinky', who operated out of Lisbon. One day he contacted the SIS station there and said: 'I've got some very valuable information for you. It's a new German code book and I want one hundred thousand US dollars for it.' After some checks, the British decided that the book was genuine and paid up. Blinky then contacted the German military intelligence representative in Lisbon and said: 'I've got some very valuable information for you worth a hundred thousand US dollars.' Since Blinky had been reliable in the past, the Germans paid. Then Blinky said, 'I've just sold your new code book to the British.' The Germans were not too angry because now they knew that the British were reading that code, they could cease using it for important communications and instead use it to plant false information that would keep the British running around in circles.

Then Blinky went too far. He figured that if the British knew that the Germans knew that the British were reading their code, it would enable the British to ignore the wrong information the Germans would try to plant on them and thus save valuable time. So he went back to the British and said: 'I have some *really* important information for you. It's got to be worth a hundred thousand US dollars – I told the Germans that I had sold their code to you.'

But the British had had enough, and told Blinky to enjoy his money today because he would not be around to spend it tomorrow – as soon as it could be arranged, he was going to have a nasty accident. Instead, within an hour the British had a telephone call from the chief of the Portuguese security police, whose permission was necessary for the British to stay in the country. He simply said: 'I understand you people have been threatening my partner.'

Philby was new to this sort of intrigue and approached his job with some trepidation. He knew nothing about counter-intelligence work, so he would have to learn as he went along. 'I was given precious little guidance from above,' he wrote later, 'and soon became indebted to my head secretary, an experienced girl who had been in the service before the war and . . . was able to keep me from the worst pitfalls.'[1] In the meantime he found himself in the middle of a bureaucratic minefield.

As we have seen, the first Ultra material to come on stream was from German military intelligence. Menzies had won the right to control the distribution of this and had delegated the task to Section Five under Felix Cowgill, the man who had employed Philby. Menzies had impressed upon Cowgill that the source of this marvellous material had to be protected at all costs – it was no use breaking the German codes if, through some indiscretion, the Germans realized what was happening. If they did, then they would change their codes, or, worse, pepper their communications with false information so as to deceive the British.

Quite properly, Cowgill took these orders seriously but he was soon at loggerheads with MI5, the Radio Security Service and several other departments within SIS. They did not understand his position and, according to Philby, accused him 'of withholding information that might have been put to effective use'. The more Cowgill was pressed, the more defensive and suspicious he became, regarding any criticism as disloyalty. This sort of feuding should have been squashed at an early stage by firm directions from the deputy chief of the service, Valentine Vivian, who was responsible for the overall control of counter-espionage. But Vivian was busy with his own feud with the assistant chief, Claude Dansey, who regarded all counter-espionage in wartime as a waste of time and its practitioners as cowards. Cowgill had seen Vivian's ineffectiveness and – to Vivian's anger – had gone over his head to get the increased appropriations needed for Section Five to hire people like Philby.

Philby noted all this and waited to use it to his advantage. He took no side, kept a low profile, worked hard, and learnt his job. He was, it is true, a rather voracious drinker, known socially for his ability to throw down the most appalling mixtures of alcohol. It is worth noting that on the occasions he became distinctly drunk he avoided the loosening of the tongue and the indiscretions that affect normal people. Philby could use alcohol to relieve the inner tensions of his double life without any fear of self-betrayal. I asked him about this in Moscow and he said: 'It often puzzled me how I could hold so much drink and never give anything away. It wasn't a trick or anything like that. It was just that something within me seemed to be aware that there was a limit to what I could say, a limit beyond which I could not go. No matter how much I drank it was always there.'

Philby's inner tensions must have been greatly relieved by the German invasion of the Soviet Union in June 1941. Since his return from Spain he had been struggling, like so many communists, to understand what had induced Moscow to sign a non-aggression pact with Germany in August 1939. Burgess was of no help to him. He had heard the news while sunning himself in the south of France and had driven back to London through the night to talk to Blunt. Another Cambridge friend, Goronwy Rees, has said that both men were extremely distressed and he suspected that Burgess was sorely tempted to give up communism.

Philby's control steadied him. No doubt he gave him the standard communist line: Stalin did not trust the Western offer of an anti-nazi alliance; he doubted the real strength of the British and French desire for such a pact; and, on the other hand, he thought it likely there could be a union between Britain, France, Germany, Italy and, perhaps, Japan, against the Soviet Union. In the event, Philby seemed far less troubled by what had happened than the other penetration agents and Germany's attack on Russia ended any doubt he might have had.

In fact his two employers, SIS and the Russian intelligence service, now shared a common goal, the defeat of Hitler. Matters might later change, but for the moment anything Philby did on behalf of Britain to thwart the Germans had the approval of his Soviet control. Philby has described some, but not all, of this work in *My Silent War* and he discussed it further with me in Moscow. It is worthwhile briefly recalling some of his cases, because they became the basis of his reputation and were to lead to his promotion.

The case of the false diary   Angel Alcazar de Velasco, of the Spanish press office, visited Britain. Since he was suspected of working for the Germans, SIS waited until he returned to Spain and then had one of its agents steal his diary. At first Section Five thought it had a major case on its hands: the diary was full of names and addresses of a network of agents de Velasco had recruited in Britain to work for German intelligence. It took several weeks' investigation to conclude that the diary was false, no spy network existed, and that de Velasco had concocted it to extract money from his German intelligence contacts in Madrid.*

But then Philby decided that the diary might be useful after all. Among its list of names were two genuine ones – Luis Calvo, a Spanish journalist based in London, and the Spanish press attaché. At Philby's suggestion MI5 arrested Calvo, and took him to its interrogation centre on Ham Common. There, stripped naked and confronted with the diary entry, he talked about espionage work that had had nothing to do with de Velasco and was detained for the duration of the war. When the Spanish press attaché was shown the diary entry mentioning him and told that the Foreign Office might consider this sufficient reason to ask for his recall, he, too, 'proved satisfactorily co-operative' and agreed to pass on to MI5 anything he could learn about Spaniards visiting Britain.

The case of the Orki companions Ultra intercepts showed that German intelligence was sending two agents to South America on board a Spanish ship. Both men were named and the senior was said in a second message to be travelling with his 'Orki' companions. Who could these be? Philby suggested that they might be dissident communists of some sort, and after passing the whole passenger list through counter-intelligence records came up with six or seven names whose careers suggested that this might be so.

When the Spanish ship stopped at Trinidad, every passenger about whom Philby harboured any suspicion was arrested. One of the two named German agents promptly confessed, but all the others denied everything and had to be detained on technical grounds to do with smuggling. A year later one of Philby's officers, reviewing the case, was hit by an idea. He got GC and CS to check something in the original intercept. Yes, indeed, said GC and CS, the word was not Orki but 'drei'. There was the senior agent and his 'three' companions – his colleague, his wife and his mother-in-law. Fortunately for

---

*Velasco later turned up in the United States, where he claimed to have organized another network – four journalists and two diplomats, all Spaniards – to spy for Japan. He said that this network was abandoned when a Canadian counter-intelligence officer caught them encoding information for transmission.[2]

Philby, by the time the others who had been detained on his orders had got around to suing the British government for wrongful arrest he had been posted to Istanbul.

The case of the cancelled operation A decision by Philby to try to use Section Five's intelligence to disrupt German operations in Spain coincided with information that German intelligence was planning something near Algeciras. From Ultra intercepts he knew that the code-name for the operation was 'Bodden'. Puzzling over the choice of the code-name, Philby recalled that the Bodden is the name of the strait separating the island of Rugen from the mainland in northern Germany. Could Bodden have something to do with another strip of navigable water – the Strait of Gibraltar? Philby's section consulted Dr R.V. Jones, head of the scientific section of SIS, who said that it looked as if the Germans planned to instal a device which would be able to detect the passage of Allied ships through the Strait at night.

Philby considered asking SOE if it was interested in blowing up the Germans' apparatus at the right moment, but rejected this in favour of a more conspiratorial approach. The idea was for the Foreign Office to make a formal protest to the Spanish government through the British ambassador in Madrid, Sir Samuel Hoare. Philby had no expectation that General Franco would force the Germans to abandon the plan. Instead he hoped that Franco would warn them that the British knew about it. German intelligence would then panic because the operation had leaked; they would wonder how SIS had learnt of it; they would consider that their Spanish network had been penetrated. This is exactly what happened, and in a few days Philby had the satisfaction of reading an Ultra intercept from Berlin to Madrid saying: 'The Bodden operation must be stopped in its entirety.'

The case of Admiral Canaris One day Philby got an Ultra intercept revealing that the head of German military intelligence, Admiral Wilhelm Canaris, was to visit Spain. He was going to drive from Madrid to Seville, stopping overnight at a small town called Manzanares. As Philby told me in Moscow, 'I knew the town quite well from my Spanish Civil War days. The only place Canaris could stay would be at the Parador. So I sent Cowgill a memo suggesting that we let SOE know about it in case they wanted to mount an assassination operation against Canaris. From what I knew about the Parador, it wouldn't have been too difficult to have tossed a couple of grenades into his bedroom.

'Cowgill approved and sent my memo on up to "C". Cowgill showed me the reply a couple of days later. Menzies had written: "I want no action whatsoever taken against the Admiral." Some time later I had occasion to see "C" and I remembered the memo and raised it with him. I said: "Chief, I was puzzled by your decision over this. Surely it was worth a go?" Menzies smiled and said: "I've always thought we could do something with the Admiral." It was only later that I learnt he was in touch with Canaris via a cut-out in Sweden.'

The significance of this last case – and, in particular, Menzies's comments – did not escape Philby. The belief that war between Britain and Germany was a tragedy that could have been avoided had not died after the outbreak of hostilities. Contacts with the German opposition to Hitler, whose spokesman had been Adam von Trott, continued in the United States.* In Rome, Vatican officials had been approached by the Germans to see if Pope Pius XII would act as an intermediary in securing a fair and honourable peace. There had been a meeting in Switzerland at which Prince Hohenlohe, a Sudeten aristocrat operating with the encouragement of the Nazi leader Goering, discussed with retired Group Captain Malcolm Christie, British air attaché in Berlin from 1927 to 1930, a compromise peace which would free Germany to cope with the threat of communism.

The Venlo incident in November 1939, when the Gestapo seized two British intelligence officers it had lured to a meeting to discuss peace terms and a united anti-Soviet front, changed the government's attitude. Churchill banned any further contact with the German opposition. And in May 1941 when Rudolf Hess, Hitler's deputy, made his dramatic flight to Scotland armed with a list of prominent people in Britain who he believed would be interested in a peace pact and an alliance against the Soviet Union, Churchill was

---

*Von Trott had sent Colonel Count Gerhardt von Schwerin of the German General Staff to London in July 1939 with an introduction to David Astor, later to become editor of *The Observer*. Astor was so impressed with what von Schwerin had to say that he arranged an appointment with SIS, hoping that it would agree to meet von Schwerin. Instead a senior SIS officer told him: 'I know who this man is; and if you want to know what I think of his coming over here, at a time when our country's relations with his are as bad as they are today, I think it's a damned cheek.'

careful to keep SIS officers well away from Hess because he believed that SIS still favoured such a move.

The Battle of Britain, the Blitz and the German invasion of Russia silenced those seeking a compromise peace and an anti-Soviet alliance. Britain swung behind Churchill's war effort with its emphasis of the role of the Red Army in the struggle to defeat Hitler. But pockets of the old attitude remained. Philby had even uncovered one.

The British ambassador in Madrid, Philby's territory, was Sir Samuel Hoare, a former Home Secretary and a leading appeaser who still cherished hopes for peace, which, he believed, might be negotiated through the good offices of General Franco. The last thing Samuel wanted was SIS operations against the Germans in Spain, or, worse, SIS plots to overthrow Franco and bring Spain into the war on the Allies' side. He had already vetoed one SIS plan – to open an office in Madrid to debrief Allied prisoners who had escaped to Spain from German prisoner-of-war camps. Hoare protested vigorously and SIS was forced to transfer the office to Lisbon.

Now Menzies's revelation that he was protecting Admiral Canaris, and the discovery that he was in touch with him via neutral Sweden, came as a shock to Philby. What could be the reason for such a contact? Philby decided that Canaris must be in touch with anti-Hitler elements in Germany and that Menzies wanted to keep a line open to them. Philby told his Russian control and was instructed to remain alert for any developments in this area.

As we shall see, keeping Moscow informed of moves for a separate peace between Germany and Britain and a switching of the war to one against the Soviet Union was to be Philby's major service for the Russians. He told me in Moscow that this area interested his control above all else and that he was urged not just to note any such moves but, wherever possible, to work actively to frustrate them. Philby did not disappoint the Russians.

Late in 1942, for example, he dealt with a paper written jointly by Hugh Trevor-Roper's department and Stuart Hampshire, a temporary SIS analyst specializing on Germany. The paper explained the background which would make approaches for an accommodation with Germany – short of unconditional surrender – perfectly rational, and set out why such approaches should be taken seriously rather than treated as a ruse. It was generally accepted as a brilliant paper, but since the peace feelers would almost certainly come in Spain or Portugal, and this was Philby's territory, the paper had to be shown to him for his imprimatur before it could go into general circulation and, perhaps, be shown to the Americans.

To everyone's surprise, Philby resolutely blocked the paper, arguing that it was 'speculative'. Trevor-Roper says:

> We were baffled by Philby's intransigence which would yield to no argument and which no argument was used to defend. From some members of Section V mere mindless blocking of intelligence was to be expected. But Philby, we said to ourselves, was an intelligent man: how could he behave thus in a matter so important? Had he too yielded to the genius of the place?[3]

In retrospect, Philby's attitude was perfectly rational. As a Soviet penetration agent he had immediately seen the danger. The German anti-Nazis did not want to stop the war against Russia. They wanted to eliminate Hitler, make peace with the Allies, and then complete the invasion of the Soviet Union in which they stood on the brink of success. Philby could not run the risk that this might prove attractive to some elements in Britain so he used his power to deal with it.

There was also Philby's role in the Otto John affair. John, a lawyer working for Lufthansa and a member of the opposition to Hitler, had made contact in 1942 with an SIS officer, code-named 'Tony', who was working from the British embassy in Lisbon. John told me:

> I was to find out the chances of getting support from the British government if we were to eliminate Hitler. I was not acting for Canaris. He never himself worked for this conspiracy, but he did cover our activities. In a walk through the vineyards outside Lisbon Tony made it clear to me that we wouldn't get a hearing in London until we had proved ourselves.
>
> In January 1944, in the midst of preparing for Stauffenberg's coup d'état [the bomb plot on Hitler's life], I tried on Stauffenberg's behalf to see Tony again to find out the attitude of the British government to Stauffenberg's plans. Tony was ostensibly away and I was able to talk only with a member of his staff, Rita. She told me that there had been strict instructions from London forbidding any contact with 'emissaries of the German opposition'. And she added: 'General Eisenhower has been appointed Supreme Commander for the invasion. The war will now be decided by force of arms.' There was no longer any chance for Stauffenberg to negotiate an armistice with Eisenhower, as he had hoped. There was nothing left for us but unconditional surrender.[4]

The instructions from London had, of course, come from Philby himself. He had suppressed Tony's report of his first meeting with John on the grounds that John was 'unreliable'. As he told me in Moscow, 'John was a difficult man. We tried to use him during the war as a double agent but he was always changing sides. The trouble with the German peace terms was that they were too demanding to take seriously. They were suggesting terms that might have been appropriate if Germany had still been winning the war instead of losing it. We rightly turned them down, so the good Germans had to go it alone, and unfortunately for them they failed.'

John vehemently denies that he was ever a double agent and has further accusations to make against Philby. John says that after the bomb plot failed and he escaped to Lisbon, Philby did his best to make certain that John was kept away from London as long as possible so that he could not report on the extent of the remaining opposition to Hitler.*

These actions of Philby's are defensible. Not only communists thought that it would be an act of betrayal to talk peace with the Germans behind the back of our Soviet ally who had borne the brunt of the war and suffered the heaviest losses. As Philby said, 'It would have been dangerous for the Russians to think that we were dickering with the Germans; the air was opaque with mutual suspicions of separate peace feelers.'

But, according to former MI5 officers who gave me the information after the *Sunday Times* articles on Philby appeared in March 1988, Philby went further. Stalin's master plan for postwar Germany, kept secret from Britain and the United States, envisaged legitimizing in Moscow a German National Committee which could serve as the basis for a communist German puppet government, ready to take over after the war. Thus Moscow was against *all* internal opposition to Hitler because it would threaten any future communist rule in Germany. In February 1944 a senior German intelligence officer and his wife, Erich and Elisabeth Vermehren, defected in Istanbul. The Vermehrens, devout Catholics, and well placed in the German bureaucracy (Elisabeth Vermehren was a cousin of Franz von Papen, the veteran German diplomat and politician), felt that they could no longer go on working for the nazi regime. After contacting the British Legation, they agreed to be spirited away to Britain, where

*Canaris was hanged on 9 April 1945 for alleged complicity in the bomb plot. John became director of security in West Germany after the war and made headlines in the 1950s by turning up in East Berlin and speaking against the West. Then after a year he escaped to West Berlin and claimed that the communists had kidnapped him.

they stayed with Philby while they were being debriefed.* According to MI5 officers, the Vermehrens revealed the extent of the Catholic opposition in Germany and provided their interrogators with a list of leading Catholic activists who could be instrumental in the postwar period in helping the Allies establish an anti-communist government in Germany.

But when, after the war, the Allies tried to contact the people on this list, most of them were dead. The MI5 officers claimed that Philby had seen the list, passed the names to his Soviet controller, and because Moscow had decided to eliminate all non-communist opposition in Germany, these Catholics had been shot. I did not hear this story until after I had seen Philby in Moscow so I was unable to ask him about it, but the MI5 officers assured me that it was true and that this was one explanation for the deep animosity many intelligence officers had for him.

This was major strategic intelligence work, but there was also 'nuts and bolts' material that came Philby's way by the very nature of his work. Section Five did not work from SIS headquarters, then in Broadway Buildings, just opposite St James's Park tube station. Wartime expansion had pushed it and other departments out of London to the suburbs and Home Counties. Section Five and Central Registry, which housed all SIS files, were located in St Albans, next door to each other. Philby soon made friends with the officer in charge of Central Registry, Bill Woodfield, and began to take out from the registry SIS source books, the top-secret lists of SIS agents operating abroad.

Philby had every excuse for needing the source books for Spain and Portugal – these countries were in his area of responsibility and it was natural that he wanted to know everything he could about all the SIS agents who had ever worked there. But the two source books for the Soviet Union were another matter. The names of SIS agents in the Soviet Union would be invaluable to the Russian intelligence service – it could plant disinformation on them or round them up and shoot them as it pleased. But if Philby were ever seriously challenged to explain why he had taken the books out, he would be in trouble. Confident that the easygoing Woodfield would not challenge him, Philby went ahead, requested the two books, worked through them noting the agents' names, and returned them.

A week later Woodfield telephoned and asked for the return

*They spent the rest of the war working for a black propaganda team and eventually settled in Switzerland under another name.

of the second book. Philby consulted his records and replied that it had been returned. But Woodfield came back to say that his staff had searched the Registry for it and could not find it. He urged Philby to make a thorough investigation, which he did and was still unable to find the book. As Philby described the incident, 'Bill and I met once or twice in the evening to discuss the mystery over a few pink gins. He told me that the normal procedure on the loss of a source book was for him to report immediately to the chief. I managed to stall him for a few days, during which my alarm grew. I doubted whether the chief would appreciate the excessive zeal which had led me to exhaustive study of the source books, especially as it had apparently resulted in the loss of one dealing with a country far outside the normal scope of my duties.'

Just as Philby was wondering whether his short career in SIS was about to be terminated, Woodfield telephoned him to say that the book had been found. One of his secretaries had tried to save space by amalgamating the two books into one volume. When the search for the missing book had been going on, she had been away from the office with influenza. On her return, told about the search, she had immediately remembered what she had done. Philby and Woodfield celebrated with many pink gins – Woodfield the fact that the book had turned up, Philby that he had survived yet another unexpected threat to his career as a Soviet intelligence officer.

In the meantime, Philby had discovered that he could volunteer for night duty once or twice a month at SIS headquarters in Broadway Buildings. The night duty officer's job was to receive and act on reports that came in from all over the world, so for twelve hours or so he was in a key position in the service. As well, several other government departments used the SIS communications network for their top-secret traffic in the mistaken belief that it was more secure, so the night duty officer had access to a wide range of government business.

One department that used SIS radio channels was the War Office, and its messages to and from the British Military Mission in Moscow were on file for Philby to read when he did his spells of duty at Broadway. The issues the mission was discussing with Moscow around this time included military aid, arrangements for the exchange of intelligence, and the British decision in June 1942 to reduce the flow of Ultra material to its Soviet ally. We must assume that Philby passed to his Soviet control all he could learn of these matters. The end result was that the Soviet authorities knew the British position *before* their regular meetings with the mission in Moscow – a great tactical advantage.

At this stage of the war, the Russian intelligence service officer in charge of the English desk must have been reasonably pleased. His principal penetration agent, Kim Philby, had succeeded in getting himself recruited for SIS and was steadily consolidating his position. But Guy Burgess was a bit of a disappointment. He had been in and then out of SIS, and although he had been useful in helping Philby's penetration he had not been able to get back in again himself. However, he maintained a wide range of friends and contacts in government and in the secret world and, if the Soviet intelligence officer Vladimir Petrov, who defected in Australia in 1954, is to be believed – other statements made by him have not proved very reliable – the volume of material Burgess picked up from these contacts was so great that 'the cypher clerks of the Soviet Embassy were at times almost fully employed in encyphering it so that it could be radioed to Moscow'.[5]

Anthony Blunt was another matter. In MI5's B branch (counterespionage) his job was to keep neutral missions in London under surveillance. This included opening their diplomatic bags and photographing the contents. Thus he was in a position to pass on to his Soviet control what he learnt about the attitudes of neutrals to the war, their assessment of the British war effort, and any intelligence that the neutrals themselves had picked up from their own sources. Blunt was unassuming and efficient. His fellow officers liked him and respected his intelligence. As he rose in the ranks his access to other secrets improved. When his boss, Guy Liddell, was otherwise engaged, Blunt represented him on the Joint Intelligence Committee and could thus report to his Soviet control not only on what intelligence the committee considered but on how it graded it.

Maclean, the Soviet agent who had penetrated the British Foreign Office, seemed to be stuck in a backwater. After his escape from France he was posted to the General Department, a recently created and not very highly rated section of the Foreign Office which dealt with shipping, contraband, and other aspects of economic warfare. Until I met Philby in Moscow in 1988, I believed that there was nothing Maclean could have done for the Soviet intelligence service during this period.

But in Moscow Philby told me the following story. 'Maclean was crossing Green Park [near the Foreign Office] one evening carrying a briefcase full of sensitive documents. An FO colleague caught up with him and said: "Walk with you, old boy?" Maclean said: "Delighted", and the colleague fell into step and walked in silence for a while. Then the colleague suddenly said: "I was wondering, Donald, how much is the Soviet embassy going to pay you for the contents of that briefcase?" Maclean's heart skipped a beat but he carried it off superbly. He simply said: "I can't say yet. But I suppose that now you'll want half." '

Philby, who must have heard the story from Maclean, told it to me as a joke, an example of the dangers likely to confront spies at unlikely moments. But it does carry the implication that Maclean, despite being in a backwater at the Foreign Office, still found material there to interest his Soviet control.

The big puzzle – until I saw Philby in Moscow – was what role the Soviet penetration agents played in telling Moscow about Ultra. Two thirds of the German war effort was expended on the Eastern front, yet the role of Ultra in relation to this has remained a mystery. Did the Allies share with the Soviet Union their 'priceless' intelligence jewel? If not, did the Russians realize it and resent being excluded? Since the first Ultra revelations, attempts to answer such questions have done little more than create new Ultra myths. The best of these is that the Russians were so mistrustful of Britain that Churchill realized that it would be no use passing Ultra material to Stalin in a normal manner. For, if he did, Stalin would automatically suspect Churchill of planting it on him for some ulterior motive. So – the myth goes – SIS disguised the Ultra material and fed it into the Lucy ring, a famous Soviet spy network in Switzerland. Only when Stalin received it from his own trusted spies did he believe it was true. This is pure fantasy.

Other versions are more credible. Peter Calvocoressi, who worked on Ultra at Bletchley Park during the war, says that there was a justifiable reluctance to give Stalin *any* Ultra material because Soviet communications were notoriously insecure and the Germans, intercepting Russian messages, might well tumble to the fact that the British were reading their Enigma codes. But when it became clear that the Soviet Union was going to put up a powerful resistance to Hitler, then both loyalty and expediency required that Britain should give the Russians everything that might help them defeat the Germans. Calvocoressi says that Ultra material of use to Stalin was suitably doctored to disguise its source, then sent to a British liaison officer in Moscow, Major Edward Crankshaw, who passed it via the British ambassador direct to Stalin. The British MP, Rupert Allason, who writes on intelligence matters, has a similar account, except that he says SIS had an officer in Moscow, Cecil Barclay, whose job was to provide his Soviet counterpart, General F.F. Kuznetsov, with selected Ultra material 'without compromising the source'.

But the whole point of Ultra *was* its source. Unless the Russians knew that the British had broken the German Enigma codes and that this was how Ultra was produced, then they would not have known how much reliance to place on the material. If the source was disguised to suggest, for instance, that the material came from SIS agents, or an Allied 'stay-behind' network of spies, or – an actual example – 'from a highly placed agent in the Berlin war office', then Stalin would have been justified in ignoring it.

And this is exactly what he appears to have done. Calvocoressi has doubts that Stalin ever used *any* of the Ultra material. 'In the case of the great tank battles of 1942, for example, when [the Russians] were warned that they were pouring men and materials into a huge German trap, it is difficult to suppose that they gave full credence to warnings which, if heeded, would have saved them terrible losses.'[6]

But there are political questions to consider here. Did the Russians learn of Ultra and its real source, and, if so what did they make of their Allies' refusal to share it with them? The most likely way the Russians could have learnt about Ultra was from their penetration agents, Philby and Blunt. In December 1979 I wrote to Blunt and asked him: 'You received in MI5 some of the Ultra material; did you know it was Ultra material and did you tell your Soviet control about it? If so, was there anything that especially interested him?' Blunt replied in January 1980: 'I never received any operational intercepts, but only those emanating from the Abwehr. My control was primarily interested in any information that I could obtain about the German intelligence services.'

Before I met Philby in Moscow it was known that he had handled Ultra material relating to the Abwehr – he mentions it in his own book. There was circumstantial evidence that he knew that GC and CS had cracked other German codes. He had told his fellow SIS officer, Leslie Nicholson, some time before the first V2 rockets that: 'The Germans have got a new weapon to hit London. I'm going to move my family to the country' – an important piece of information that came largely from the intercepts of messages from the Japanese ambassador in Berlin to his superiors in Tokyo, not from Abwehr intercepts. And a secretary who worked in Philby's office recalls: 'There was a special room where material was available on application to sections which needed it for their work. It was common knowledge among the staff that the material was largely derived from Enigma intercepts.'[7]

I discussed Ultra with Philby. He said he got the impression –

'It was nothing more than that' – from his control that it was not a major concern of the Russian intelligence service. This tallies with what Calvocoressi felt:

> They must have captured Enigma machines and cypher books and they must have supposed that we did so too. They were not lacking in mathematicians and chess-players capable of appreciating what was involved in breaking cyphers. They may have been without an organization like BP [Bletchley Park] capable of making the most of such skills, but it would have been natural for them to harbour at least a suspicion that we possessed a precious advantage which we were withholding from them . . . Yet neither directly nor indirectly did they probe Eden [the British Foreign Secretary] or anybody else on the subject of Ultra.[8]

The only reason for this attitude that makes sense is that the Russians *did* know the origins of the Ultra material and suspected that there were political divisions in Britain over whether to share it with them. On one side were those who had been adamant against collective security before 1939 and who were hard at work after 1941 to ensure that the war would end with the Soviet Union bled to death. They had as allies those security officers with whom secrecy had become a way of life and who were determined that Ultra be confined to as small a group as possible, preferably all Englishmen.

Against them were the penetration agents who saw in the attitude of the others confirmation that their country was not doing enough to help a hard-pressed ally, and Churchill, who had not only directed GC and CS to stop working on Russian cyphers so as to concentrate on German ones, but who was temperamentally in favour of giving the Russians more information rather than less. Calvocoressi notes: 'He was not the only one in this frame of mind, but he had on occasions to be restrained by others who feared that he was taking too many risks.'[9]

In 1943 it would appear that the Russians decided to put Britain to the test. Late the previous year Soviet code-breakers had cracked their first military Enigma traffic, and in January 1943 they captured some twenty-six Enigma machines at Stalingrad.[10] Well on their way to being independent of the disguised Ultra material from Britain, they simply instructed their intelligence liaison officer in London, Colonel I. Chickayev, to ask the British to tell them all about Enigma. What happened next is not mentioned in any of the official histories of the war and remained secret until 1986.

Then James Rusbridger, of St Austell, Cornwall, an author and an indefatigable researcher of archives, managed to bully the

Ministry of Defence into producing a 'Most Secret' receipt recording that on 15 July 1943 a Colonel Shukalov, of the Soviet Naval Mission, had accepted from Paymaster Lieutenant R. Hutchings, 'One German Cypher Machine, "Enigma" No. "M.2520" [and] One photostat copy of Instructions for Use in German (31 pages).'[11] Rusbridger released this astonishing news through the columns of Peterborough in the *Daily Telegraph*. It created instant controversy.

The argument centred on whether the machine and instructions by themselves were of any use to Moscow without, as the official historian of the intelligence war, Sir Harry Hinsley, put it, 'any information bearing on the problem of decrypting Enigma keys'. Rusbridger believes they would have been – when used with the information supplied by the Soviet penetration agents.

To settle the dispute we need to know who made the decision to give the Russians the Enigma machine, and, more important, *why* did we give it to them? As Peter Calvocoressi says, 'Were we trying to get some kind of return help, or were we trying to fool the Russians that the machines were of no use to us?'[12] My own belief, after talking to Philby and others, is that the Russians knew all along that Britain had Ultra. Apart from Philby and Blunt, the Russian intelligence service also had John Cairncross actually *inside* GC and CS until 1944, when he transferred to Section Five of SIS. In 1964, then living in Rome, Cairncross admitted to MI5 that he had had regular meetings with his Soviet control *while at CGC and CS*. It is inconceivable that three such highly motivated Soviet spies as Philby, Blunt and Cairncross could know about Ultra and not tell their Soviet controllers about it.

I believe that the Soviet Union began to crack the Enigma codes by late 1942 – they had a long tradition of code-breaking going back beyond the Revolution – and by mid-1943 had a lot of Enigma material on stream. Even the Germans, who had previously not thought this possible, now agree it was so. 'It is absolutely certain that the Russians succeeded in deciphering Enigma messages in certain instances,' a former German intelligence officer wrote. 'The reason for this, besides the usual mistakes in cyphers, was the sending of too many messages with the same basic key.'[13]

I further believe that, knowing Britain had Ultra and now possessing similar material themselves, the Russians asked Britain for an Enigma machine to see what the British attitude to the request would be. Unfortunately, our response was an unsatisfactory compromise. We gave the Russians a machine – but only because we were reasonably confident that it would be of no use to them. Moscow noted Britain's attitude and drew its own conclusions.

Kim Philby's father, St John Philby, as a King's Scholar of Westminster school in 1902, aged seventeen.

The Philby clan: (from right to left) Kim Philby's grandmother, May; his sister, Pat; Kim himself, aged eleven; his mother, Dora, his cousins Frank and Averil and his sister Diana.

Above: *Kim aged eight. He had arrived in Britain for the first time a year earlier.*

Right: *Head of the school: Kim, aged twelve, in the uniform of Aldro preparatory school, Eastbourne.*

Kim Philby, just down from Cambridge. At twenty-one, already a Communist, he was soon to sign up with the Russian intelligence service.

Litzi Friedmann, the vivacious
Viennese girl, who confirmed him in
his beliefs and became his first wife.

The actress, Frances ('Bunny')
Doble. Philby met her during the
Spanish Civil War and they
became lovers.

Philby, war correspondent for The Times, lines up to meet George VI
at British headquarters in France during the Second World War.
Philby is third from the left, partly obscured by the King.

Philby, the charming intelligence officer, after his posting to Washington in 1949.

Aileen, Philby's second wife, aged forty-five, at the Philby flat in London.

Reporters crowd Dora's flat to interview Philby after the British government clears him of being the 'third man'.

Above: *FBI 'wanted' notices for Burgess and Maclean, distributed throughout Europe after the two men disappeared in May, 1951.*

Right: *Donald Maclean and his wife Melinda, attend the funeral of Guy Burgess in Moscow.*

Guy Burgess, shortly before his death.

James Jesus Angleton, the crack CIA counter-intelligence officer. Philby said he became "too embattled" to function properly.

Top: *Philby, the bottle empty, relaxes at a picnic in the hills outside Beirut.*

Above: *Happy times in Beirut. Eleanor Philby (centre) and Philby (in sun glasses) entertain friends at Harry's Anzac Bar.*

St John Philby, with Eleanor and Kim's youngest son, Harry, on the terrace of Kim's Beirut flat.

Kim, with his father and his two step-brothers, Khalid and Faris, in Saudi Arabia.

Philby, happy and at home in the Moscow winter.

A spy's picnic: Philby at a dacha outside Moscow, looks at his fourth wife, Rufa. George Blake sits in front of his Russian wife Ida, with his son, Mischa, on his lap.

Top: *Kim Philby in his Moscow study early in 1988. He usually read* The Times *but was trying out a new London paper.*

Above: *Philby studies his Order of Lenin at the desk where he did most of his KGB work.*

Philby in his Moscow study. On the wall are two manuscript pages from one of his father's books and a photograph of the Soviet ice-hockey team with Philby (motivation manager) after it had won the world championships.

Top: *Philby explains a point to the author during their six-day interview.*

Above: *Moscow dinner: Philby, his mother-in-law, his wife, and Yvonne Knightley.*

*Philby's own favourite picture of himself and Rufa,
'the woman of my life'.*

Above: *Philby's grave with its simple headstone*
'Kim Philby: 1.01.1912–11.05.88'.

Below: *The funeral: a KGB guard of honour stands at the head of*
Philby's coffin as mourners file past.

MASTERSTROKE
FOR MOSCOW
9

During the winter of 1942–3, the first American intelligence officers arrived in Britain for training. They were members of the Office of Strategic Services, an American-style SOE, set up by General William ('Wild Bill') Donovan, an unconventional lawyer who had that appealing, if naïve, American belief that anything is possible, and that an inspired amateur can often do it better than the professional. One of his 'boys', he often said, was worth ten conventional soldiers.

Donovan mistakenly thought that the Germans were particularly adept at secret warfare and concluded that an organization like OSS was the only way to counter this menace. He then compounded this error by imagining that the British held the key that could unlock all the secrets of the great game for his boys; so he turned to his friends in Britain for the expertise and sophistication that his organization needed to become truly operational.

The British welcomed the opportunity. They wanted American manpower, money and supplies. They saw the relationship as one in which they would exercise complete if indirect control; the Americans would be junior partners in a largely British concern. As Malcolm Muggeridge put it, 'How well I remember [the Americans] arriving like *jeunes filles en fleur* straight from a finishing school, all fresh and innocent, to start work in our frowsty old intelligence brothel. All too soon they were ravished and corrupted, becoming indistinguishable from the seasoned pros who had been in the game for a quarter century or more.'[1]

Philby was one of the few who saw things differently. He saw that cooperation with the Americans in the intelligence field would, in the long run, doom the British to junior status – as indeed it has – that American power and resources would eventually outweigh British expertise, that the Americans, itching for action, would not be content forever to be under British control. What began as friendly cooperation soon degenerated into outright hostility.

Some British SIS officers complained about American security. Henry Kerby, an MP who had worked for SIS in the 1920s, remembered, 'The Americans had no intelligence service to speak of. OSS was an exact parallel to SOE, drawing on the ethnic dregs of America for skill in languages and knowledge of foreign countries. Their security was non-existent, but they were in constant liaison with SIS and SOE. Thus *our* security was bitched at one remove.'[2]

Other SIS officers objected to OSS's operational methods. OSS wanted to establish its own relationship with European governments in exile; the British argued that contact should be made only through them. OSS wanted to be able to put agents into the field independently; the British insisted that they should be informed and their approval sought. SIS wanted to impose its codes and communications system on OSS; the Americans refused to accept this, arguing that this would enable SIS to know all about OSS activities while keeping its own operations secret. Early in 1944, the two organizations clashed over missions which OSS in Algiers was sending to Occupied France, the British using their monopoly of aircraft available for covert operations to control OSS plans, much to Donovan's disgust.

Although Philby was in the thick of much of this in-fighting – a lot of it took place in areas under his control – it did not prevent him from developing quite close relationships with some of the Americans who came to St Albans. One, in particular, became a friend. This was James Jesus Angleton, a tall lean man, interested in poetry, orchid growing, and fishing, an intelligence officer of deep patriotism and powerfully held beliefs. Philby was one of Angleton's instructors, his prime tutor in counter-intelligence; Angleton came to look upon him as an elder-brother figure. Philby's betrayal of this relationship was later to tip Angleton into a state of permanent suspicion and have profound effects on the intelligence world. In 1943, however, they worked together for a common end – the defeat of Nazi Germany.

Life at St Albans was dedicated to this end. By now SIS had attracted some quite high-powered talent. Philby's fellow officers included Tim Milne, the old schoolfriend from his Westminster days and his predecessor on the Iberian desk, Graham Greene, Hugh Trevor-Roper, Charles de Salis, Desmond Pakenham and Richard Comyns-Carr. But Philby still stood out. What was it that made him such a good officer? Sir Robert Mackenzie, a Foreign Office security expert who knew Philby well, recalled:

One of the most impressive things, although a superficial one, was the beautiful English of his reports. He wrote them out in longhand, in neat, tiny writing; he never did a draft first, yet the English was magnificent – never a word too many, never a

118

statement open to two interpretations. And, of course, there was this attractive personality. Philby had inherited from his father that same sense of dedicated idealism in which the means did not matter as long as the end was a worthwhile one. Although he had a façade on other matters, this sense of dedication and purpose to whatever he was doing gleamed through and inspired men to follow him. He was the sort of man who won worshippers. You didn't just like him, admire him, agree with him; you worshipped him.[3]

But one of the secretaries in the typing pool noticed a side to Philby's character at this period that disturbed her. 'You were either completely taken in by him or you disliked him,' she said later. 'His secretary, Catherine Gange, was devoted to him, but I didn't like his single-mindedness, what I saw as his calculating ambition, and his cold-hearted way of handling his staff. If you made a blunder in the typing, old Cowgill would snort and bellow but you knew he didn't mean it and it didn't hurt. Philby would call you into his office, point to the error and say coldly: "Would you correct that, please." I used to shrivel up like a worm. He used it on the men too, just as effectively. I can remember walking into Graham Greene's office and he was gripping the chair and his eyes were glinting with anger. I asked him what was the matter and he said: "I've just had a caning from the headmaster." '[4]

In the summer, the office social life could be quite pleasant. There was a decent restaurant called the Chalet within walking distance where Philby and Milne could often be seen sitting over a couple of pints of beer 'talking shop'. On long, fine evenings, there would sometimes be a pick-up cricket game in the nearby fields between two SIS teams.

It all came to an end in the winter of 1943–4 when Philby's section moved to an old house in Ryder Street near Piccadilly. Although some officers in Section Five were reluctant to leave the countryside for London, Philby was anxious to get back to the capital. For one thing, he and Aileen had been sharing a house just outside St Albans with the Milnes, but two small children – Josephine, born in 1941 and John (1943), and another on the way (Tom, born 1944) were going to make things a little crowded.

At first they all stayed with Philby's mother, Dora, in her flat in Drayton Gardens, off the Brompton Road, but they soon scraped together the mortgage for a house in Carlyle Square, taking in a lodger and arranging a nursery school in the dining room which Aileen ran with the help of a friend and a professional teacher. This seems to have been the best stage of their married life. 'They lived in cheerful disorder amidst children, friends, books, music and alcohol,' says Patrick Seale.[5]

Philby's drinking companions at his local, the Markham Arms, had no idea what he did. If they thought about it, they would probably have put him down as a schoolteacher, or a civil servant in some obscure government department – which, in a way, he was. Most times he wore corduroy trousers, an old tweed jacket with leather patches at the elbows, and a check flannel shirt. He got around London in a battered old taxicab which could often be seen parked outside the most unlikely places, not because Philby was there, but because he had been on one of his twenty-four-hour drinking bouts and could not drive.

Aileen was surprisingly tolerant of these bouts. She had got over her suspicion at his long absences from the house, which he never explained except to say that they had to do with his work. She was ignorant even of the exact nature of his job; only that it had something to do with the Foreign Office and the war effort. Her contribution to the marriage was to provide a relaxed domestic atmosphere, to bear Philby's children, and to accept his dictum that they should not receive any sort of religious education. She did occasionally press him to marry her, usually without result, Philby arguing that he did not have the time to chase up Litzi to get a divorce. But he accepted that once the war was over they would really have to do something to legitimize their relationship.

With his colleagues, Philby was careful to keep his distance. After he had defected to the Soviet Union some of these officers looked back and realized that they had only thought that they knew him well, that they had made assumptions about him which he had been careful not to deny. Trevor-Roper remembers thinking that Philby had a first-class mind which he surrounded with a barrier of 'a tough, flexible and active set of defences'. Muggeridge claims to have detected 'a quality of suppressed violence' but another colleague says he thought Philby was 'a sensitive man trying to make himself out to be tough'.

The one person Philby might have been able to engage with on a reasonably frank basis would have been Graham Greene – as their many meetings later in Moscow testify, they had a lot in common, even at that time. As Philby recalled, 'When Graham first came to work in my department we had a long talk. Of course, I couldn't talk to him as a Communist, but I did talk to him as a man of left-wing views and he was a Catholic. But at once there was human contact between us.'[6] The two began to lunch together frequently and their friendship grew. But Philby went down in Greene's estimation over what Greene later described as 'a piece of [Philby's] office jobbery', over which he resigned. 'I attributed it then to a personal drive for power, the only characteristic in Philby which I thought disagreeable,' Greene wrote in the introduction to Philby's book. 'I am glad now that I was wrong. He was serving a cause and not himself, and so my old liking for him comes back.'[7]

Philby displayed a remarkable aptitude for office politics. He foresaw that when peace came most of the wartime 'amateurs' would be returned to civilian life. In order to be asked to stay on he would need not only a record based on hard and productive work but one that showed he understood the way SIS functioned and, above all, that he knew how to protect its future. With a masterstroke, one that turned an SIS failure into an outstanding triumph, Philby virtually ensured his future in the secret world.

On 23 August 1943, a German Foreign Ministry official, Dr Fritz Kolbe, arrived at the British Legation in Berne, Switzerland, and asked to see the military attaché, Colonel Henry Cartwright, who also represented MI9, the organization which helped and debriefed escapers from Germany. Cartwright's cover role was well known in neutral Switzerland and German intelligence had several times tried to plant an agent on him. This had made Cartwright very suspicious of 'walk-ins', so when Kolbe virtually came in off the street and said he wanted to help the Allies, Cartwright was immediately on his guard.

Kolbe said that he was highly placed in the German Foreign Ministry but that he was anti-nazi, so he had taken advantage of his position to steal copies of secret documents from his office in Berlin. He had brought some of them with him to Berne and had hundreds more hidden away. Cartwright did not even bother to read them. He decided that Kolbe was an Abwehr plant and showed him the door. Kolbe, amazed at the British reaction, mentioned the matter to a friend who suggested that he try the Americans. The next day Kolbe called on Allen Dulles, the Office of Strategic Services' (OSS) representative in Switzerland, and left 183 flimsy file copies of German Foreign Ministry telegrams, promising to return with more when he had a chance.

During the next sixteen months Kolbe delivered more than 1,500 secret German documents which provided a useful insight into the intentions of the German Foreign Ministry. According to one American intelligence officer, Kolbe was 'one of the best secret agents any intelligence service ever had'.* Unfortunately for the British, this was not only an American triumph but – since SIS had turned Kolbe away – an embarrassment.

Then events gave Philby his chance. OSS duly passed copies of the Kolbe material to SIS. There Dansey, who had always regarded Switzerland as his special territory, backed Cartwright's belief that the whole operation was a German plant and handed them over to Cowgill's counter-intelligence section, where they eventually reached the section's brightest, hardest-working officer, Kim Philby. Philby was only too happy to check the documents' authenticity, which he did by asking GC and CS to compare the contents of the documents with the Ultra decrypts of German Foreign Office messages for the same period to see if they matched. They did, and GC and CS excitedly asked for more. As Philby described it:

> When about a third of the material had passed through [GC and CS] hands with a steadily increasing tally of matches, and never a suggestion of anything phony, I felt that I had no choice but to circulate the documents as genuine. Accordingly I passed them on to our sections dealing with the service departments and the Foreign Office, purposely playing down their significance, as I did not wish Dansey to get premature wind of anything unusual.
>
> The reaction of the service departments was immediate. Army, Navy and Air Force – all three howled for more. The Foreign Office was more sedate, but also very polite. I asked the sections concerned to get written evaluations of the material from their departments. I also asked Denniston for a minute explaining the cryptographic reasons for supposing the documents to be genuine. I needed all the ammunition I could get for the imminent confrontation with Dansey . . . With some trepidation, I asked when I could conveniently pay him a visit.

As Philby had expected, Dansey was furious and read Philby a lecture. Even if the documents were genuine, what of it? Philby was encouraging OSS to foul up the whole intelligence field in Switzerland and perhaps blow the entire SIS network there. He should keep out of things which did not concern him and, since he

---

*He remained in place and above suspicion until April 1945 when, as Germany collapsed, he managed to slip over the border into Switzerland.

had never worked in the field, were beyond his experience. Philby continues:

> When Dansey had exhausted his reckless improvisation, I asked him with puzzled deference how OSS came into the business at all. I had not circulated the material as OSS material. Not even our own circulating sections, let alone the departments, knew that OSS were involved. They regarded it as *our* stuff, they were asking *us* for more. It seemed that the credit would be ours. When I faltered to an end, Dansey gave me a long, long stare. 'Carry on,' he said at last. 'You're not such a fool as I thought.'[8]

Here we can see Philby at his conspiratorial best. While maintaining his reputation of refusing to engage in office intrigue, he had enhanced the respect that many officers in sister services held for him, manipulated Dansey into accepting what he had done, and exacerbated the friction between Cowgill and his colleagues. He soon put all this to good use.

As the war continued to go the Allies' way, the German intelligence assault on Britain slowed down and with it the work of British counter-intelligence. By 1944 Section Five was no longer directly concerned with the war and now dealt with counter-espionage only in unimportant areas, such as South America or Arabia. This decline coincided with the first indications of how SIS's priorities would be re-ordered after the war.

Until 1944, being a member of the Communist Party had not automatically excluded someone from secret work. James Klugman, who had joined a communist cell with Donald Maclean at Cambridge in 1931 and remained a communist until his death in 1977, made no secret of his beliefs and yet served with SOE in Cairo during the war. But early in 1944 Churchill ordered a remorseless weeding out of every single known communist from all of Britain's secret services. He said he had decided to do this 'after having to sentence two quite high-grade people to long terms of penal servitude for their betrayal of important military secrets to the Soviet Union.'[9]*

---

*This was probably a reference to the cases of Douglas Frank Springhall and Captain Ormond Leyton Uren. Springhall, national organizer of the British Communist Party, was sentenced to seven years in July 1943 – after a secret trial – for having obtained details of the jet engine from an Air Ministry clerk. Uren, a captain in SOE, received seven years in November 1943 for giving Springhall a description of SOE headquarters.

SIS took notice and considered reviving a scheme to have a separate counter-intelligence section devoted to anti-communist operations. Actually, Cowgill had been recruited in 1939 to run just such a section but wartime work against Germany had kept him busy elsewhere. Now a modest stop-gap project was launched. Jack Currie, a retired MI5 officer, was brought in to head the new section, to be called Section Nine, until Cowgill was free.

When Philby informed his Soviet control about Section Nine he was told that he must do everything possible to ensure that he became its boss. As Philby told me in Moscow, 'First I reviewed the situation. Currie hadn't been doing much, just going through the archives to see what we had from our prewar operations and to get an idea of what we could re-create. Frankly it wasn't very effective and after about a year of this, towards the end of 1944, the word around the office was that the Chief wanted to expand the section – more people, more resources. The job was rightfully Cowgill's but I had to make certain that I got it.'

Philby mounted a two-pronged assault – to get rid of Cowgill, who certainly deserved the job, and to ensure instead that it was then offered to him – the office jobbery that so disturbed Greene. First he took advantage of the resentment Colonel Vivian harboured for Cowgill by suggesting that Vivian arrange a meeting between someone from MI5 and Christopher Arnold-Forster, who, as SIS's Principal Staff Officer, had the ear of the 'Chief', General Menzies. The idea was to get over to Arnold-Forster the fact that Cowgill and MI5 were hardly on speaking terms. Vivian arranged the meeting, where he must have also conveyed to Arnold-Forster that if appointing Cowgill as head of Section Nine posed problems, then Philby would be a suitable candidate. For, soon afterwards, Philby was invited to a meeting with Arnold-Forster at which the two had a long discussion on SIS's peacetime role.

Next, while Philby was casting around for a way to get the Foreign Office on his side, Cowgill drafted for Menzies a letter of complaint to the head of the FBI, J. Edgar Hoover. The hostile tone of the letter upset the Foreign Office adviser attached to SIS, then Patrick Reilly, and he asked Vivian to redraft it. Vivian got Philby to do so and then took the opportunity to tell Reilly his concern about Cowgill and his confidence in Philby. Vivian probably also checked with GC and CS on its attitude to Cowgill and learnt of several clashes which would virtually ensure that the cryptographers would not make a stand over Cowgill's departure.

In Philby's own words:

The ordeal virtually ended one day when Vivian summoned me, and asked me to read a minute he had written to the Chief. It was of inordinate length and laced with quotations from Hamlet. It traced the sorry story of Cowgill's quarrels, and argued that a radical change must be made before a transition to peacetime conditions. My name was put forward as a successor to Currie. Cowgill's candidature for the appointment was specifically excluded. My own suitability for the post was explained in flattering detail. Strangely enough, the recital of my virtues omitted my most serious qualification for the job – the fact that I knew something about communism.[10]

Philby had one last card to play. When Menzies called him in to offer him the job, Philby sowed in the Chief's mind the thought that it would be better if, before the appointment was announced, MI5 agreed to put it on record that they approved. Menzies, who at once saw the bureaucratic advantages of doing so, wrote to the then head of MI5, Sir David Petrie, and got a friendly reply. Philby had thus ensured that if he fell under suspicion in his new job, MI5's reaction would be handicapped by the fact that they themselves had had a hand in his appointment.

Cowgill's immediate resignation when he heard that he had been shunted aside completed Philby's triumph. As one of Philby's former colleagues writes, 'Philby at one stroke had got rid of a staunch anti-Communist and ensured that the whole post-war effort to counter Communist espionage would become known in the Kremlin. The history of espionage records few, if any, comparable masterstrokes.'[11]

What was the nature of this new department Philby was to head? The fact that it was created so soon after Churchill's decision to weed out communists from secret organizations, and that Currie came from MI5, suggests strongly that the original plan for Section Nine was that it should be a *counter*-espionage organization, working to protect Britain from communist penetration. But the section ended up also carrying out offensive espionage operations – that is, it sought to penetrate communist countries and mount espionage operations there. The irony is that the very man appointed to head Section Nine was Kim Philby, the KGB penetration agent. This put him in a position not only to protect all Russian penetration agents, including himself, but to reveal to Moscow all British operations mounted against the Soviet Union.

We must therefore consider the likelihood that it was Philby himself who changed the nature of Section Nine. To begin with, Philby persuaded his boss, Menzies, to allow him to draft the broad charter for the section. This gave him responsibility, under Menzies, for 'the collection and interpretation of information concerning Soviet and Communist espionage and subversion in all parts of the world outside British territory'. The wording was so vague it gave Philby the right to do just about anything. He could have argued, for instance, that the best way of collecting information about Soviet espionage plans was to penetrate the Russian intelligence service – an offensive operation.

There is further evidence of Philby's intentions. Since the size and scope of Section Nine involved financial implications and questions of cover for its officers in British embassies, the Foreign Office had to be consulted on Philby's plans. In February 1945 Philby submitted his ideas to Menzies's personal assistant (PA/CSS), since 1942 a Foreign Office appointee, at that time Robert Cecil. Cecil remembers:

> I was shocked, both at the size of the operation and its aims. It included a substantial number of overseas stations to be held by SIS officers under diplomatic cover and who would be directly responsible to [Philby]. I sent it back to Philby with a note suggesting he might scale down his demands and adding, 'I don't think that this is the Foreign Office view of post-war Europe or our part in it'. Within hours Philby had descended on me upholding his requirements and insisting that these be transmitted to the F.O.
>
> With hindsight it is easy to see why Philby pitched his demands as high and why he aimed to create his own empire within SIS. Quite apart from his covert aims, it is also clear that he foresaw more plainly than I the onset of the Cold War, bringing with it more menacing surveillance and making necessary more permanent use of diplomatic cover.[12]

But there are other reasons why Philby wanted to change Section Nine from a purely counter-espionage department into an aggressive intelligence-gathering one. As Cecil says, Philby did foresee the onset of the Cold War and knew that this would mean that the West would soon be mounting intelligence and subversion operations against the Soviet Union. Better then that he should stake an early claim for his department to be in control of such operations, so that he could sabotage such operations where possible, or at least keep Moscow informed about them.

Furthermore, if his section managed to include in its duties intelligence *gathering* from the Soviet Union, his Moscow masters would be in a position to pepper the intelligence gathered with nuggets of disinformation. In short, they would be able to control SIS's perception of the Soviet Union and its aims and thus influence British policy.

Small wonder that Philby's Soviet control was so insistent that he should fight to become head of Section Nine and was so delighted when he achieved it. Small wonder that Philby was adamant that Cecil must not interfere with his plans for the size and scope of the new department. Small wonder that Philby pushed ahead with the expansion of his section as fast as he could: within eighteen months, he had transformed a one-man, one-room section into a major department occupying a whole floor and employing a staff of more than thirty.

In the winter of 1945–6, Philby visited France, Germany, Sweden, Italy and Greece to brief SIS station chiefs on what Section Nine planned to do and what it would require. The first task would be to recruit agents in newly liberated Europe in order to re-establish and expand its prewar anti-communist network. The spy business being what it is, SIS was not surprised to discover that some of its agents, arrested by the Germans in the general round-up of 1939–40, had been recruited to work in Eastern Europe against the Soviet Union. With a typical display of pragmatism, some of these agents were now rehired by SIS, which argued that their anti-Soviet experience would be invaluable. Other former German intelligence and security officers were recruited because they were considered to have intact organizations behind the Iron Curtain. If they were wanted for war crimes, so much the better – this gave SIS a tighter hold over them.

Of course, these agents never had much success. They went behind the Iron Curtain and, betrayed by Philby, they vanished. Until now we have been able only to guess at their fate. Then in June 1988 the Russians surprisingly produced one of them for an interview. His name was Felikss Rumniceks. He had been recruited by Section Nine in May 1945 to take part in an operation to penetrate Soviet Latvia. Rumniceks, who had worked for German intelligence during the war as an agent in Sweden, was passed to SIS by the anti-Soviet Latvian underground. He was briefed in a series of interviews in the British embassy in Stockholm and finally met Philby himself.

As Rumniceks told it:

He was slender, fair and very well-spoken. He gave me a mission to organize an underground network in Latvia so that we could provide safe houses for the other agents when they came in. The network was also to provide information on the Latvian economy and on the Soviet army. If war broke out we were to build a resistance force to carry out sabotage and subversion. We were supplied with arms and money. I was to communicate with Philby once a month at an address in Stockholm using a written code called, if I remember right, Silenge. I was taught it there, on the spot, in the British embassy. It took me a day to learn. I was not the only one recruited. I know others were because I later met them.

I then crossed back into Latvia as a refugee from Finland and began at once to set up a network of agents. Eventually I had ten, mostly men. The network was quite successful for a while but after about two years we were all arrested and I was charged with high treason. I was sentenced to twenty-five years' hard labour. I served fifteen years, some of it in Riga and some in Siberia doing coal mining. Then there was a special decree signed by Brezhnev and I was released without serving the last ten years. I didn't know until later that Philby was an agent for Soviet intelligence. I now believe that it was Philby who betrayed me. My trouble was that I was on the wrong side at the wrong time. Now I am no longer anti-Soviet.

Rumniceks was lucky: at least he was not shot, as were some of the other agents Philby first recruited and then betrayed. The fate of men like these will come up again. Philby mounted other anti-Soviet operations but it offers a convenient point at which to note Philby's feelings about this side of his work for the Russian intelligence service. When I saw him in Moscow I did not know the whole story of his involvement in the Latvian operation and the question I asked him had to do with the agents he had sent into Albania some years later. But his answer applies equally well.

'The agents we sent into Albania were armed men intent on sabotage, murder and assassination. They were quite as ready as I was to contemplate bloodshed in the service of a political ideal. They knew the risks they were running. I was serving the interests of the Soviet Union and those interests required that these men were defeated. To the extent that I helped defeat them, even if it caused their deaths, I have no regrets. Don't forget that I was also responsible for the deaths of a considerable number of Germans and did my modest bit towards helping to win the war.'

We argued over this. I said I could not imagine being so devoted to a political ideal that I would be prepared to shed blood for it. Philby said: 'Well, that's where we differ. I have always operated on a personal level and a political level. When the two have come in conflict I have always put politics first. Contrary to what people believe I have felt badly about the necessity for this. But then a decent soldier would feel badly about the necessity for killing the enemy in wartime.'

In these last days of the war the new battle lines in the intelligence struggle were being drawn. Moscow knew that of its major penetration agents Philby stood the best chance of remaining in place. In fact there were already indications not only that Philby would be asked to stay on in SIS when peace came, but that his youth – he was still only thirty-three – gave him an excellent chance of rising to high rank. Then, with the war in Europe already over, two Soviet defectors threatened to wipe out everything that Philby had achieved.

THE MURDER OF A
NASTY PIECE OF WORK
10

Throughout the *Sunday Times* investigation in 1967 into the life and times of Kim Philby we were picking up tantalizing references to a Soviet defector at the end of the war who brought the first substantial clue to Philby's treachery and whose reception in the West left a permanent mark against Philby's name. Some former SIS or MI5 officer would drop into the conversation a remark like: 'Of course, it was that defector in 1945 who put us on to Kim. After that you only had to look at the files to see it all.' But when pressed for further details he would invariably clam up: 'Better leave it at that, old boy. Don't want to get into trouble with the OSA [Official Secrets Act].'

At first we thought these officers were referring to the defection in September 1945 of Igor Gouzenko, a twenty-five-year-old cypher clerk who had been based at the Soviet embassy in Ottawa from 1943 to 1945. Gouzenko sought asylum from the Canadian authorities who, unused to this sort of thing, considered handing him back to the Russians to avoid a diplomatic incident. It was only the intervention of Sir William Stephenson, a Canadian, head of British Security Coordination in New York during the war, who persuaded the Royal Canadian Mounted Police (RCMP) to hide Gouzenko at a wartime special training school on the north shore of Lake Ontario, that saved him from being seized by his embassy colleagues.

Gouzenko was questioned, at first by RCMP officers, later by an SIS officer, Peter Dwyer, and then by Sir Roger Hollis, then head of MI5's section dealing with political parties in general and the British Communist Party in particular.[1] Gouzenko's value was that he had brought with him clues to the identity of Russian spies working in the West. Some of these clues he had obtained during his Ottawa posting, the others, he said, while doing routine duty in Moscow.*

*The so-called 'need to know' rule in intelligence agencies – no one is given more information than he needs to know to do his job – means that defectors rarely know a spy's name. At best they will know his code name. But they may be able to pick up clues to his identity, both from

From Gouzenko's clues, the Canadian authorities amassed evidence which led to the arrest and conviction in 1946 of Dr Alan Nunn May, the British scientist who had worked at Chalk River, Ontario, on the Allied atomic bomb project during the war, and who had passed information about his work to the Russians. In fact, Gouzenko brought so much material that the Canadian government set up a Royal Commission on espionage, and eventually eighteen people were prosecuted, nine of whom were convicted. One of these was Kathleen Willsher, who worked in the British High Commission's registry. She was arrested on 15 February 1946, pleaded guilty to passing secrets to the Russians and, since they were minor secrets, given only three years' imprisonment.

The clues that led to Willsher included Gouzenko's information that she worked in 'administration' and that her code name was 'Elli'. But Gouzenko later claimed that he knew of yet another spy for the Russians who was also called 'Elli'. Unlike Wilsher, this second 'Elli' was of great importance. He said that he had learnt of the second 'Elli' when he was doing night duty in 1942 in the main military intelligence cypher room in Moscow. A colleague called Liubimov had passed him a telegram from this Soviet intelligence source in Britain. Pressed by his interrogators, Gouzenko offered a number of clues to the second 'Elli's' identity: he was a man, despite the female code name; he was in British counter-intelligence; he was so important he could be contacted only through messages left at pre-arranged hiding places; and, finally, he had 'something Russian in his background'. (This could mean, explained Gouzenko, no more than that he had visited the Soviet Union, had a wife with a Russian relative, or had a job to do with Russia.) Gouzenko said that Liubimov had told him that the second 'Elli's' information was so good that when his telegrams came in, there was always a woman present in the cypher room to read the decrypts and, if necessary, take them straight to Stalin.

If Gouzenko were to be believed, this meant that Moscow had a spy in Britain at the heart of Western intelligence (the CIA was not formed until 1947), and a hunt began to identify this second 'Elli'. The trouble was that Gouzenko kept changing his story. The exact place where 'Elli' worked was obviously very important. At first Gouzenko said that 'Elli' worked in 'five of MI', which could have been either MI5, or Section Five of MI6 (the other name for

---

the type of information he sends and from gossip within the service. Much counter-intelligence work consists in trying to find the person who fits all the clues.

SIS) – Philby's section. Later he was confident that 'Elli' worked in MI5, but then became less certain and accepted the possibility that he worked in counter-intelligence in SIS.

There were other, independent clues to Elli's identity. In 1944–5 the FBI had recorded radio messages sent from the Soviet consulate in New York. After the war its code-breakers started work to try to read these messages and in 1948 they began to get results. One message – to the Soviet embassy in London – advised that Gouzenko had defected and asked that 'Stanley' be warned of this fact 'as soon as he returns to London'. MI5 interpreted this as meaning that a highly placed Russian intelligence officer was in danger of being exposed by Gouzenko and that he could not be warned at that moment because he was abroad and out of contact. But was 'Stanley' also 'Elli'; or were there *two* Russian agents in British intelligence; and if there were, why had the Russians wanted to warn only one, Stanley?

Over the years the possibilities were whittled down. When Maclean's defection in 1951 exposed him as a long-serving Soviet agent, it was realized that he could not be either 'Elli' or 'Stanley' – he was in Washington at the relevant time and in regular contact with his Soviet control. It could not have been Burgess because he was in London. It might just have been Blunt, who was abroad at the relevant time. The file has never been closed and today, in the late 1980s, there are two schools of thought in Western intelligence.

The first, led by Peter Wright, the former MI5 officer in exile in Australia, holds that 'Elli' was the late Sir Roger Hollis, director general of MI5 from 1956 to 1965, and that Hollis was a Soviet penetration agent of status equal to, if not higher than, Philby. Although an investigation by a joint SIS-MI5 committee could not find any conclusive evidence against Hollis and although a former secretary of the Cabinet, Lord Trend, reviewed this investigation and could find no substance in the allegations, this school defiantly sticks to its belief.

The second school, which includes at least three former heads of the services, rules out Hollis as 'Elli' and believes that 'Stanley' was almost certainly Philby, and that Philby could well have been 'Elli' too. He was abroad at the relevant time, on a mission in Istanbul (of which more later); he worked in 'five of MI', and he was certainly an important Soviet penetration agent. True, he did not have 'something Russian in his background' but Gouzenko was very vague about what this meant. Gouzenko in his old age (he died in 1982) said that he felt that Roger Hollis was 'Elli'; but in one of his last interviews before his death he said it was possible that Charles

Ellis, an Australian-born SIS officer who had a Russian wife, was 'Elli'.

In the hope that Philby could end all this speculation and clear Hollis's name, it was one of the first subjects I raised with him in our conversations in Moscow. I began with a broad question: 'Can you cast any light on the Hollis affair?' Philby replied: 'I honestly cannot. Such a matter is not within my area of knowledge over here. All I can say is that I knew him, not well, but I did know him. And any idea that he was a Soviet penetration agent seems to me to be unlikely. I thought he was an upright if slightly stodgy Englishman.'

I believed Philby's reply for the simple reason that it would have been in the interests of the KGB to have encouraged the idea that Hollis was indeed a Soviet agent so as to create suspicion and uncertainty in the British services, to demean them in the eyes of the British public, to sow dissension between the British and American services, and to inflate the reputation of the Russians as brilliant spymasters. On the other hand, for Philby to have hinted to me that Hollis *was* a Soviet agent would automatically have been suspicious, so perhaps this was the only reply he could have made. Even if true, his answer did not take us much further, so I pressed him by saying: 'You must know something about Gouzenko and the Elli business.'

Philby replied: 'Certainly. The first information about Gouzenko and Elli came from Stephenson. "C" called me in and asked me my opinion about it. I said Gouzenko's defection was obviously very important and we treated it as such. But it was a disaster for the KGB and there was no way I could help. The Mounties had Gouzenko so well protected that it was impossible for the Russians to do anything about him, bump him off or anything like that. So he was able to give away a big Canadian network, and the telegrams he brought with him when he defected would have been of great help to Western decrypters.'

Philby paused at this stage and grinned. Then he went on: 'It was a bit of a comfort to learn later that Gouzenko nearly bankrupted the Mounties when he discovered the joys of the capitalist mail order system. He'd order all sorts of consumer durables from the catalogues, whether he needed them or not, and send the bill to the Mounties. His basement was apparently full of unopened television sets and so on.'

'And Elli?' I said.

'Well, trying to identify Elli certainly occupied a lot of people's time in the British services. I remember one day Blunt and I were in Hollis's office. Hollis and I were chatting and Blunt was idly turning the pages of some report or other. There was a break in the conversation and suddenly, without warning, Hollis turned towards Blunt and called: "Oh, Elli." Blunt didn't bat an eyelid. He just went on turning the pages as if nothing had happened. And Hollis for his part, resumed the conversation with me as if it hadn't been interrupted.'

I pondered for a moment whether this anecdote was meant to imply that Blunt was 'Elli' and that Philby had told it to me to illustrate Blunt's coolness under pressure. But what he said next discounted this idea. 'Elli's identity will probably never be satisfactorily resolved. Elli appears in the Gouzenko telegram story and never before or since. I am not Elli – as far as I know. An officer or agent does not necessarily know his own code name.' And then Philby moved on to other topics.

The most logical explanation for the mystery of the second 'Elli' is this: Gouzenko invented him. Realizing that the first 'Elli' was a comparatively small fish and anxious to impress Western security services, Gouzenko created a second, making up the story of Liubimov and the telegram to give his story substance. It is significant that Gouzenko did not seize the first opportunity to say to his interrogators: 'Look, strange as it may seem, there are two Soviet spies in the West with the same code name – "Elli". One is here in Canada and the other is in Britain.' Instead, the possible existence of a second Elli emerged, almost as an afterthought, in Gouzenko's evidence before the Royal Commission:

Q: Do you know whether Elli was used as a nickname or cover name for any person other than Miss Willsher?
A: Yes, there is some agent under the same name in Great Britain.
Q: Do you know who it is?
A: No.

It did not take the *Sunday Times* team long to realize that the references to the defector who compromised Philby could not have meant Gouzenko. Who then could it have been? Despite our best efforts we had got no closer to unravelling this part of the Philby story when we went to press with our first article on 1 October 1967. Then that old maxim of journalism – 'Publication provokes information' – worked, and on the following Tuesday there was a letter from the heart of England waiting on the editor's desk. It read:

I am wondering whether next week's issue will mention an incident which occurred in Istanbul in August 1945 and in which both Philby and I were involved. If so, and I am mentioned by name, I should be grateful for a preview of the text before it is published. The incident convinced me that Philby was either a Soviet agent or unbelievably incompetent and I took what seemed to me at the time the appropriate action.

The letter was signed by John Reed, at that time the Sheriff of Shropshire. We all agreed that the incident Reed mentioned could well be one involving a defector and that Reed might be able to solve the mystery for us. Accordingly I set off the following day, found Reed's great house set in acres of forest, ate a magnificent lunch and then retired to his study. Reed said he was a former diplomat and was concerned that the Foreign Office might not approve of his talking to us; but he was willing to tell me all he knew if, for the moment, he could remain anonymous. His recall was excellent and his story enthralling.

'I was serving in our embassy in Turkey in 1945,' he said. 'First secretary. In those days we used to move from Ankara in the summer and go down to Istanbul and work from the old consulate building, a lovely place. One morning this Russian walks into reception looking very nervous and asks to see the acting consul-general, Chantry Page. The Russian is Konstantin Volkov, Page's opposite number in the Soviet embassy. I'd done my Russian exams so I get the job as interpreter.

'Anyway, it turns out that Volkov is really an NKVD officer [forerunner to the KGB] and he has decided to defect. He says he wants a laissez-passer for himself and his wife to Cyprus and £27,500 [an odd sum but possibly a conversion from a round figure in roubles]. In return he is offering the real names of three Soviet agents working in Britain. He says two of them are working in the Foreign Office, one the head of a counter-espionage organization in London. There was some other stuff as well – addresses of NKVD buildings in Moscow, the burglar alarm systems, key impressions, guard schedules, a list of Soviet agents in Turkey. He'd obviously been preparing for his defection for some time.'

Reed decided that the Ambassador, Sir Maurice Peterson, had to be told of Volkov's approach, so he asked him to wait. Peterson was horrified. He had for some time been trying to prevent what he regarded as an 'invasion' of his embassy by SIS men under cover and he saw Volkov as a step in the same direction. 'No one's going to turn my embassy into a nest of spies,' he said. 'If you must go ahead with this business do it through London.' This decision effectively cut the SIS head of station, Cyril Machray, right out of the affair, with disastrous results.

Reed told Volkov that his approach would have to be referred to London and warned him that it would take time to get a decision. Volkov said if that was necessary then so be it, but he made three conditions: the outline of his proposals would have to be handwritten by Reed and not typed because there was a Russian agent in the British embassy; communication with London would have to be by diplomatic bag because the Russians had cracked some of the British cyphers; and he would wait only twenty-one days for an answer. He left after making elaborate arrangements for re-establishing contact with him.

Reed wrote a report and the embassy respected Volkov's wishes – it sent it, securely but slowly, in the diplomatic bag to London. Reed told me the rest of the story as seen from his point of view in Istanbul. It was only when Philby's book, *My Silent War*, was published in 1968 that I learnt his side to events. It began in London where, ten days after Reed had written the report of his meeting with Volkov, it landed on Philby's desk.

After the first wave of shock and fear as he read the material, Philby was no doubt able to appreciate the irony: two Soviet agents in the Foreign Office and one of them *the head of a counter-espionage organization* in London. He immediately understood this to be him (although, as we shall see, Peter Wright and his followers believe that Volkov, too, was referring to Hollis). So Philby had been given the job of investigating his own case – on the face of it a great advantage for him. However, he soon realized that any decision he took had its dangers.

'I rejected the idea of suggesting caution in case Volkov's approach should prove to be a provocation. It would be useless in the short run and might possibly compromise me at a later date. The only course was to put a bold face on it,' Philby wrote later. 'I told the Chief [Menzies] that I thought we were on to something of the greatest importance. I would like a little time to dig into the background and, in the light of any further information on the subject, to make appropriate recommendations for action.'[2]

Philby was, of course, stalling for time. He knew that once he had made his recommendations – and what else could they be but to accept Volkov's offer and get him out of Turkey and on to British territory as quickly as possible? – the case would be conducted by the SIS station head in Istanbul. Philby himself would have no hour-by-hour control of the situation. Yet he would need time to alert his control, then time for the control to tell Moscow and for Moscow to act against Volkov. So Philby would have to run the whole case himself in order to slow it down, even if this meant going to Istanbul. The first thing to do was to alert the Russians. As he rather chillingly puts it, 'That evening I worked late. The situation seemed to call for urgent action of an extra-curricular nature.'

The next day Philby suggested to Menzies that someone should be briefed in London and then sent to Istanbul to handle the Volkov case. Menzies did not react as Philby had hoped and reply: 'Yes. I think you had better go yourself.' Instead Menzies said he knew just the man; he had met him the previous evening in his club: Brigadier Douglas Roberts of Security Intelligence Middle East (SIME). Roberts, who had been enjoying the last days of his leave, had a formidable reputation and was particularly suited for this job – he spoke fluent Russian and had worked in Turkey.

One of the reasons for Philby's success as a spy was his luck. When Menzies asked Roberts to take the case Roberts said no: he could not stand flying and went abroad only by boat. Philby now took a chance and suggested diffidently that he had better go himself. Menzies agreed. By the time he had called on the Foreign Office to complete the necessary protocol, collected his cypher pads from the SIS coding section and had a quick refresher course on their use, briefed his deputy on outstanding business, packed and arranged a seat on a plane to Cairo, his first stop, three days had passed. Philby's luck held: storms over Malta diverted his aircraft to Tunis and the flight eventually arrived in Cairo too late to catch that day's connection to Istanbul. When he finally did arrive, the British community's habit of maintaining the British weekend helped Philby still further.

He arrived on a Friday and saw the Minister, Knox Helm, a stickler for protocol, the same afternoon, only to be told that the Ambassador would have to be consulted first. On Saturday morning Helm said that Peterson would see Philby on the ambassadorial yacht during a cruise the following day. Meanwhile he was to do nothing. After a pleasant weekend, on Monday morning Philby briefed Reed, who was to accompany him to the meeting with Volkov, on what should be said. So it was not until Monday afternoon that they made the first attempt to contact Volkov again.

This was done through Chantry Page, the acting consul-general, who frequently had routine consular business with Volkov and could therefore telephone and invite him over to his office for a talk without arousing anyone's suspicion. Page got through, asked for Volkov and spoke briefly. Then he turned to Philby and said: 'I asked for Volkov and a man came on saying he was Volkov. But it wasn't Volkov. I know Volkov's voice perfectly well, I've spoken to him dozens of times.' Page tried again but did not get past the telephone operator. 'She said he was out. A minute ago she put me on to him.'

Page tried a third time the following day. It was the briefest call of all. This time the operator told him: 'Volkov's in Moscow.' Then Page, reporting to Philby, added: 'Then there was a sort of scuffle and slam, and the line went dead.' Philby asked Page to make one last attempt to reach Volkov by calling at the Soviet consulate-general in person. He was back in an hour. 'It's no bloody good,' he said. 'I can't get any sense out of that madhouse. Nobody's ever heard of Volkov.'

Philby advanced his view that Volkov's own insistence on diplomatic bag communications had brought about his downfall. Nearly three weeks had elapsed from Volkov's first approach until these abortive attempts to contact him. Reed, angry that the whole affair had gone wrong and feeling some responsibility for Volkov, turned on Philby and asked him why the hell someone could not have come out from London sooner. Philby brushed the question aside with a flippant: 'Sorry, old man. It would have interfered with leave arrangements.'

Reed pressed him as to what had gone wrong in London but Philby would not give him a direct answer; he tried to change the subject, and behaved in an evasive manner. 'I finally made up my mind,' Reed told me, 'that either Philby was criminally incompetent or he was a Soviet agent himself.' Later Reed took the opportunity at a diplomatic reception to pass on his suspicion to a colleague from the American embassy in Ankara, but this was before the CIA had been created, OSS was winding down, and Reed's American colleague had no intelligence contacts, so it is unlikely that the story got back to Washington in a form that could do Philby any harm. SIS itself accepted Philby's theory about Volkov's insistence on bag communications, so his luck held again.

Some weeks later a Soviet military aircraft made an unscheduled landing at Istanbul airport. A car raced out to the plane on the tarmac and a heavily bandaged figure on a stretcher was lifted on to the aircraft, which immediately took off. It seems likely that this was the departure of the unfortunate Volkov. I reminded Philby of this in Moscow, but apart from saying that Volkov was 'a nasty piece of work' and deserved what he got, he did not want to talk about it. All the same, he left me in no doubt that he had taken such risks to silence Volkov because he was convinced that Volkov could unmask him, that Volkov's 'the head of a counter-espionage organization in London' referred to him.

The Peter Wright theory, that it actually referred to Roger Hollis, depends on the English translation of the Russian words used by Volkov to describe the job the Soviet penetration agent held at that time, and raises issues not only of the subtleties of the Russian language but of the bureaucratic and intelligence jargon in use then. For example, does the Russian for 'fulfilling the duties of a head of section' really mean the '*acting* head of a section'? Does the Russian word for 'section' mean just that (part of a larger establishment) or could it also mean 'department' (in the sense of 'Department of Trade and Industry' i.e. an organization in its own right)? Depending on which view you take – and assuming that Volkov knew what he was talking about – the clues could point to Philby or to Hollis.

This dispute alone has kept many MI5 officers occupied for many man hours over the past twenty-five or so years. And yet it has been sterile pursuit. There is no verbatim record of the meeting with Volkov. John Reed took notes and wrote up a report that night but Reed agrees that he was not familiar with Russian intelligence idiom and cannot be absolutely certain of the fine details of what Volkov said.[3]

And what about the most alarming possibility of all: that Volkov was, after all, a plant; that consciously or unconsciously, he was being used to launch a masterly deception operation, designed either to protect other Soviet penetration agents, or, more likely, simply to bring MI5 to a grinding halt chasing bogus clues to mythical master spies. If this was the Russian aim, then it would appear to have been notably successful.

This did not concern Philby. He firmly believed that Volkov had fingered him and he had been forced to act to save himself. With something of a shock, he realized now that the Russian intelligence service was not invulnerable: information about him could leak to people like Volkov; a defector could bring him down. Until he went home to Moscow in 1963, he never felt secure again.

GROOMED FOR 'C'
11

The New Year's Honours List for 1946 was long and extensive – the country's grateful recognition of the work many of its citizens had done towards winning the recently concluded war. One of the names on the list was that of Harold Adrian Russell Philby, made a Commander of the Most Excellent Order of the British Empire, the third of the grades of the order and only two ranks below that of a knight. Philby had arrived. Not only was he one of the few wartime recruits asked to stay on in SIS, the fact that he had been the only 'amateur' to be honoured meant he was on the upward path; the higher echelons of the service were now open to him.

In Moscow Philby told me that he had an interesting anecdote about his CBE, one that clearly was important to him. 'I've just been reading Anthony Cave Brown's book about Menzies,'[1] he began. 'He tells a marvellous story about my investiture. Apparently I invited James Angleton, who was on leave from his American intelligence posting post in Rome, to come with me to Buckingham Palace on the big day. Brown then quotes Angleton as remembering that as we walked away from the Palace, I suddenly said: "What this country needs is a good stiff dose of socialism." Angleton is supposed to have told Allen Dulles [director of the CIA, 1953–61] that I sounded like a "Commie" and that he had a feeling in his bones about me from that moment on.

'It's a nice story, but there's one rather big flaw in it. I never went to Buckingham Palace with Angleton or anyone else to get my CBE. It was delivered to me at home. There were so many wartime honours being handed out that it seemed the sensible way of doing it. You can see the purpose of the story though – Angleton was suspicious of me early on and yet didn't do anything about it. Why? Because he wanted to use me for his own deception plans. It's an attempt to save face.'*

*Buckingham Palace press office confirmed on 31 March 1988 that Philby's CBE had been sent to his residence in Carlyle Square.

In keeping with his new image of a responsible peacetime professional SIS officer, Philby set about tidying up his private life. The main problem was that he was still married to Litzi, and although Aileen had changed her name by deed poll to Philby, their three children had all been born out of wedlock. This was not a handicap for a young SIS officer in the relaxed moral atmosphere of wartime, but for a permanent civil servant who wanted to make his way to the top it could count against him. By now Litzi was living in East Berlin with her wartime lover, Georg Honigmann, a known communist. Philby was certain that she would agree to a divorce, but if he contacted her to arrange it all and somehow or other MI5 later got to hear of the contact, it could be made to look very suspicious: why had Philby, a British counter-intelligence officer in charge of the anti-Soviet desk, been in touch with a communist living in a communist bloc country? If he then told the reason, he could well be asked why he had not mentioned before that he had been married to a communist.

Philby took the bold way out. He asked Vivian for permission to contact Litzi so as to arrange a divorce that would enable him to marry Aileen. And he got in first by describing how he met Litzi during a youthful escapade in Vienna and had married her to save her from imprisonment or death at the hands of the fascists. Vivian listened sympathetically and instantly gave his permission. Nevertheless he got MI5 to make a routine check of its records for anything it had on Litzi and must have been rather surprised to read the reply that Alice (Litzi) Kohlman/Friedmann/Philby/Honigmann was a confirmed Soviet agent.[2] Although Vivian must have pondered over this, he did nothing about it. To begin with, he was Philby's patron in the service and to make a fuss about Philby's marriage would end up reflecting badly on Vivian as well. It would not have been hard to convince himself that the MI5 trace added little to what Philby had already told him. As well, the marriage had really ended ten years earlier, before Philby had joined SIS, so there appeared little point in resurrecting a brief indiscretion that might stain the career of such a promising and much-liked officer.

So Philby got in touch with Litzi, and it was agreed that she should petition for a divorce on the grounds of Philby's adultery with Aileen. The decree was made absolute on 17 September 1946 and Philby and Aileen were married a week later. He was thirty-four; she was thirty-five and seven months pregnant with their fourth child, Miranda. The witnesses were Tommy Harris and Flora Solomon, Aileen's former boss and a longtime friend of the Philby family. The reception, a noisy, hard-drinking affair, was held in the Philby house in Carlyle Square.

Talking about it in Moscow, Philby expressed surprise that so long after the event the story that he had committed bigamy was still given credence: (Anthony Cave Brown had written: 'That Philby had married Miss Furse bigamously was an astonishing development . . . One wonders why Philby took this dangerous step, for 'C' would certainly have sacked Philby had he known that his chief of counter-espionage was a bigamist.')[3] 'Does anyone really think that I would have been foolish enough to marry Aileen without first getting my divorce?' Philby asked me. 'Bigamy carried a prison sentence in those days. I would have been out of the service on my ear in no time at all.'

In February 1947 Kim Philby was posted to Turkey. He was to be station chief of SIS in Istanbul, working out of the consulate-general under cover as a first secretary. There were two reasons for the move: Turkey was in the front line of the rapidly deepening Cold War and an ideal place from which to run operations into the Soviet Union's southern flank; and Philby, excellent intelligence bureaucrat though he might be, had had little experience in the field.

There had been a shake-up of SIS at the end of the war and the committee which had conducted it had plumped for versatility rather than specialization. All officers were to be able to conduct defensive and offensive operations both at home and abroad. Philby could claim to be able to handle both sorts of operations but he had done so mostly from his office in London. The time had come to bridge the gap between those who go and those who send them. The posting was considered a promotion, and Philby was happy to accept.

He went out ahead of his family, both to find a place to live, and because he wanted to stop off in Saudi Arabia to see his father and had decided that it would be easier all round if he did not have to introduce Aileen to his father's Saudi wife, Rozy al Abdul Aziz (by whom St John was to have two children). St John seemed to have settled back into life at the Saudi court as if the war had never intervened, and he was as optimistic about business opportunities as he had ever been, especially, he said, when oil eventually began to flow.

In our conversations in Moscow Philby was quick to defend his father against accusations that he had made a fortune negotiating these oil deals for the Saudis. 'Let's get this clear,' he said. 'My father did not sell off oil concessions to the Americans. He played a part in negotiating one Arabian oil concession on behalf of the Standard Oil Company of California, the acorn from which Aramco grew. For his services, he was paid one hundred dollars a month for the period of negotiation, five thousand dollars on signature of the contract, and five thousand dollars on the discovery of oil in commercial quantities. Less than twelve thousand dollars for one of the richest concessions in the world. Incidentally, the reason my father was able to convince King Saud that he should allow the Americans to prospect for oil was the possibility that while doing so they would strike water. In those days the Saudis were more interested in water than in oil.

'The picture of my father as a shifty businessman selling useless stuff to the Arabs is completely wrong. Between the wars my father was representative in Jidda of the Marconi company. When he died I received one hundred and twenty-six letters – they're in my desk over there – from people all over the world; one of them was from a senior executive of Marconi. Let me read you a bit of it: "One of the Sunday papers described [St John] as a businessman. He may have tried to be one and had he been willing to put his scruples aside he would undoubtedly have become wealthy and I for one would have gained indirectly – but, thank God, he was not a businessman." '

Since we were talking about his father, I asked Philby if he would like to comment on other accusations. Malcolm Muggeridge had said, for example, that the secret of Philby's motivation could be found in his father: 'Philby is an adventurer. He liked to think that he was following in his father's footsteps. Russia was his Arabia and Stalin his Ibn Saud.'[4] Or John le Carré: 'The avenger [Philby] was an embittered solitary with the arrogance of a man familiar with the terrain of personal philosophies: the Arabian desert.'[5]

Philby said: 'I first saw the Arabian desert, from an aeroplane, at the age of thirty-five when my character was surely formed. Since then I've spent perhaps twenty-one days in that "terrain of personal philosophies". Have a look at what I wrote about Saudi Arabia in my book; the time I stopped off there to see my father.'

Philby had written:

He [St John] met me in Jidda and took me briefly to Riyadh and Al Kharj. It was my first acquaintance with the country to which he had devoted the greater part of his life. Neither then, nor thereafter, did I feel the slightest temptation to follow his example. The limitless space, the clear night skies, and the rest of the gobbledygook are all right in small doses. But I would find a lifetime in a landscape with majesty and no charm, among a people with neither majesty nor charm, quite unacceptable. Ignorance and arrogance make a bad combination and the Saudi Arabians have both in generous measure. When an outward show of austerity is thrown in as well, the mixture is intolerable.[6]

In Istanbul Philby found a charming villa in Beylerbeyi, on the Asian side of the Bosporus. It commanded a fine view: from the minarets of Hagia Sophia in the distance to an ancient fortress on a bend of the Bosporus. The house itself was huge and the garden and orchard ran nearly down to the water. It was almost right alongside the landing stage which enabled Philby to commute daily to the European side, where the consulate was located, by ferry boat. The rent even included a private lobster harbour.

Aileen and the four children soon joined him, coming out by boat. The children found life in Turkey one long holiday. They played in the garden, swam in the Bosporus, and in summer turned so nut-brown that if it had not been for their fair hair they could have been mistaken for Turks. Soon, to all outward appearances, Philby settled down to life as a diplomat in one of the more exotic postings available to an officer of his rank. There was the round of diplomatic parties, dinners, picnics and cruises. 'I wonder why they don't hire the same bus to take the same people to all the same parties,' he wrote to a friend in London.

His secret life was different. Turkey has a long border with the Soviet Union and another with communist Bulgaria. In the 1940s Stalin was claiming a slice of eastern Turkey, plus the right to put Russian bases on the Bosporus and the Dardanelles – main thoroughfares for Soviet shipping. The Turks, to protect their independence, were clamouring for Western military aid. A civil war was raging in nearby Greece, which looked as if it might easily go communist. Istanbul is a city of many communities, including Armenians, Georgians, Bulgarians and Albanians, all with direct links to the homeland communities behind the Iron Curtain. So the city should have been a spies' paradise, yet it is hard to find anything really worthwhile that Philby achieved during his three years in Turkey, not because he was lazy or had lost interest in espionage, but because the nature of the work at that time and in that place turned out to be singularly unrewarding.

The Turkish authorities were no problem. They had a simple and straightforward attitude to all the foreign espionage officers who wanted to make their base in Istanbul: they welcomed the currency that their activities brought to Turkey and they allowed them to get on with whatever they wished to do – as long as they did it discreetly. In their eyes Philby behaved admirably. When a reporter on the Istanbul newspaper *Cumhuriyet* called on him, said he was writing a feature article to be called 'The Spies of Istanbul', and asked if he could interview him, Philby refused.

The Turkish authorities noted that Philby seemed to spend a lot of time with 'students' from the Balkan states, and travelled a lot, especially in the Lake Van area, close to the Soviet border. But Philby had established good relations with the head of the Istanbul office of the Security Inspectorate, a man he nicknamed 'Aunt Jane', and took care to tell him what he was doing, so there was seldom any difficulty.

The trouble was that the quality of intelligence was so poor. The Turks insisted as a matter of national pride that only they could debrief refugees from communist countries and interrogate those smugglers whose cross-border activities they tolerated. They then passed on what information they had gleaned to Western intelligence officers. But, according to Philby, the Turks never asked the right questions and seemed always to believe the answers.

Another possible source of information were the exile groups. But they quickly learnt that espionage can be a money-spinner, so nearly every Bulgarian or Romanian exile turned out to have taken the trouble to establish a spy network before he left his country and was willing to put this network at Philby's disposal if the money was right. 'Much of our time was spent in devising means of smoking such operators into the open, so we could judge what price to put on their work,' Philby wrote. 'We rarely succeeded, and I am pretty sure that, in spite of the care we took, several of the exiles made regular monkeys of us.'

When the exile front was quiet, Philby adopted standard SIS procedure and tried to recruit as agents members of the British expatriate community. Other SIS officers have suggested to me that there is something in the personality of the British businessman abroad that makes him more susceptible to this approach than other nationalities. Sir Dick White, a former director general of SIS, once told a French colleague that SIS was inundated with offers from British businessmen abroad who wanted to do a little espionage on the side. His French colleague was surprised. 'When a French businessman goes abroad,' he said, 'it's not a bit of spying he wants on the side.'

But Philby found that the British businessmen who might be in a position to get him useful information were not interested. 'They have too much to lose; they have duties to themselves, to their families; they even have duties to their damned shareholders. They would usually agree to pass on anything that "came their way" – invariably valueless gossip. But patriotism was not enough to induce them to take the risks involved in the systematic search for intelligence; and I could not offer them anything like the inducements they received from, say, the oil companies or civil engineering firms. My patience would be tried by requests from headquarters for information about Turkish harbours which had actually been built by British concerns.'7

This is a fascinating outburst from a man who was working at the time for the Russian intelligence service. He is angry at the fact that he cannot convince *British* businessmen to spy for the *British* service he is in the process of trying to destroy. Could it be that the professional intelligence officer in Philby was annoyed that his fellow countrymen showed so little patriotism and so much commercial caution? Many things that Philby said in our conversations in Moscow suggested to me that this would have been so. He respected strong views strongly held – even when they did not agree with his own. Of course another factor would have been his desire to do well in SIS so as to help his prospects of promotion. As Hugh Trevor-Roper has said, 'Philby . . . knew that solid and conscientious work was the only real way to rise.'8

So most of Philby's work in Turkey was for the British, consolidating his reputation. He recommended to London that he should undertake a long-range photographic reconnaissance of the Soviet frontier, 'Operation Spyglass'. Equipped with a camera 'as big as a tram', and escorted by a Turkish security officer, he started at the eastern end, where the frontiers of the USSR, Turkey and Iran meet, and worked his way westward, stopping every two or three miles and swinging the camera in a wide panorama across Soviet territory. Philby managed half the job and then postponed the remainder until the following summer.

His only other operation was an attempt to infiltrate Western agents into Georgia. Philby decided that it would be useless to look for such agents on the Turkish side of the frontier; he needed sophisticated and trained men. The task of finding them was given to the Georgian community in exile and when two suitable candidates had been found in France, they were trained in London and sent to Philby. Whether they knew the dangers they were running or whether they were cynically exploited is impossible to tell. As far as SIS was concerned, the men were going on a reconnaissance mission. They were to find out whether safe houses could be located, identity papers obtained, and a reliable means of communication established. They probably had an additional assignment from the Georgian community in Paris and a third from Turkish intelligence.

The operation was a disaster. The two volunteers had been born in Paris, knew nothing of the Soviet Union, and, on Turkish insistence, were put over the frontier right opposite a Red Army garrison town. One was shot within minutes of crossing the border. The other escaped and was last seen disappearing into a wood. Since he never established communication, the conclusion had to be that he had been caught. But it is unlikely that Philby betrayed the two men. He had his sights on bigger targets and would have been reluctant to risk his plans for two such innocuous agents.

There remains a puzzle about Philby's Turkey period. How close were his relations with his opposite number at the Soviet consulate in Istanbul? Turkey was as important for the Russian intelligence service as it was for the West, and it had a strong presence there. It is not unusual for rival intelligence officers to seek each other out, try to get to know each other, score off each other, and, in general, enter that moral twilight of the double game in the hope of slicing the fat and leaving the opposition with the lean, or of persuading one's opponent that his future lies with your service and not his own.

In 1967 we were told that Philby, like many field agents, had been given permission to try the 'full double'. If an opportunity arose to convince the Russian intelligence service that he was willing to betray his own service and work for the other side, then he had permission to seize it. Such was the faith the British service had in its star officer that it was prepared to trust him to feed the Russians genuine material in the hope of scoring off them. We could find no evidence that Philby actually did this, and in Moscow he declined to discuss it with me for operational reasons. But the fact remains that later when things did go wrong for Philby and MI5 became convinced that he was a traitor, many of his fellow SIS officers defended him with an extraordinary determination that can have only one explanation. To an outside observer, the behaviour of an SIS officer playing the double is indistinguishable from that of a traitor. Only his colleagues know the truth. At some stage in his career Philby must have been involved in double operations, and when he was attacked by MI5, his fellow SIS officers felt obliged to defend him. Turkey remains the most likely place for this double game to have occurred.

In the spring of 1948 Guy Burgess turned up in Istanbul to spend a holiday with the Philbys. His career had picked up under the Labour government – he was now in the Foreign Office hoping to become established. He was in the mood for fun, and who better to enjoy himself with than his old friend Kim Philby. Philby welcomed him. They went for long walks; they drove off for days on end in Philby's office jeep; they dined at the fashionable Moda Yacht Club, where they shocked the English members with the extent of their drinking – one night Guy, Kim and two friends drank, apart from wine with their meal, two bottles of brandy with their coffee.

It is clear that Philby did not merely tolerate Burgess because they both worked for the Russians, but that they shared a deep and genuine liking for each other. 'All my troubles can be put down to an injudicious friendship,' Philby said several times in Moscow, leaving no doubt that he was referring to Burgess. He had said much the same to other people. Yet two men could not be more different. Guy was a slob, untidy and often dirty. Philby dressed casually but was almost obsessively clean. Women did not exist as far as Guy was concerned. He ignored them and had no sensitivity about their feelings. Kim was charming with women, attentive, interested in their conversation, and curious about their attitudes.

The friendship between the two men was based on an intellectual affinity, and their mutual commitment. Each admired the other's dedication to their cause – no backsliding, no equivocation, no doubt. And only alone in each other's company could each truly relax, with no need to maintain a front, create a mask, or conceal an idea. Small wonder that Aileen bitterly resented the relationship her husband had with Guy Burgess – in many ways it was closer than her own.

Other wives have coped with their husband's best friend by ignoring him, seducing him, or by blackmailing the husband into choosing once and for all. Aileen did not have the strength to try any of these methods. Perhaps if she had been more aware of what her husband did, even if not of his true loyalties, she would have been more understanding. But as Philby said in Moscow, 'I never told Aileen anything, anything at all.' So she reverted to methods her family said she had used as a child when she felt neglected – she had 'accidents'.

Soon after Burgess had gone and Philby was away from Istanbul on a trip, Aileen arrived at the house of a British diplomat covered in blood. She said that she had been driving along a lonely road and had stopped briefly. Someone had jumped on to the running board of her car and had struck her several heavy blows on the head. A police investigation got nowhere and Aileen, instead of recovering quickly, contracted an infection. Philby, alarmed, arranged for her to be flown to a clinic in Switzerland. He went too, and stayed with her until she was out of danger and convalescing. Aileen told him that she did not want to return to the house at Beylerbeyi, so he went back to Istanbul and moved everything to a large flat in a villa owned by friends in Moda.

Six weeks after Aileen's return, Philby had to go to London. While he was away Aileen somehow managed to set their living room on fire, and before servants could put it out she was badly burned. Once again Aileen contracted an infection and had to return to the clinic in Switzerland. There her doctors decided that there was something beyond mere chance in these two accidents, and their physical effect on Aileen, because they advised her not to return to live in Istanbul. Her recovery was slow, but when she was well again she went briefly to Turkey to help Philby pack up and then she and the children returned to London to live.

Whether this would have meant a permanent separation we shall never know, because in August 1949 Philby received a telegram from London offering him the SIS representation in the United States, working in liaison with the CIA and the FBI. He accepted immediately. As he wrote in his book, 'The intention was to upgrade the job for a significant reason. The collaboration between CIA and SIS at headquarters level (though not in the field) had become so close that any officer earmarked for high position in SIS would need an intimate knowledge of the American scene.'

But there was more to it than this. After the *Sunday Times* articles appeared in 1967 there were denials that Philby could ever possibly have become head of SIS. His former boss, Sir Stewart Menzies, mantained that Philby held only minor posts. Other officers said Philby's drinking would have disqualified him from the job. Some believed that the Foreign Office would have exercised its veto to prevent his appointment on the grounds that he was his father's son; others said that MI5 was, by this time, already suspicious of him.

Hugh Trevor-Roper takes a different view:

I was convinced (and still am) that he was destined – indeed that he was being groomed – to head the Service: that he would have been, in the 1950's, the new 'C' . . . First, Philby was undeniably competent: the most competent and industrious man in that generally lax organisation. Secondly, although conspicuously abler than they, he never showed any trace of impatience or disrespect towards the established leaders of SIS. Consequently he was regarded by them as the hope of the future. Thirdly, his successive posts in the Service gave him, as no one else, a direct understanding of all the branches of it and thus fitted him to command it all.

Finally, who else, of his generation, was there? . . . I looked around the world I had left, at the part-time stockbrokers and retired Indian policemen, the agreeable epicureans from the bars of White's and Boodle's, the jolly, conventional ex-naval officers and the robust adventurers from the bucket-shop; and then I looked at Philby. I was reminded of Tiresias among the ghosts of Hades. He alone was real; they flitted like the shadows in their crowded *coulisses*.[9]

In Moscow I asked Philby for his own assessment of the likelihood that he would have been 'C' – Sir Harold Philby, KCMG, director general of Her Majesty's Secret Intelligence Service. He thought for a while and then he said: 'Frankly, I don't think I would ever have been the Chief. The plan was for Menzies to retire and then hand over for a brief period to Jack Easton [his assistant]. Then I would have been on the short list for the next 'C'. I don't think I would have got it, mainly because I was not a good committee man, which was Menzies's greatest attribute. But I had a good chance of being VCSS [vice-chief of the Secret Service] or ACSS [assistant-chief]. Getting the Washington job was the indication that I was definitely going to be on the short list for 'C'.'

The Russian intelligence service must have been delighted when Philby's control reported on his agent's new appointment. From the moment Philby had been given his lifetime assignment it had taken him only seven years to achieve the first stage – the penetration of SIS. Nine years later he had been given one of the top jobs in the service, in Washington, at the centre of Western intelligence operations. Only the last step remained. And if Philby did pull it off and become 'C', he would be invulnerable, and SIS would pass to Soviet control. Small wonder that he packed and left Istanbul in a hurry. He could not wait to get to Washington.

THE WASHINGTON PENETRATION
12

Philby spent a few weeks in London being briefed on what was expected of him in Washington. Apparently SIS felt that Philby's predecessor, Peter Dwyer, had leaned too far towards the FBI at the expense of the CIA. One of Philby's jobs, while being careful not to offend J. Edgar Hoover, was to turn this around. He took all the meetings, instructions and warnings in his usual cool, controlled manner until his briefing from Maurice Oldfield, later to be director general of SIS. Oldfield told him about the hunt for 'Homer'.

The same FBI cryptographers who, working on radio transmissions from the Soviet consulate in New York, had turned up 'Stanley' (see p. 132) had also come across the code name of another Russian spy, 'Homer'. What the FBI knew about 'Homer' strongly suggested that there had been a leakage from the British embassy in Washington during the years 1944–5 and that among the material that had found its way out of the embassy had been the telegraphic traffic between Churchill and Truman.

Oldfield told Philby that, working in tandem, the FBI and MI5 had been narrowing down the list of people who had been working at the embassy at that time and who might have had access to such material. Soon, and certainly during Philby's spell of duty in Washington, the case would come to a head and Philby should prepare himself to handle the British end of it. As soon as he could Philby contacted his KGB control in London and told him about the 'Homer' case. He needed an answer from Moscow; shortly before he left Istanbul his contact there had asked him if he could discover what the British were doing about an investigation in Washington involving the British embassy; were this and the 'Homer' case one and the same? Within a few days Philby had the answer: they were. Philby now knew who 'Homer' was – Donald Maclean.

Maclean has been posted to the British embassy in Washington in 1944 as first secretary and at one time had been acting head of Chancery. His career in the British diplomatic service was on a steep upward curve – he was the 'golden boy of the FO', as one of his colleagues described him, on his way to eventual ambassador in somewhere like Bonn or Rome. He was also doing very well for the Russians. By providing them with the main exchanges of views between Churchill and Truman in the closing days of the war he enabled Stalin to be one up in his negotiations with the West.

Then in 1947 Maclean became joint secretary of the Anglo-American Combined Policy Committee on atomic energy. This gave him access to material which enabled him to tell Moscow about political differences between Britain and the United States on atomic energy matters and to provide details about both countries' atomic programmes.

He must have provided useful information to Moscow in 1948 when he was part of an embassy team which accompanied Gladwyn Jebb, then serving in the Foreign Office, to a specially convened Anglo-American-Canadian meeting at which the first discussion took place of the project that was formalized a year later as NATO. This was a highly secret matter: the meeting was held in the Pentagon rather than the State Department and no notes were taken. The news that the West was considering constructing a united front against communism would have been very important for the Russians.

But his double role began to tell on Maclean. Melinda Maclean puzzled over her husband's excessively long hours of work and bouts of drinking which either put him in a morose humour or brought out the homosexual streak in him. She put it down to the demands of official duties; perhaps a quieter posting would help solve Donald's obvious psychological problems. It must have been something of a relief to her when, in October 1948, Maclean was posted to Cairo as head of chancery.

His realization that Maclean was 'Homer' posed something of a problem for Philby. He was in the fortunate position that he could control the investigation and act when it looked like getting too close to Maclean. But with Maclean now in Cairo, it would not be so easy to get Maclean away if the need should arise. And if the investigation got bogged down for any reason, then it might not conclude before Philby was moved elsewhere. 'Something drastic would certainly have to be done before I left Washington,' he wrote later. 'Heaven knew where my next appointment would lie; I might well lose all control of the case.'[1]

So Philby tucked the 'Homer' case away in that part of his mind where he filed his duties as a Russian intelligence officer and concentrated on his immediate task in Washington – getting to know the Central Intelligence Agency and its officers. He was under no illusions about what type of organization he would be dealing with. The CIA had grown out of the Central Intelligence Group (CIG) which had, in turn, grown out of the OSS. Philby had met OSS officers during the war and had formed strong views about their politics. We discussed these in an exchange of letters in 1984. Doing research for my book, *The Second Oldest Profession*, I had been impressed by the stance OSS officers had taken during the war over Britain's treatment of its colonies. Philby wrote: 'I was taken aback by your assessment of OSS as radical, realistic and anti-colonialist. It was the latter only in the narrowest sense that it wanted the Open Door extended to the British, French and Dutch empires, for the same reason that successive US administrations pressed for it in China: economic domination. Realistic, perhaps, but not radical.'[2]

Truman had disbanded OSS at the end of the war and did not intend to have a peacetime intelligence agency. But in January 1946 he gave the go-ahead for the formation of the CIG to collate and distribute material collected by the Army, Navy and State Department. It was meant to be a mere clearing house, a way of ensuring efficiency and preventing rivalry between the intelligence arms of the services. But right from the beginning, the CIG showed the ruthlessness and hunger for power that were later to be associated with the CIA. Within eighteen months it had extended its role to include the *collection* of intelligence, and from then on it became unstoppable.

It confronted and defeated the FBI, outmanoeuvring that master of conspiracy, J. Edgar Hoover. It abolished the FBI's foreign networks, seized control of the intelligence organizations of the very three government departments it was meant to report to: State, War and Navy. It uncovered the existence of a secret intelligence service which had been founded in the War Department in October 1942 and was known throughout the war only to the State Department and President Roosevelt himself, and wiped it out.

In one year the CIG expanded six times over, absorbing in the process all the bits and pieces of OSS that had managed to survive. And it so won over Truman that from 1948, when the CIG had become the CIA, his first caller of the day was invariably the director of central intelligence. By the time Philby arrived in Washington, the CIA was well on the way to becoming the huge bureaucracy that we know today, with its own revenue and banks, its own airline and its own policies. Its secret slogan in 1947 was 'bigger than State by forty-eight' – and it was.

As it grew, so its conception of its own role changed. It saw its duty not merely as collecting information about what was happening in the world, but as making things happen that would benefit

America. It became a major instrument of foreign policy operating in semi-independence. In short, Philby was to liaise with what was really a government within the government of the United States.

Philby later blamed this expansion, and the direction the CIA had taken, on Allen Dulles, its deputy director when Philby was in Washington, and its director from 1953 to 1961. He said in a letter to me:

> OSS was the product of the hot war, CIA of the cold war. So the real question is not how OSS turned into the CIA, but how the pre-Dulles CIA (it was formed more than five years before he took over) turned into the raving beast . . . A few ideas. Dulles, through JFD [John Foster Dulles, Secretary of State, 1952–9, and Allen Dulles's brother], had far too much power, which Ike couldn't curb and JFD wouldn't. (Ike probably knew very little about it.)
>
> AD, for his part, was the genial chairman who could never get his mouth around the essential 'No'. So, side by side with a lot of very sensible chaps, a lot of maniacs were allowed to go off every-which-way and do more or less what they liked. The dirty tricks multiplied of their own momentum. Naturally, if you think in terms of global struggle, dirty tricks are inevitable; but without control and purpose, they become incredibly wasteful and too often counterproductive. The Mad Mullah succeeds Mossadegh. Not very helpful I'm afraid, but I'm not writing your book.[3]

Philby seemed fascinated by Dulles and Dulles by Philby. When the author Leonard Mosley was writing his definitive work on the Dulles family he found among Allen Dulles's writings a half-finished sketch of Philby. Part of it read: 'In some ways, in temperament, in his attitude to people, his love of womankind and good living, he is not unlike myself.' Mosley sent this sentence to Philby in Moscow and provoked a long response, interesting because of the picture it gives of one of the leading lights of the CIA at that time, as seen through Philby's eyes.

> I hope I have not been too deprecatory about AD [Allen Dulles]. I liked him a lot. He was nice to have around: good, comfortable, predictable, pipe-sucking, whisky-sipping company. A touch of [Richard] Hannay, perhaps; definitely not Bond (detestable fellow!) . . . I first met Dulles in 1950, when he became DDI to Bedell Smith and met him frequently for a year, professionally and socially.
>
> I had known him much earlier by reputation, from his days in Switzerland where he acquired his legend. (All intelligence

people who achieve fame or notoriety, *quorum pars minima fui*,* are elevated to legendary status – by their own side.) Dulles did nothing to play down his legend; his unprofessional delight in cloak-and-dagger for its own sake was an endearing trait. It sank him finally, in the Bay of Pigs . . .

I would meet AD, usually with two or three colleagues, for lunch or dinner at the usual Washington eating places, the Colony, La Salle, Mayflower, Shoreham etc. (Harvey's was off-limits because of Hoover's addiction to the place; it is nice to have found out that he never paid for his meals.) I would often call at AD's office late in the afternoon on business, knowing that he would soon suggest drifting out to a friendly bar for a further round of shop talk . . .

Your prodding has caused me to think more deeply than for many years about AD. I find recurring, with inexorable insistence, the adjective 'lazy'. Of course AD was an active man, in the sense that he would talk shop late into the night, jump into aeroplanes, rush around the sophisticated capitals and exotic landscapes. But did he ever apply his mind *hard* to a problem that did not engage his personal interest and inclination; or was he basically a line-of-least-resistance man? . . . I put it to you that Dulles enjoyed what he did and did what he enjoyed, no less, no more. Quite enough, you may retort, for a nice guy. Yes, but not for the post that he held.[4]

In Washington, Philby rented a house off Connecticut Avenue and the SIS officer he was succeeding, Peter Dwyer, began to introduce him around. The first thing Dwyer told him was that the FBI would bug his house for the first three months, just as they had bugged Dwyer's. In Moscow Philby explained this to me: 'It wasn't because there were any suspicions about me – I'd have never got the Washington job if there had been – but because Hoover trusted no one until they proved they were clean. Hoover hated and distrusted just about everybody – Slavs, Jews, Catholics, homosexuals, liberals, "niggers" and the rest. They blinded him to his real job, luckily!'

Philby slipped easily into his new duties. He worked from the British embassy but spent a lot of time in the offices of the CIA and the FBI. In the CIA the two divisions he had most to do with were the Office of Strategic Operations (OSO), the intelligence-gathering section, and the Office of Policy Co-ordination (OPC), whose innocent-sounding name concealed that fact that it dealt in

*'Of whom I was a small part.'

155

covert operations and subversion. His contacts in OSO were James Angleton, his counter-espionage friend from wartime London who now became a fairly regular luncheon partner, and Bill Harvey, a tough former FBI agent, whom Hoover had sacked for drunkenness on duty. At the FBI he dealt mainly with Micky Ladd, one of Hoover's original G-men in Chicago.

These were hectic times as the world seemed to stagger from one international crisis to another. First there was the shock of the Soviet atomic bomb, exploded on 29 August 1949. This had brought an outcry against the CIA, which had said that it would be at least mid-1953 before the Russians could build a bomb – the greatest miscalculation of the Cold War. (The then director, Admiral Roscoe Hillenkoetter, took the blame and was eventually replaced by General Walter Bedell Smith.)

The scandal was followed by a massive spy scare as the FBI sought to explain away the failure by suggesting that American estimates of anything from ten to twenty years before the Russians got the bomb were correct, but had been invalidated by Soviet espionage rings in the United States which had, Hoover said, 'stolen the most important secrets ever known to mankind and delivered them to the Soviet Union'.*

In June 1950, the Korean War broke out, again with recriminations about the CIA's failure to foresee the North Korean attack, even though the agency had been carrying out covert operations in Korea for at least two years prior to the invasion. And all the while the two super-powers confronted each other around the world as the CIA implemented its policy of trying to defeat Soviet subversion with covert action. The CIA intervened in Greece, France and Italy to check the power of the Communists there. It mounted anti-Communist operations in Iran and Guatemala and, later, Indonesia, Angola, Cuba and Chile.

Philby was at the centre of the early CIA operations and when we assess what he was able to do for the Russians during his two years in Washington, we have to think not in terms of 'nuts and

---

*This is an exaggeration. The atomic spies – Julius and Ethel Rosenberg, Klaus Fuchs, Bruno Pontecorvo, Alan Nunn May and, perhaps, Donald Maclean – did not give the atomic bomb to the Soviet Union. Soviet physicists developed it themselves. The spies, particularly Fuchs, may have advanced the date of the first Soviet bomb but even this remains debatable and it would appear to be a matter of a year or eighteen months at the most. There is no evidence that the Rosenbergs, executed for treason in 1953, ever told the Russians anything of value about the atomic bomb.

bolts' intelligence like the thickness of the armour on an American tank, but political will, or the lack of it, long-term military intentions, divisions in decision-making bodies, and relations between allies – the West's grand strategy. His days were crowded with meetings, hearing the American view, presenting the British one, negotiating compromises, planning operations, reporting back to London. He had access to every level of the CIA, including the director, Bedell Smith, whom he saw frequently.

To illustrate the calibre of Bedell Smith's mind, Philby wrote in his book about the time he took him a document of twenty-odd paragraphs for his scrutiny and comment. Knowing of the director's 'precision-tool brain', Philby had spent the whole morning learning the document by heart. Bedell Smith read it through once and engaged him in a close discussion about it, referring to the numbered paragraphs without looking at the document again. But Philby omitted in his anecdote the most important fact – the nature of the document. In Moscow he told me what it was – a detailed account of how SIS and CIA would cooperate in the event of war with the Soviet Union. Philby passed it on to his Soviet control, dictating it to him from memory, which was the real reason he had learnt it by heart in the first place.

The McMahon Act of 1946, preventing as it did the sharing of atomic military information with America's allies, made it difficult for Philby to learn anything directly of the debate in the winter of 1949–50 on whether the United States should go ahead with building an H-bomb. But his indirect access to the pros and cons enabled him to find out all he needed to know. Lyman Kirkpatrick, later an inspector-general of the CIA, told me: 'Intelligence officers talk trade among themselves all the time. Philby was privy to a hell of a lot beyond what he should have known.'[5] Since Britain was equally interested in the H-bomb debate, and as much in the dark about it as the Soviet Union, Philby passed on what he could learn to both his masters.

This does not mean, however, that every officer in the CIA and FBI told Philby everything, or even that Philby was able to use everything he *was* told. In the secret world of intelligence not even close friends are entirely trusted. Philby made a major play soon after he had arrived in Washington to persuade the CIA to use SIS's worldwide communications system, at that stage faster and more efficient than that of the Americans. He would turn up at meetings with an operational report from a British source which he knew the Americans would not have yet received from their own man, toss it casually on the table with a tight smile and say: 'Wonder what you make of this, old boy?' And then, not too often and with the right degree of diffidence, he would suggest that SIS would be delighted to allow the CIA to use its communications any time it liked. But senior CIA officers, led by Angleton, were against the idea because they did not want SIS reading their messages.

Angleton and Philby also fenced over where the point of liaison between SIS and the CIA should be – the CIA office in London, or the SIS office in Washington? Angleton wanted it to be London.

> By doing so he could exert maximum pressure on SIS's head-quarters while minimising SIS intrusions into his own. As an exercise in nationalism, that was fair enough. By cultivating me to the full, he could better keep me under wraps. For my part I was more than content to string him along. The greater the trust between us overtly, the less he would suspect covert action. Who gained most from this complex game I cannot say. But I had one big advantage. I knew what he was doing for the CIA and he knew what I was doing for SIS. But the real nature of my interest was something he did not know.[6]

There are two points worth making about this. One is that struggles in the secret world are not always James Bond exploits but are often the same sort of bureaucratic battles that take place in industry, commerce or government. The other is that Philby may have underestimated the advantage he had over Angleton, as we shall soon see.

There was other information which Philby did receive, but could not use because so few people had access that if the Soviet Union acted on it, the CIA would be bound to be suspicious of him. And there was information on which it could act only by covering Philby by duplicating it from other sources. This appears to have been the case with the number of covert operations which SIS and the CIA mounted jointly in the late 1940s and early 1950s, both to penetrate the Soviet Union and to destabilize Soviet bloc countries. The most notorious of these, and the one which caused the heaviest loss of life, was the Albanian operation.

In 1948, the British and American governments had sanctioned in principle the idea of trying to splinter a Soviet bloc country away from Moscow's control. The theory was much like the domino one which later obsessed American planners in South-East Asia – one country topples, others follow. The tactics were to plant enough well-trained agents inside the country to organize a maquis-style campaign which might provoke a full-scale civil war. The trouble which this would cause the Russians would alone be sufficient justification, with the added possible bonus of other Soviet bloc countries following the example. The planners, in their most optimistic moments, saw the whole base of the Soviet empire beginning to crumble.

Much preliminary work went into choosing a country for the experiment. Finally it was decided that Albania, the weakest and smallest of the socialist states, offered the best prospects for success. The communist regime under Enver Hoxha was not firmly established. The Germans had been driven out in November 1944, but in the early postwar years the communists were still struggling with their reconstruction programme. King Zog was in exile in Cairo but many loyalists remained. Albanian émigré groups were confident that the majority of the population was only waiting for a little encouragement from the West to rise in counter-revolution.

Plans advanced rapidly. The British provided Malta as a base and small boats for seaborne missions. The Americans supplied the money and the weapons and Wheelus Field, Libya, as a supply depot and for airborne drops. The operation was run by an SIS-CIA committee in Washington with James McCargar and Kim Philby as joint commanders. On paper and over the conference table it all seemed feasible, so until 1952 carefully trained agents were parachuted into the mountains of Albania, landed on the coast, or infiltrated over the border from Greece.

The logic was this: the communist rebels in Greece were on the point of collapse, Yugoslavia had broken with Russia, and Soviet technicians and advisers had been brought in to run Albania. So the hawks in the State Department, CIA, SIS and the Foreign Office thought they could remould the face of Eastern Europe. But the plan turned out to be one of the great débâcles of the Cold War.

Hundreds of émigrés were trained in an old fortress in Malta, equipped with weapons, explosives, radios, and a supply of gold sovereigns, and sent to their deaths. In 1973 I located one of the SIS officers who had helped train one group of Albanians. He recalled:

We set up our forward base on Corfu because the Albanian coast is only three miles away. We took over a large villa just west of Dassia Bay. Early in December 1949, we sent over the first six by motor launch. Two days later we got a WT signal from the group saying that they had made contact with loyalist elements and had been welcomed. All was safe for the other groups to follow as soon as possible.

Four went across without incident but the fifth was fired on by an Albanian gunboat. It got safely away in the darkness. Three days passed without any word, then a week. By now our WT operator was manning our receiver in Corfu on a twenty-four hours a day basis. They continued to do this for nearly a month before a message from the military mission in Athens reported a rumour from Albania that every team had been wiped out or captured within minutes of landing.

One of the men managed to get back across the border to Greece and then we had a lot of trouble with the Greek security authorities. They wanted to shoot him, partly because they thought he might now be an Albanian agent and partly to show us that in future they'd like to be informed of what we were up to in their territory. We were all recalled to London where there was an inquiry and then 'C' told us that for the moment the operation was declared 'abandoned'.*

Later the Albanian Ministry of the Interior announced that police and troops had engaged groups of 'émigré saboteurs' who had landed by sea and parachute. Twenty-nine had been killed in resisting capture. In October 1951, fourteen survivors were tried in Tirana, the Albanian capital. Two were shot and the others sent to jail for from seven years to life.

There is no doubt that the strategic aim of the Albanian operation was betrayed by Philby. He admitted it to me in Moscow. We were discussing John le Carré's introduction to *Philby, the Spy Who Betrayed a Generation*, and Philby said: 'He makes a rather nasty innuendo. He asks if I *proposed* the Albanian infiltrations which sent a lot of agents to their deaths. Now if I had proposed such an operation and forced it successfully up to the highest level, and if I had then scotched it, thus postponing for a couple of decades a Western-inspired bloodbath in the Balkans – perhaps killing it for ever – then, for heaven's sake, I'd claim full credit for a coup of such brilliance.

'Instead, I only claim credit on a much reduced scale for having played a part in frustrating a scheme thought up by others. Incidentally, those others, as the nature of the scheme shows, were quite as ready as I was to contemplate bloodshed in the service of a political ideal. Yet I'd hesitate to damn them as innately bloodthirsty men. So why do people damn me as having an inexhaustible appetite for blood?'

*The fort in Malta where the agents were trained still stands. The villa in Corfu has been turned into a hotel. The few Albanian agents who survived were found work in Britain with the Forestry Commission. Most of them eventually emigrated to the United States.

So Philby certainly betrayed the *existence* of the Albanian operation to the Russians – valuable enough information. But he cannot be blamed for all the operational failures. For the last two years of the operation he had nothing to do with it, having been recalled from Washington, as we shall see, in the aftermath of the flight of Burgess and Maclean. And even when he was in Washington, the Russians would not have used him to obtain details of the infiltrations. It would have been too risky for him and he was too valuable an agent to endanger. For what it is worth, Enver Hoxha says it was the vigilance of his security police and their 'radio game' which caused the débâcle 'and not the merits of a certain Kim Philby, as some have claimed'.[7]

This gives us a clue to what really happened. Philby told the Russian intelligence service about the operation in principle. Moscow told Tirana. The Albanian security service then penetrated the Albanian émigré organizations – if they had not already done so – and one or more of these penetration agents managed to be selected for the CIA-SIS operation. Once infiltrated into Albania he handed over his team to the Albanian security authorities who then forced the team's radio operator to work for them. From that moment, Albanian security would have controlled the whole operation and could have played a 'radio game' in order to lure the rest of the CIA-SIS teams to their doom.

Ironically, it only emerged in the early 1980s that the CIA was not as committed to the operation as it made out. It knew it could not work. Mike Burke, the CIA officer in charge of the Italian side of the operation, has said: 'The operation would not have succeeded regardless of Philby.'[8] The Albanian exiles were dupes, sent to make a noise, to show that the CIA was active in the fight against communism. They were sacrificed for wider political interests. As it turned out, Albania soon formed a close friendship with China anyway, and in so doing probably became a bigger headache for the Soviet Union than if the West's splinter operations had actually worked.

There were other covert actions during Philby's time in Washington. The Latvian operation, which Section Nine had started in 1945, continued and was expanded to include Lithuania and Estonia. It had become swashbuckling stuff, involving dashes across the Baltic at night in high-speed patrol boats, with young SIS officers handing out cyanide tablets to the would-be anti-Soviet Pimpernels, along with radios and explosives.

The exiles were recruited in 'displaced person' camps in the British zone in Germany and taken to Britain for training. Former German patrol boats were converted by the Vospers company in

Britain and, operating under the guise of the British Control Fishery Protection Service, landed the agents along the Baltic coast. Once ashore the agents buried their radios and weapons and then tried to make contact with local anti-Soviet groups.

There were attempts at deeper penetration. The RAF dropped British-controlled agents into Poland and the Ukraine, including members of the fiercely nationalist White Russian organization, NTS. The CIA, for its part, recruited Lithuanians, Estonians, White Russians, Ukrainians and some Armenians for a series of drops that went on until 1953. It had US Air Force ground support but ran its own two planes – a Hungarian pilot crew and a Czech pilot crew – which went into Soviet air space at 5,000 to 8,000 feet. They were tracked by Soviet radar and shot at but the CIA never lost one.

These operations had varied aims. The Ukrainian one was to support a Ukrainian resistance group, originally about forty thousand strong, in and around the Carpathian Mountains. Until 1953 when the Red Army finally wiped them out, these insurgents were supplied with food and weapons by the CIA. A second CIA penetration operation, using agents drawn from a similar pool of émigrés, defectors and deserters from the Red Army, got under way in 1948. The agents were trained in the use of radio and codes, given forged identities and dropped in various parts of the Soviet Union with only one instruction – to look for evidence of preparations for war. This operation also lasted until 1953. And finally, there were a few agents dropped in 1950 with orders to obtain a vial of water downriver from a number of suspected uranium processing plants, both to confirm that the plants were processing uranium and to determine what process they were using.

Harry Rositzke, a senior officer in the CIA Soviet bloc division, who was involved in all these operations, summed up the outcome:

> We lost, in the long run, most of the agents who went in. We had no expectation that any of the resistance groups they went to support would ever pose a real threat to Moscow, or that the agents themselves would cover the Soviet Union the way it was later covered by the U-2 flights and the satellites. But we were all scared of the Russians then and we had to do what we could.[9]

But why did the operations go so badly wrong? Philby certainly betrayed some of them. He writes: 'A first party, equipped by the British with W/T and other clandestine means of communication, was sent into the Ukraine in 1949, and disappeared.

Two more parties were sent the following year, and remained equally silent.' He goes on to recount that in 1951 the British dropped three six-man parties, the aircraft taking off from Cyprus. One was dropped midway between Lvov and Ternopol; another near the headwaters of the Prut, not far from Kolomyya; and a third just inside the border of Poland, near the source of the San.

Philby then writes: 'In order to avoid the dangers of overlapping and duplication, the British and Americans exchanged *precise information about the timing and geographical coordinates of their operations* [emphasis added].' The exchanges were, of course, conducted through Philby, as the British liaison officer with the CIA. According to Rositzke, at some of the meetings held to discuss the operations, Philby actually took the minutes. So we can appreciate, but not condone, the hidden meaning in what Philby concludes: 'I do not know what happened to the parties concerned. But I can make an informed guess.'[10]

This story accounts for only one particular operation. No doubt Philby betrayed the general outline of others but he was not responsible for the failure of them all. Rositzke says: 'The general notion that Philby knew everything that the CIA knew about our operations into the Soviet Union is simply not true because we had many operations about which we told the British nothing whatever. Philby might have been able to tell Moscow: "The Americans are planning two drops in the spring." Well, the Russians were terribly alert for that kind of thing anyway, so I don't think Philby's information helped them that much.'[11]

Another former CIA officer, George Muslin, has a convincing explanation for the failure of those missions not betrayed by Philby. 'The British were running an operation called "Broadway", dropping agents into Poland. It got too expensive for them and they passed it on to us,' he said. 'It never succeeded because the whole agent-training programme in Germany had been infiltrated by the communists before we took it over. We learnt this when one of the agents managed to get back out of Poland and told us we'd been had. We closed down the whole operation, abandoned it on the spot. I had a friend running a similar operation into Russia and much the same thing must have happened there. He told me that every agent they sent into the Soviet Union was never heard of again.'[12]

For what it is worth, this tallies with what the Russians themselves have to say on the subject. In 1982 they published *CIA Target: The USSR*, in which the following paragraph appears:

In the confusion that followed the collapse of the Nazi Reich, the NTS managed to assure the chiefs of the Secret Intelligence Service that they had left a network of agents behind in the Soviet Union. The British nibbled at the bait . . . And the CIA, learning of the British breakthrough, also made eager contact . . . [Agents] were smuggled into the Soviet Union with CIA and partly Secret Intelligence Service aid. In 1951–4, the Soviet Security rendered harmless the following American and British agents smuggled into the Soviet Union.

There then followed a list of names. This section concludes:

On February 28–29, 1956, the Secret Intelligence Service and the CIA met in London to discuss the future of the NTS . . . The British conclusion is that the British-NTS partnership has been largely unproductive . . . The British service has therefore decided to terminate this partnership in all sectors of activity.[13]

My own view is that all these operations were doomed from the start. Covert action has turned out to be little more than a gimmick, effective only when the internal forces of a country were already moving in the direction the CIA wished to push them. (There have been exceptions, such as Chile.) When this was not so, covert action has either failed or has even been counter-productive, as in the Ukraine, where CIA intervention hindered rather than helped the resistance movements. Furthermore, the Western penetration operations of Soviet bloc countries in the late 1940s and early 1950 were to leave an awkward legacy. Many of the émigrés that the Americans had recruited for these operations were former nazi collaborators who were smuggled into the United States. It was only in the 1970s that evidence began to emerge that a number of nazi war criminals had safely lived out their final years as American citizens with the connivance of the CIA.

The last person anyone in Washington suspected of having a role to play in the failure of these anti-Soviet operations was the bright, charming, urbane, relaxed, informal, companionable British diplomat, Kim Philby. 'He was obviously knowledgeable and educated enough to be a welcome member of Washington society,' Rositzke remembers. 'He was the kind of man any hostess would pick out. He was the kind of man American non-intelligence personnel would find a plus. This is all beyond the business of the general liking of the British by people in Washington.'

Everyone enjoyed his informal style of entertaining. Philby had moved from his first house when Aileen and the children arrived and had taken a spacious, ramshackle two-storeyed place at 4100 Nebraska Avenue. Here he gave a lot of parties. A CIA colleague, James McCargar, remembers: 'The furnishings were sparse – Kim exhibited a noteworthy disregard for the décor of life. Luxury chez Philby was a full martini pitcher and several bottles of whisky; it mattered not a whit who served them or from what one drank.'[14]

But as the months passed the drinking – not only Philby's but Aileen's too – seemed to get heavier, and the birth of a fifth child, Harry, who suffered from convulsions, produced tensions in the family that Aileen seemed to have difficulty in handling. Right in the middle of these difficulties, Guy Burgess arrived in Washington and went to the Philbys' to stay. Aileen wrote a distraught letter to friends in Turkey: 'Who do you think has arrived? Guy Burgess. I know him only too well. He will never leave our house.'[15]

Burgess's posting to Washington with the rank of first secretary is difficult to explain. The Korean war had started in June 1950 and there was some sensitivity in Washington over British reservations about the conflict. The posting called for someone able to explain British policy in the Far East to the Americans. Since Burgess was violently against the war and Britain's involvement, it is hard, therefore, to think of anyone less suited for such a job at such a time. In our 1968 book we suggested that Burgess must somehow have convinced his patron, Hector McNeil, that he should use his influence to get him the posting. But there is later evidence that McNeil, the head of personnel at the Foreign Office, George Middleton, and Burgess himself all had considerable reservations about the move.

The Foreign Office advised Sir Robert Mackenzie, then its regional security officer for North and Central America, that this was a last-chance posting for Burgess. He had been in too many scrapes and if he did not make good in Washington then he would be sacked. Mackenzie, who knew of some of Burgess's escapades, protested but was overruled. The Foreign Office, which had a reputation then for looking after its own, explained that Burgess's 'eccentricities' would be more easily overlooked in a large embassy than in a small one. It then listed some of these eccentricities and warned that worse might be in store. 'What do they mean "worse"?' Mackenzie said to Philby. 'Goats?' According to Mackenzie, Philby replied: 'Don't worry. He's an old friend of mine and he's going to stay with me. He's on the drink now, but I'm going to straighten him out.'[16]

By any reckoning, Philby's decision to allow Burgess to stay with him was extremely foolhardy. Although each knew that the other was working for the Russians and so they had nothing to hide, the very idea that two agents should associate so openly was totally against all intelligence practice. Philby has attempted to explain the lapse. 'I genuinely thought that Burgess would be less likely to get into trouble if he stayed with me,' he said in Moscow. 'I was going to keep an eye on him, keep him in check.'

No doubt he also felt an obligation of friendship – as he admits, an injudicious one – and wanted to help Burgess moderate his drinking. But both Burgess and Philby were in touch with their Russian controls while they were in Washington. *They* must have known that the two men were sharing a house. So the question becomes: why did the Russian intelligence service allow Philby and Burgess to commit such an elementary breach of security?

There are several likely answers. There is the simple one: the Russians agreed with Philby's assessment of the situation, that Burgess was safer with him than roaming the streets of Washington. There is the cock-up explanation: the Russians knew the danger of the circumstances but had not got around to doing anything about it. And there is the conspiratorial theory. This is that far from Philby helping Burgess, Burgess had come to Washington to help Philby. The Korean war was occupying a lot of Philby's attention. Indeed, his work for Moscow on the war may well have been more important than his information on CIA/SIS covert action operations. Harry Rositzke certainly thinks so.

'The positive value to Moscow came out of Philby's political reporting from Washington in the fall of 1950. That was a crucial period in terms of what was going to happen in Korea. Stalin was as cut off as he could be from what was going on in the West, but here was a bright, alert, politically aware intelligence officer who could tell him what was the American thinking on, for example, whether the UN forces would go up to, or cross, the Yalu River. And, obviously, Stalin could tell the North Koreans and the Chinese.'[17]

In the middle of this period, with Philby working day and night, Burgess gets a still unexplained posting to Washington and moves in with his fellow Russian agent. We cannot rule out the suggestion, therefore, that Burgess manoeuvred the posting to help Philby cope with his extra duties for Moscow caused by the Korean war.

Whatever the reason, the two of them made a mess of it. Burgess drank enormously, came home at all hours and soon destroyed what little discipline Aileen had managed to impose on the household. He then fell out with his immediate superior at the embassy, Sir Hubert Graves, and soon ceased to attend the office for large parts of the day. He could instead be found, often with a bottle of whisky at his side, making repairs to John Philby's electric train set, which occupied most of the floor space in Burgess's room in the basement of the Philby house.

When Burgess did attend the embassy, he infuriated the security officer, Squadron Leader 'Tommy' Thompson, by leaving classified documents on his desk overnight, and then by losing the pink slips Thompson gave him to complete to explain these lapses. Thompson complained: 'The man was in an alcoholic stupor most of the time.'[18] To those Americans who crossed his path Burgess was overbearing, rude and aggressive. He took a delight in displaying his utter contempt for the entire American way of life. When, occasionally, he met one who stood up to him and whom he considered worthy of engaging in debate, he poured out a stream of invective about Korea, and the role there of General Douglas MacArthur.

Burgess's attitude soon infected the Philbys:

He brought to the surface a hatred of America until then concealed. Aileen started running down everything to do with the country, but from the basis of prejudice and ignorance . . . Burgess's influence over Kim was more radical. It was as if he had been able to regain something of the ascendancy that at Cambridge the dazzling Apostle exerted over the timid Westminster schoolboy. Kim insisted on taking Burgess everywhere and making much of their friendship in the hopeless endeavour of persuading the Americans to like Guy as much as he seemed to. He was attempting to control Burgess but instead was swept along in his dangerous wake.[19]

One incident was to turn out to be very damaging. It has been told before, but the version Philby gave me in Moscow was particularly vivid. 'We were giving a party, mostly for the FBI, but there were CIA people as well. A lot of drinking was going on. Bill Harvey was there with his wife who was called, if I remember correctly, Libby. Both were fairly well away. In the middle of the party Guy came home. He would have been all right if only the Harvey woman had left him alone, but she'd heard that Guy was a brilliant quick sketch artist and she kept pestering him to draw her.

Finally Guy said: 'Oh, all right then.' He got his pad and dashed something off. He'd done this terrible caricature of her and when she saw it she was deeply hurt. I rang Bill the next day and took him to lunch and apologized on Burgess's behalf. Bill said: "Forget it," but clearly he didn't.'*

How long Burgess would have been able to hang on in Washington is debatable. Thompson had already decided to do all in his power to get rid of him. Aileen might well have decided that enough was enough and kicked him out – Philby's protests notwithstanding – and it is unlikely that he would have survived on his own. Hoover had been getting reports on Burgess's homosexual activities and would gladly have deported him if it had been in his power to do so. But in the end Burgess blew it himself, in his usual flamboyant way, and unwittingly won a role in the Russian intelligence service's desperate effort to save its whole penetration operation from falling apart.

*Philby's description of the drawing is mild compared with others. The American writer David Martin says that Burgess's sketch showed Libby Harvey 'legs spread, dress hiked up above her waist, and crotch bared'.[20]

TERMINATED WITH
PREJUDICE
=== 13 ===

Philby's headquarters were in an annexe to the embassy, but he also had a small office in the FBI building where he would go to read FBI material too sensitive to be allowed out. A lot of this related to what became known as the 'Venona decrypts' – the radio traffic from the Soviet consulate in New York in 1944–5 which, as we have seen, American code-breakers had been working on since the end of the war.

This work had its origins in the recovery on a Finnish battlefield of the charred remains of a Soviet code book. The book by itself was useless because all it gave was the Russian word and a number which represented that word. The Soviet practice at that time was first to turn the original message into a series of numbers, then to add to each group in this series another set of numbers which was changed regularly for every Soviet station around the world. A simplified example will show what difficulties such a system created for code-breakers.

The word *atom* might be listed in the code book as 1,000. The number to be added at that moment, the additive, might be 500. The clerk encyphering the message would add the 500 to the original 1,000 and get 1,500. He would then send the message. At the receiving end, the clerk decyphering the message would look up the current additive, subtract it from 1,500, get 1,000 as the answer, look this up in the code book and read the word *atom*. If anyone intercepted the message – even if they had the code book as the Americans did – and they then looked up 1,500, they would read, say *rifle*. So unless the code-breaker had both the code book *and* the additive, all he would get would be gobbledegook.

But each additive was meant to be used only once, and in 1944 someone in Moscow made a mistake. He sent out a set of additives that had already been used before. One of the Russian installations to receive one of these duplicate additives was the Soviet Purchasing Commission in New York. When the FBI burgled the Commission, it photographed some of the messages the Commission had sent to

Moscow before they had been encoded – when they were still in plain text.

The American codebreakers now had all the ingredients they needed to open a small window on the uncrackable Soviet code: they had the plain text of some messages later sent in code, they had the encoded text, a code book, and because of the repeated use of an old set of additives, a chance to work out what these additives might be. It was still time-consuming and laborious work, involving years rather than months, but the results were worth the trouble. David Martin, who has studied the Venona story, says that this one code break became responsible for nearly all the major spy cases of the postwar period.

Here we are concerned only with the effect on Philby. As he sat in his tiny FBI office and read the Venona material he saw the FBI steadily closing in on Maclean as the Soviet agent code-named 'Homer'. This happened not because any one message referred to Maclean by his real name but because clues to his identity crept into even the most carefully worded message. For example, one message said that although 'Homer' was in Washington he was able to continue to report to his control in New York because he could use a visit to his wife as an excuse. At that time Maclean was going to New York regularly because Melinda was pregnant and staying with her mother there.

This was nerve-racking for Philby. Not only was a Russian intelligence service comrade in danger of being exposed, but Philby knew that what was happening to Maclean could happen to him. There was every likelihood that somewhere in other Verona traffic his own code-name would surface and the FBI searchlight would begin to swing in his direction. Then how long would it be before some clue to his identity also emerged? Philby took the Maclean problem to his Soviet control.

> From discussions with my friends at meetings outside Washington, two main points emerged. First it was essential to rescue Maclean before the net closed on him. That was accepted as an axiom. No question was raised about his future potential to the Soviet Union in the event of his escape. It was quite enough that he was an old comrade . . . Second it was desirable that Maclean should stay at his post as long as possible.[1]

Here the difficulties began. Maclean was no longer in Washington. In October 1948 he had been posted to Cairo as counsellor and head of Chancery, a considerable promotion because at thirty-five he thus became the youngest counsellor in the Foreign Service.

But, almost from the beginning, Maclean seemed determined to throw it all away. It was as if he could no longer maintain the mask, as if his true beliefs and feelings were surging through the façade which his role as a Soviet agent required him to maintain.

At embassy parties, drunk and aggressive, he drew comparisons between life on the diplomatic circuit and the miserable fate of ninety per cent of the Egyptian population. His binges became more frequent and more dangerous. He wrecked the interior of his house at Gezira and refused to pay the landlord for the damage. On a Nile boating picnic he tried to throttle Melinda, had a fight with an Egyptian watchman, then fell on top of an embassy collague, Lees Mayall, breaking Mayall's leg.

In May 1950 during what was to be his last week in Cairo, he went on a forty-eight-hour drunken spree during which he broke into the flat of the US ambassador's secretary, dumped her clothes in the lavatory, chopped up her furniture and smashed her bath – all because 'the bloody girl's an American'. Then he somehow made his way to Alexandria, where he was arrested and placed in a special jail for drunken sailors. For two days his condition was so bad that he was unable to identify himself. When he finally did so, the embassy picked him up and put him on a plane to London, hoping to keep the Egyptian press away from the story. Maclean, the embassy announced, was suffering from a nervous breakdown brought on by overwork.

In London Maclean went to a Foreign Service psychiatrist who recommended six months' break and treatment for alcoholism. It did not work. While Melinda remained in Cairo, Maclean went from one disaster to another. When he was drunk his personality differed so radically from when he was sober that his friends christened the fighting drunk Maclean 'Gordon' and took to making remarks like: 'My God, Gordon was pretty bloody last night, wasn't he?' Maclean was clearly going through some sort of crisis. Once in a sober moment he told a friend that he longed for the leap of faith that would convince him that communism was right. As well as doubt he was also apparently beset by despair. Writing from Oxford, where he was staying with another friend – a diminishing band – he said: 'There are two men in a car waiting outside. They've been there for hours. Are they after me?'[2]

If he had been a Catholic, Maclean might have found peace in confession. He was evidently anxious to tell someone everything. After a Chelsea dinner party he cornered Mark Culme-Seymour, one of his set, and had the following conversation with him:

Maclean:	What would you do if I told you I was working for Uncle Joe?
Culme-Seymour:	I suppose I'd be very embarrassed.
Maclean:	Well, wouldn't you report me?
Culme-Seymour:	I don't know. Who to?
Maclean:	Well I am. Go on and report me.

The next day Culme-Seymour told the critic and journalist Cyril Connolly, who said Maclean had probably been testing Culme-Seymour's friendship and, anyway, if Maclean *was* working for the Russians, no doubt MI5 already knew about it. Their slight unease was put to rest when the Foreign Office decided that Maclean was fit to return to work and in November 1950 made him head of the American department in London; if there were any suspicion attached to Maclean, Culme-Seymour reasoned, then surely he would not have been given such an important post. This was true. Officially Maclean was still regarded as a first-class officer who had health problems, now overcome.

This is why Philby's control in Washington told him that Maclean had to be kept at work as long as possible – he was in a position again to provide first-class information. Philby himself has written:

> After his departure it was said blandly that [Maclean] was 'only' head of the American department of the Foreign Office, and thus had little access to high-grade information. But it is nonsense to suppose that a resolute and experienced operator occupying a senior post in the Foreign Office can have access only to papers that are placed on his desk in the ordinary course of duty.[3]

Other evidence shows that Maclean had access to very high-grade information indeed. The man who succeeded Maclean after he defected was Robert Cecil. He says:

> [Maclean's] post entitled him to receive a wide distribution of telegrams to and from missions abroad, as well as secret material circulated in boxes, of which keys were held by heads of departments and their seniors. No doubt once suspicion against Maclean had hardened, he would have received only a meagre supply of boxes, sparsely filled. But to have withdrawn his key would only have put him on his guard at a time when it was hoped to catch him red-handed.

What did these secret boxes contain in the period *before* suspicion against Maclean hardened in March 1951? Cecil says:

> When I succeeded to [Maclean's] post I found in the filing cabinet

reserved for the head of the department [i.e. Maclean] a numbered copy of the Cabinet paper containing Prime Minister Attlee's account of his hasty visit to President Truman in December 1950, the aim of which was to ensure that General MacArthur should not be permitted to use the atom bomb in the Korean war.[4]

As we now know, Truman did give Attlee such an assurance: 'Truman flatly told Prime Minister Attlee that the United States did not intend to use nuclear weapons in Korea.'[5] Four months later Truman sacked MacArthur, saying that one of his reasons was the pressure exerted by MacArthur to make him use the bomb. It is inconceivable that a Russian agent of Maclean's calibre, deeply concerned over the course of the Korean war, would not have passed this highly important intelligence to Moscow. The knowledge that the American President did not want to use the atom bomb in Korea can only have been an enormous advantage to the communists and they had Maclean to thank for it. Small wonder that Moscow was determined to get Maclean safely away.

The key man in the escape plan had to be Philby. Only he could follow the progress of the 'Homer' investigation and choose the right moment to rescue Maclean – not too soon but not too late. Philby was due to be recalled from Washington in the autumn of 1951; he might then be posted anywhere and be out of touch with the case, so it seemed safest to get Maclean away in the middle of 1951 at the latest. There are several versions of what happened next, all flawed in various ways.

The generally accepted account, based in part on Philby's story as told in his book, goes as follows. With the permission of his control, Philby told Burgess all about Maclean's troubles. Philby says that an idea then emerged – 'I do not know whose' – that Burgess could help in the rescue. 'If Burgess returned to London . . . it seemed natural that he should call on the head of the American Department. He would be well placed to set the ball rolling for the rescue operation.'[6] Burgess could not simply resign and return, however, because that would look suspicious. The story continues with Burgess deliberately getting booked for speeding three times in one day, the governor of Virginia protesting at this abuse of diplomatic privilege, the State Department complaining to the embassy and Burgess being ordered back to London. There he contacted Maclean at the Foreign Office and they later met for lunch at the Royal Automobile Club.

Meanwhile at a meeting on Thursday 24 May 1951 of officers of SIS, MI5 and the Foreign Office it was decided to apply to the

Foreign Secretary, Herbert Morrison, for permission to interrogate Maclean the following Monday. Morrison signed this permission on the Friday. Somebody – Philby is the most popular choice but Peter Wright believes it was Roger Hollis – learnt of this decision and tipped off Burgess that Maclean was about to be questioned. Burgess, who had booked a two-berth cabin on the cross-Channel steamer *Falaise*, due to sail from Southampton at midnight on the Friday, met Bernard Miller, the American friend he had said he would take with him, and told him at 10.30 that morning, Miller remembers clearly: 'A young friend of mine in the Foreign Office is in serious trouble. I'm the only one who can help him.'

Burgess ordered a hire car, packed a suitcase, said goodbye to his live-in friend Jack Hewit, and drove to Maclean's house in the country. He dined with the Macleans, then drove Donald to Southampton, arriving at 11.45 pm. They rushed on board the steamer, leaving the car on the dockside unlocked. When a sailor noticed it and shouted after them, one of them called 'Back on Monday', and they were gone. (Although it was quickly assumed that they had gone to Moscow, it was not until 1956 that the Russians produced them for the Western press.)

This account suffers from one major flaw: the involvement of Burgess. The role he plays as outlined above simply does not make sense. Burgess's escape with Maclean proved a disaster for the Russian intelligence service because it 'blew' Philby, Moscow's white hope, the penetration agent who might have become head of SIS and who, even as it was, had proved a most valuable officer in a most rewarding post. Once Burgess went, and in so doing revealed himself as a Soviet agent, Western counter-intelligence officers naturally looked at all his close associates. And who had been so close a friend that the two had shared a house in Washington? Kim Philby, the crack counter-intelligence officer. Either Philby was not as good as had been made out, or else he too must be a Soviet agent or sympathizer.

Philby's version of Burgess's role as set out above is mischief-making because anyone looking closely at it must quickly conclude that the 'tip-off' which galvanized Burgess on that Friday morning could not have come from Philby because there was insufficient time for him to have heard about Morrison's signing of the permission to interrogate Maclean and then to have got the news back to Burgess in London – only some forty-five minutes.

George Carver, a former CIA officer who analysed the tip-off account, commented:

Since the witting circle of those who knew that Morrison had signed was terribly small, to me a much more logical explanation is that someone in that witting circle passed the information along. Now, you can't really chalk it off to Blunt because Blunt had left MI5 several years before . . . My thought has always been that the sequence of events on that day alone certainly raised the possibility that there was yet another person in the net *who presumably has not been discovered to this day*, who occupies a very senior position, possibly in Six [SIS] , but more likely in Five [MI5].[7]

Thus Philby's account of the tip-off sows suspicion that even after he, Burgess, Maclean and Blunt had been uncovered there remained yet another Russian penetration agent in place, and the hunt for him, led by Peter Wright, was to divert the energies of MI5 from more rewarding tasks for many years.

When I put all this to Philby in Moscow he was quick to agree that his account, 'while truthful as far as it goes', was not the whole truth. From what he told me and from what I had learnt from senior SIS officers (all retired) who had known Philby, I was able to reconstruct an account of the escape of Burgess and Maclean which, I believe, is as close to what really happened as we are likely to get, and which offers other reasons why Philby muddied the waters.

Once it became clear that Maclean would eventually be identified as 'Homer' – a great success for Western counter-intelligence – the Russian security service set its mind to examining ways its other agents might survive the disaster. One of Moscow's ploys in such circumstances is to allow one of its other agents to point the finger at the one who is about to be uncovered anyway. This causes no harm to the first agent, providing he is spirited to safety in time, and it enhances the reputation of the second agent for loyalty and diligence and diverts attention from his own guilt. So it was decided that when Maclean's escape plan was formulated and his exposure imminent, Philby should improve his own image by subtly steering the investigation in Maclean's direction. In *My Silent War* he describes accurately and truthfully how he did this:

Now that the rescue plan was taking shape there was no reason why I should not give the investigation a nudge in the right direction. To that end I wrote a memorandum to Head Office . . . I recalled the statement of Krivitsky to the best of my ability from memory. He had said that the head of Soviet intelligence for

Western Europe had recruited in the middle thirties a young man who had gone into the Foreign Office. He was of good family and had been educated at Eton and Oxford. He was an idealist, working without payment. I suggested that these data, such as they were, should be matched against the record of diplomats stationed in Washington between the relevant dates in 1944–45 of the known leakages.[8]

This was done, and produced a list of names that included Roger Makins (Chairman of the Atomic Energy Commission), Paul Gore-Booth (later Permanent Under Secretary at the Foreign Office) and Donald Maclean. Maclean had not been to Eton and Oxford, but as Philby pointed out, 'MI5 did not attach too much weight to that detail, on the ground that foreigners often assume that all well-born young Englishmen must go to Eton and Oxford.'[9] In no time Maclean was at the top of MI5's list and, according to messages from London to the FBI, passed on through Philby, he was already under surveillance.

Now Philby and his Russian control in Washington realized that they might have bungled Maclean's escape plan by moving too soon. Philby had underestimated the speed with which MI5 would act on his Krivitsky tip. He hints at this in *My Silent War* when he writes of 'disconcerting speed' and how he was 'alarmed by the speed with which the affair was developing'. But in Moscow he told me more. 'It was a nightmare. Everything was unravelling.. All we could do was to work out schemes for getting us all away if it blew up. We had the long-standing plan to get Maclean away from London but we had to abort it when MI5 put Maclean under surveillance. In the new plan Burgess was supposed to coordinate everything and steel Maclean for what he had to do.'

We can see now how Philby juggled with the time sequence in his version in his book. He placed Burgess as part of the escape plan *from the beginning* – brought into it because 'Guy's special knowledge of the problem might be helpful'. What special knowledge? Philby then recounts the story of Burgess's deliberate speeding offences as a ploy to have him sent back to London forthwith. This had always struck me as implausible. How could they be certain that it would work? What if the governor of Virginia had *not* complained to the State Department? What if the Ambassador had let Burgess off with a caution?

My suspicion of this account increased when I learnt that Burgess, far from being delighted that his ploy had worked, was, according to the head of his department, Denis Greenhill, 'boiling with rage' when told he was being sent back to London.[10] Next, the timescale is all wrong. Burgess's speeding offences were on 28 February. The State Department lodged its complaint about him on 14 March. Burgess was sacked a few days later, but he hung on in the United States for a further *six weeks*, not arriving in London until 7 May. Hardly a case of 'a pressing need for haste', as Philby writes.

A much more likely version goes like this. Moscow's long-standing plan to get Maclean away did not involve Burgess. Why should it? He had nothing to offer that the Russian intelligence service did not already have. But everything began to go wrong when Philby, anxious to protect himself, made his Krivitsky intervention too soon. MI5 moved more quickly and more efficiently than Philby had expected and the escape plan had to be abandoned because of the surveillance on Maclean. Forced to improvise, Philby and his Soviet control in Washington decided to give Burgess a role in the new plan because Burgess was about to return to London, having been sacked for his genuine speeding offences. A date was set for Maclean's flight: Friday 25 May, because he would not be missed from his office until the Monday morning.

But in all this concentration on Maclean no one took a really hard look at Burgess. Just before Burgess left Washington he had a chance meeting with Michael Straight. Straight, an American who had been at Cambridge in the 1930s, had been recruited for the Russians by Anthony Blunt. But Straight had had second thoughts – he eventually unmasked Blunt – and, according to his account of this meeting, he threatened to turn Burgess over to the security authorities: 'If you aren't out of government within a month from now I swear to you I'll turn you in.'[11]

When Burgess arrived in London and contacted Maclean, the danger of what he had undertaken was brought home to him. He would have to face an MI5 interrogation after Maclean's escape. By itself this had not previously worried him, but coupled with Straight's threat it made him realize that his future looked very bleak. Even if he escaped prosecution he would never get an important job in Britain again. Philby told me in Moscow: 'Burgess suddenly came to the end of his tether. He was close to a total nervous breakdown, closer than anyone realized. His career in Britain was finished, and this would have made him of little use to the KGB. We were all so worried about Maclean that we didn't notice what had happened to Burgess. He was under enormous stress.'

So Burgess turned to the person he most trusted in London, his Soviet control, 'Peter'. Since Burgess was worried that he was already being watched by MI5, he did not contact 'Peter' himself but asked Blunt, who had also been controlled by 'Peter', to act as an intermediary, and we have Blunt's confirmation that he did so. We know something of 'Peter's' rule for an agent who feels the law closing in on him: play it safe. Blunt has said that when he told 'Peter' about his own interrogation when he came under suspicion, 'Peter' advised him to make a quick escape.[12] He would have given the same advice to Burgess, who was clearly in no state to bluff his way out of trouble. And since Maclean's escape had already been planned, the easiest solution was that Burgess should go with him.

But all this happened so quickly that there was no time for consultation with Moscow or with Philby or Philby's control in Washington. 'Peter' did not know how closely Burgess had been connected with Philby in Washington; he would never have imagined that two Russian intelligence agents could have broken the elementary rule against living together. Philby's Washington control could have told him, but for his part he had no idea that Burgess would want to escape with Maclean. I put this to Philby in Moscow.

'In retrospect it's easy to see where we went wrong,' he replied. 'It was a mistake for anyone to have gone, including Maclean. I had seen the evidence against him and I knew that there was nothing that would stand up in court. He could have brazened it out, threatened to have sued the Foreign Office. They would almost certainly have retreated.* Then, when everything had died down in a couple of years, if he had wanted to he could have gone to Switzerland on a holiday and then on to Moscow.'

I said: 'Perhaps the tip-off was not just about the date of the interrogation but that something really damning had turned up for them to confront him with?' Philby replied: 'There was no tip-off, except in the sense that I had written to Burgess warning him that the hunt for "Homer" was really hotting up. [The warning was disguised as a reference to a car Burgess had left behind in the embassy car park.] When he went he foolishly left this letter behind in his flat and Blunt had to rush around there and get it before anyone else did.'

I said: 'But the two of them did flee on the very day that Morrison signed the permission for Maclean's interrogation.' Philby replied: 'Coincidence. Burgess had been working on that part of the arrangements for some time and the date for the actual getaway had been set well before Morrison signed the permission for interrogation.' This appears to be confirmed by the recollections of Jack Hewit,

*Philby was probably right. In 1962, amid rumours that Maclean was considering returning to Britain, Special Branch officers contacted potential witnesses for any case against him. The officers were gloomy about their chances of mounting a successful prosecution.

Burgess's live-in friend. He said on television that Burgess told him on the *Wednesday* – that is the day *before* the SIS/MI5/Foreign Office meeting at which it was decided to approach Morrison – that he would be going abroad on Friday, helping a friend in trouble.[13]

Philby continued: 'The unplanned part was that Burgess went too. We knew that Burgess's going put us at risk but Blunt and I decided to stay and stick it out. The whole thing was a mess, an intelligence nightmare, and it was all due to that bloody man Burgess. The KGB never forgave him. They kept us apart in Moscow to avoid recriminations over what had happened. I could understand that but I was sorry about it when I heard that he had died. He'd been a good friend.'

Philby's account in his book can now been seen for what it really is – an attempt to cover up a Russian intelligence mess in which his own blunders played no small part and, by sowing suspicion in Western intelligence services that further penetration agents remained in place, to salvage something from the disaster. Later in our talks when I asked Philby the general question, 'Do you have any regrets?' he gave general answers and then suddenly said: 'Professionally I could have done better. I made mistakes and I paid for them.' He left no doubt that he was referring to his friendship with Burgess and the whole 'Homer' affair.

Philby heard of Burgess's flight from Geoffrey Patterson, an MI5 colleague in Washington. Philby has described the incident. ' "Kim," he said in a half-whisper, "the bird has flown." I registered dawning horror (I hope). "What bird? Not Maclean?" "Yes," he answered. "But there's more than that . . . *Guy Burgess* has gone with him." At that my consternation was no pretence.'[14] Philby acted quickly. As soon as he was able to get away from the embassy, he drove home, collected his copying camera and all its accessories and buried them in a wood at the side of the Potomac. He then considered his position.

He had no doubt that his relationship with Burgess would compromise him so deeply that the upward curve of his career in SIS was over. But he still might manage to hang on in the service. His advantages were that he knew the rules of evidence and was confident that there was no real case against him, and that his friends in SIS would not take kindly to any efforts to sack him because of an unwise friendship. He decided to sit tight and wait for developments in London.

These were not long in coming. A hand-delivered letter from the assistant chief of SIS, Jack Easton, told Philby that he would soon be receiving an official telegram recalling him to London in connection with the Burgess-Maclean case. This was puzzling. As Philby says, why should Easton warn him in a private letter of an impending official summons? The obvious explanation, lent credence by the way SIS chiefs behaved to Philby later in Beirut, was that he was being tipped off to run, either as a ploy to make him incriminate himself, or because SIS wanted to avoid the scandal that his arrest would provoke.

When the official telegram arrived, Philby called on CIA and FBI officers to tell them he would be away for a while. He was touched by the solicitude which the FBI officer, Micky Ladd, showed over his recall and remembered Ladd in our conversations in Moscow as 'a nice guy and a good friend'. He had a curious meeting with Angleton, not recounted in his book. As he told it to me in Moscow: 'Angleton rang me and arranged for us to meet in a bar before I went to the airport. He began by asking me how long I was going to be away and I said about a week. We chatted on for a bit and then he said: "Can you do me a favour in London?" I said I would and he handed me an envelope addressed to the head of counter-intelligence in London. He said he had missed the bag and wanted London to get the message as soon as possible.' Philby paused to see I had got the point and then went on to confirm it. 'Now that's an unlikely act for a man who was already supposed to be suspicious of me.' Then Philby grinned. 'Unless, of course,' he said, 'the envelope contained a blank sheet of paper and Angleton wanted to see what I would do with it.'

There is another mystery here. Teddy Kollek, who had known Philby in Vienna, was now an Israeli diplomat in Washington, opening the first formal links between the American and Israeli intelligence services. Kollek says he saw Philby in the corridors of the CIA one day and later mentioned to Angleton that he knew Philby had once been a Communist. The trouble is, as Kollek told Philip Jacobson of *The Sunday Times* in November 1979, he cannot remember whether he did this in 1951, before Philby was recalled, or in 1952, after Philby was back in Britain.

In fact, in 1951 Angleton went on record at the CIA as one of Philby's defenders. The director, General Bedell Smith, asked every officer on his staff who had met Burgess to write a memorandum about him. Angleton's, dated 18 June 1951, reported several encounters with a drunken Burgess and said that Philby had acted as an apologist for him even when Burgess's behaviour had caused him embarrassment, explaining it away 'on the grounds that the subject had suffered severe concussion in an accident which had continued to affect him periodically'.[15] But the tenor of the memorandum was that Philby could not be blamed for what Burgess had done and that there was no suspicion attaching to Philby.

But the memorandum from Bill Harvey was another matter. Dated 13 June 1951, it drew together all the coincidences in Philby's career: he had been in charge of the Volkov case; he had been joint commander of the disastrous Albanian operation; he knew all about the hunt for 'Homer'; and he had shared a house with Burgess. Harvey, with his FBI training, decided that these constituted too many coincidences to allow an innocent conclusion. Kim Philby was a Soviet agent.

Bedell Smith read both memoranda and decided to act on Harvey's. He wrote to Menzies in London and told him that Philby would no longer be welcome as the British liaison officer. The letter had been largely drafted by Harvey himself, who must have considered, as he did it, that Burgess's insulting drawing of Libby Harvey in Philby's house was now truly avenged.

In London, even before the Bedell Smith letter, Philby had been undergoing something of a grilling by Dick White, then a senior officer in MI5. White took Philby through his career and pounced on the fact that Philby had been to Spain *before* he became a *Times* war correspondent there. This was a sensitive area for Philby because the Russian intelligence service had paid for the trip and had topped up Philby's funding by sending more money to him with Burgess as courier. White shook Philby with his questions because unless Philby could show how he had funded the visits to Spain it put him right into the slot reserved for 'the young English journalist sent to Spain by the Russians' as described by Krivitsky back in 1937. Philby's explanation – that the Spanish trip was an attempt to break into journalism, so he had sold all his effects to pay for it – was rather thin but had the advantage of being impossible to disprove.

At first White was in two minds. His instincts told him that there was something odd about Philby, but as he later confided to fellow officers, 'Philby seemed impregnable because no one in SIS would hear a word against him. We had to go it alone.' And that is what MI5 did. It compiled a dossier on Philby, listing his left-wing youth, his time in Vienna, his marriage to Litzi, his sudden move to the political right, his work in Franco Spain, the Krivitsky warning, the Volkov affair, and the Burgess-Maclean defection. 'I have totted up the ledger and the debits outweigh the assets,' Dick White told the CIA.[16]

But first MI5 told the FBI. Robert Lamphere, an FBI counter-intelligence officer specializing in Soviet cases, remembers: 'Dick White and Arthur Martin [the senior MI5 officer on the Maclean case] came over to Washington together. We were more than a little unhappy with MI5 because it had held out on us over Maclean. So when I sat down with Arthur Martin to discuss things in detail, I let him know about my unhappiness. But then he showed me this document on Philby. From that day in the summer of 1951 forward, there was never any doubt in my mind that Philby was a Soviet spy. Also from that moment, lecturing to FBI in-service classes, I openly named Philby as a Soviet spy and I continued to do so until I left the FBI in 1955. I never understood why SIS refused to do anything about him. I can only think that it had to do with the old-boy network and its refusal to believe an individual of the upper classes would betray its own.'[17]

Lamphere was not quite right. Many of Philby's SIS colleagues believed he was guilty only of an unwise friendship with Burgess, to whom he had shown admirable loyalty. They thought he was a victim of the McCarthyism then sweeping America. (One of the most zealous and persistent defenders of Philby against 'McCarthyite suspicions' was Malcolm Muggeridge, later one of his harshest critics.) These officers expected the service to stand by Philby and to ignore the anger of the FBI and the chill in relations with the CIA. They felt that the club should hold fast and show the cousins what SIS was all about.

But these officers overlooked the new reality of the Anglo-American intelligence relationship; the British were now the poor cousins. Menzies knew what he had to do. He called Philby to his office and asked for his resignation. (One report has Philby, the master tactician, getting in first. 'I'm no good to you now, and I never will be again. I'll put in my resignation. I think you'd better let me go.')[18] Philby would get £4,000 in lieu of pension; £2,000 down and the rest in half-yearly instalments of £500. As Philby has written, 'The ostensible reason for the deferred payments was the fear that I might dissipate all in wild speculation, but, as I had never speculated in my life it looked a bit thin. A more likely reason was the desire to hedge against the possibility of my being sent to gaol within three years.'

There has been some confusion over what Philby resigned from. Later official statements spoke only of his resignation from 'the Foreign Service' and this has been taken to mean that he was still in SIS. The use of the euphemism 'the Foreign Service' was to avoid mentioning SIS, which did not officially exist, but it is true that Philby remained on the books of SIS. This is partly because 'once in

SIS, always in SIS', and partly because of the practice of keeping someone under suspicion still technically attached to the service for up to five years because it often takes that long to build a case against them.

In Philby's case it did not look as if he would remain out of jail long enough to draw the rest of his payments. MI5 had by no means given up and by November 1951 thought that it might now have sufficient information to test Philby's responses and to gauge how its accusations and his defence might stand in a court of law. To this end it arranged to play a dangerous game with him. Philby was summoned from his newly found house at Heronsgate in Hertfordshire to come to London to appear at a mock trial. The charge: high treason.

HOOVER BUNGLES, PHILBY CLEARED
14

The trial of H.A.R. Philby was held at MI5 headquarters in Leconfield House, Curzon Street, Mayfair, in November 1952. Philby would have been perfectly within his rights to refuse to attend; MI5 had no legal powers to compel him to do so. But he had decided that his best hope of remaining in touch with his old service was to cooperate, to show that he was as anxious as anyone to get to the bottom of the Burgess-Maclean business. The officer detailed to conduct what MI5 chose to call 'a judicial inquiry' was Helenus Milmo, later a King's Counsel and a judge, who had worked for MI5 during the war as an interrogator. His bluff, forceful manner had won him the nickname 'Buster'. His approach to Philby was to attempt to bully him into a confession.

From the beginning it was apparent that this was not going to work. Milmo needed rapid-fire questions and rapid-fire answers to corner his quarry. Philby fell back on his intermittent stammer to slow the cross-examination to a pace to suit him. In 1968 *The Sunday Times* spoke with an MI5 officer who was present at the inquiry and he gave this hypothetical example of the type of exchange that drove Milmo to fury. Milmo: 'Was it a fine day?' Philby: 'Yes.' Milmo (pouncing): 'How do you know?' Philby: 'Well . . . there wwwas a temperature of about ffffifty-eight degrees, I suppose. And there wwwas a sssssslight wind from the sssouth. It sssseems to me that constitutes a ffffffine day.'

As we wrote in 1968, 'Not only can a bad stammer be highly destructive of the rhythm and tension of an essentially verbal performance like a cross-examination, it also engenders, however irrationally, a certain sympathy, or at least involuntary queasiness, in even the most hostile listeners.'[1] We decided that Philby had triumphed easily over Milmo and we quoted one of the lawyers present as saying: 'It began to look like the stupidest man in the world cross-examining the cleverest.'

In retrospect, that was a harsh conclusion. For one thing, a former MI5 officer I spoke with in 1984 made the point that although the inquiry failed to produce sufficient evidence to justify a legal action against Philby, 'there was not a single officer who sat through the proceedings who came away not totally convinced of Philby's guilt.' And then, in Moscow, Philby himself complained that accounts of the mock trial made it appear that he had got off lightly.

'It was not like you made out,' he said. 'In the introduction to your book, le Carré argues that the trial was a farce because of the way it was conducted. What does he say. Here it is: "A good interrogator never specifies the charges, never reveals the extent of his knowledge, does not give the suspect the comfort and security of being accompanied by his colleagues, nor the fillip of an examination before an appreciative audience." Well, I was not accompanied by a single one of my colleagues who supported me. The audience was distinctly hostile. Don't forget that Milmo had a highly successful wartime career behind him and he had a very able junior, an MI5 officer, assisting him. Both were notably unfriendly. I don't know who gave you your information, but I've always assumed the course of the interrogation was recorded in some other room, so what I'm telling you can be checked out.

'You have to understand the rarity of the case. For eleven years I had been right inside the service, mostly on the counter-espionage side. I had studied the files in minute detail. I knew all about the procedures. How could Milmo have specified charges which I had not long before anticipated? How could he have revealed knowledge not already in my possession? He did, in fact, slip me one or two surprises, but nothing to signify.

'Now whether the MI5 authorities were right or wrong to confront me with Milmo is a question verging on the moot. They must have known I was exceptionally well armed for the test. The unknown factor was my nerve. They probably hoped that I would break under Milmo's thundering, or at least that it would soften me up for a subsequent probing by the dangerous Skardon [William Skardon, the wartime MI5 interrogator who later broke Fuchs]. Happily my nerve held, as I suspected it might. But if it had broken, the authorities would have been vindicated.'

I asked Philby what the surprises had been and how he had handled them. 'What Krivitsky actually said about the young English journalist sent by the Russians to Spain, was that he had been sent to kill Franco. I've no idea why Krivitsky said that. Anyway, Milmo roared at me: "You went to Spain to kill Franco, didn't you?" I said: "Given all the people the Russians could use to kill Franco, do you really think that they would choose me?" The proposition was so absurd that it was obvious to everyone present.

'My big worry throughout the inquiry was that there would be something new that they had found about me, something not in the files. Eventually it came: radio traffic.'

Philby was referring to the fact that MI5 had checked the volume of radio traffic between the Soviet embassy in London and Moscow about the time of the Volkov defection and again during the 'Homer' investigation. Russian intelligence service transmissions were monitored and recorded daily, largely for the code-breakers. Even if the codes could not be broken at the moment, there was no telling when this might change. In the meantime, simply by measuring the volume of the traffic the counter-espionage services could assess how busy the Soviet service was.

MI5 had found from records of the wireless traffic that two days after the Volkov material reached London there had been a spectacular rise in messages between Moscow and London. When the duration of this traffic, measured to the second, was compared with the traffic between Moscow and Istanbul a few hours later, the length of the transmissions almost matched. MI5's conclusions were that, at the time the authorities in London were getting excited about the Volkov material, the Soviet embassy also became excited about something and communicated that excitement to Moscow. Moscow, in turn, passed on whatever it was to its station in Istanbul.

MI5 looked at this and said: 'Philby learnt of Volkov, and told his London control. He radioed Moscow and Moscow passed on the information to Istanbul with orders to fix Volkov.' As we know, this was a correct *assumption*, but it was not evidence. Nor was the fact that there had been a similar jump in Russian intelligence service traffic between London and the Soviet Union soon after Philby had been officially briefed about the 'Homer' investigation. But all this did give Milmo some ammunition to try to shake Philby.

In Moscow I asked him how he handled it.

'I realized that if I tried to give explanations or advance my own theories it would only look more suspicious. So when Milmo laid it all out and then said: "Now, how do you account for this? Why did this happen?" I simply said "How would I know?" and left it at that. It was an unsatisfactory reply but one that an innocent man would make. And, in truth, I didn't know for certain that MI5's interpretation was the right one. It was only an educated guess, not evidence.'

Philby said that most of Milmo's other points were fairly flimsy. He had accused Philby of entrusting 'intimate personal papers' to Burgess. This referred to Philby's Cambridge degree, which MI5 searchers had found in Burgess's flat folded inside a book where Philby had placed it years earlier. Philby said that the charge was so nonsensical that he did not have to feign bewilderment.

Milmo gave up – his report concluded: 'We have nothing on this man which would stand up in any court of law' – and MI5 handed Philby over to Skardon. Skardon, a most ordinary-looking man with a slight stoop and a pipe clenched firmly between his teeth, had learnt the basis of his interrogation techniques in the murder squad at Scotland Yard. He had refined them in MI5. His relentlessly polite questions, returning time and time again to a small point as if begging for elucidation from someone he considered his intellectual superior, tended to produce a still only partially explained psychological break-down in the person being interrogated. This technique had worked with Fuchs, but whether it would have worked with Philby is another matter, and it is unlikely that SIS would have allowed MI5 the repeated access to Philby which Skardon would have required. For working in Philby's favour all this time was the basic philosophical difference between MI5 and SIS officers.

MI5 officers are the upholders of law and order. In that their job is to *catch* spies, they tend to have a policeman's mentality. They work with a mixture of hunch – a policeman's nose for a guilty man – and a painstaking examination of the files. Their moral attitude does not allow for grey areas, or changes of mind; the slots into which they file people are rigid and locked. I once met William Skardon after he had retired from MI5 and was working part-time for SIS, helping in the positive vetting of recruits. In the course of our conversation he made two remarks that have remained crisp in my memory. He said that even a person's hobby gave him a clue to that person's suscep-tibility to treason. He had divided hobbies into 'constitutional' and 'non-constitutional'. Gardening was 'very constitutional'; ski-ing was 'doubtful'; motor racing 'very suspect.' Then he said he had left the murder squad at Scotland Yard after the government had abolished the death penalty: the lowering of the stakes had taken the point – and the satisfaction – out of his work.

It is thus easy to see that neither the type of officer who served in SIS, the sort of work he did, nor the grey areas in which he operated, won much sympathy with the traditional MI5 man. He believed that it must be possible to examine an officer's work over a reasonable period of time and to reach some profit and loss balance – as Dick White told the Americans he had done with Philby. But an SIS officer would argue that an operation could take a working lifetime to bring to fruition, years and years spent building up the opposition's confidence to make possible the final 'sting'. If an officer conducting such an operation were, at some stage before the denouement, to have his actions examined by an outsider then, however meticulous the examination, it would be difficult not to conclude that he was a traitor. His only protection at this time is the loyalty and trust of his colleagues.

So SIS was deeply unhappy about Philby's mock trial, and those friends he told about it were even unhappier at the bouts he now had with Skardon. Skardon accompanied Philby home from the inquiry to collect Philby's passport, a tactic to leave him in no doubt that the investigation of his activities was by no means over. In the following weeks Skardon would turn up at the Philby household at fairly regular intervals. He and Philby would talk in the living room or go for a walk. Skardon devoted his time to winning Philby's confidence. Philby concentrated on keeping him at a safe distance. It was not easy.

> He was scrupulously courteous, his manner verging on the exquisite; nothing could have been more flattering than the cosy warmth of his interest in my views and actions. He was far more dangerous than the ineffective White or the blustering Milmo. I was helped to resist his polite advances by the knowledge that it was Skardon who had wormed his way into Fuchs's confidence with such disastrous results. During our first long conversation, I detected and evaded two little traps which he had laid for me with deftness and precision. But I had scarcely begun congratulating myself when the thought struck me that he may have laid others which I had not detected.[2]

After a month or so, Skardon stopped coming. There was another interrogation, this time by two senior SIS men, Jack Easton and John Sinclair. 'I enjoyed my duel with Easton,' Philby wrote in *My Silent War.* 'After my experiences with White, Milmo and Skardon, I was moving on very familiar ground, and I did not think he could succeed where they had failed. He didn't.' And this was the core of the matter. Skardon complained later that the case against Philby had been mishandled. Hauling him before the judicial inquiry had allowed him to rehearse his defence, to learn what MI5 knew about him, and to gain confidence because the evidence against him was not conclusive. Skardon would much rather have been let loose on Philby from the very beginning. It would have been one of the great matches in the history of interrogation.

Philby now entered his period in the wilderness. It was emotionally and financially draining. From being the rising star of British intelligence, a possible future 'C', Sir Harold Philby; from the comfort of a job and colleagues whose company he enjoyed, he went virtually overnight into a harsh and lonely world. His former colleagues in SIS split into three camps: a small group which thought he was probably guilty and wanted nothing further to do with him; a larger group which thought he was probably innocent but considered it better to have nothing further to do with him; and a small but important group which was convinced of his innocence and was determined to do what it could to get him back into the service and to take care of him in the meantime. But here Philby decided that it would be better if *he* had as little contact with his SIS friends as possible, so as not to endanger their careers. 'After the Milmo trial I broke my friendship with Graham Greene,' he said in Moscow. 'I didn't want to cause him any trouble.'

At this time a word of comfort from his Soviet control would have revitalized him, but this was, of course, impossible. The case against him was suspended, not closed. MI5 felt cheated of their prey and for all Philby knew might well have him under intermittent surveillance hoping to get the one piece of evidence that would put him in Wormwood Scrubs for the next twenty years – a meeting with a known Soviet intelligence officer.

Cut off from both sides, Philby tried to put the intelligence world out of his mind and concentrate on making a living. He immediately ran into a difficulty which besets all SIS officers in Britain who leave the service before their time – what do they tell prospective employers they have been doing for the past ten years or so? Philby tried the often-used cover for SIS, that he had been in the Foreign Service, but this only provoked the question, why did you leave?*

Philby told me in Moscow: 'After a while the only thing I could think of was journalism. Could I break into Fleet Street again? I'd done it once in Spain so I thought I'd try there again. I got my passport back and tried it for five weeks without much success.' (Philby submitted articles to several London papers, including *The Observer*, but no one offered him a staff job or even a con-

---

*A former SIS officer wrote a persuasive paper arguing that the service should provide officers who retire early a 'cover CV' so as to enable them to find employment in civilian life. SIS, so brilliant at creating false identities and backgrounds for its agents, resolutely rejected the suggestion.

tract. The *Observer* contact was, however, to prove useful later.)

'Then I was offered a job in the City in a company run by a friend, an export-import agency. Really. We imported fruit and vegetables from Spain and sold castor oil to the United States. But it was terribly boring work and I was rather relieved when he went bust after about a year. Especially as it wasn't my fault. The ship chartering side over-extended itself during the Korean war and got wiped out when the war ended.

'Then there was an abortive book deal. André Deutsch signed me up to write a book about my intelligence experiences. I was quite keen on it at first, but when I tried to write it it soon became clear that it was going to be a very anodyne creature. I decided I couldn't go on with it and repaid the advance. Tommy Harris repaid two hundred and fifty pounds of the six hundred pounds advance and I managed to raise the rest from friends.'

This is not quite how Deutsch himself remembers it, and not how it appears in his accounts. He says the late Nicolas Bentley, the cartoonist and a director of André Deutsch Limited, was approached by Harris, a friend since childhood, with the idea for the book. Bentley and Deutsch arranged a lunch at L'Escargot in Greek Street. 'Harris came with Philby and introduced him. I found him witty, charming and intelligent and we agreed to sign a contract for the book. It was to be written quickly and, unusually, we were to pay the advance in monthly instalments, six of forty pounds and six of sixty pounds. We had a second lunch a few months later and Philby was still enthusiastic. But at a third lunch a year later I found him greatly changed. He seemed depressed and a little shabby and he told us that he had decided not to go ahead.'

Deutsch's accounts reveal however that Harris, unknown to Philby, was a partner with Deutsch in the project. Every first of the month when Deutsch paid Philby £40 or £60, Harris paid Deutsch £20 or £30 in cash. And on 5 April 1955, when the contract was terminated, Harris paid Deutsch the balance of the whole advance of £600 (about £12,000 in today's values). The only conclusion is that Harris was subsidizing Philby, probably unknown to Philby himself, and was doing it in a manner that was unlikely ever to be traced back to him.

There was another incident in this period where Philby's recollection of it differs from the other party. In *My Silent War*, Philby writes that he had a letter from a Conservative MP who asked him to tea at the House of Commons.

He told me candidly that he was gunning for the Foreign Office in general and Anthony Eden in particular . . . He had heard that I had been sacked from the Foreign Service, and had surmised that I must be suffering from a sense of grievance. If I could give him any dirt to throw at the Foreign Office, he would be most grateful . . . I replied that I fully understood the reason behind the Foreign Office's request for my resignation, and left abruptly.

But in 1968, Captain Henry Kerby, an MP who had worked for SIS in the Twenties, told us a different story. 'I had got to know Philby towards the end of the war. He was a weird mixed-up character, nervous and jumpy, and could really knock it back. He gave the impression that he was going places and knew it. Personally, I thought he was a shit so I was rather surprised when sometime in 1954 he sought me out two or three times at the House. I had a room downstairs in the dungeons and I used to whisk the bugger down there as fast as I could. He was not the sort of man you'd want to be seen talking to. Well, what he wanted was work – of any kind. Of course, I couldn't give him any and he behaved so strangely that I smelt a rat and I told Marcus Lipton [a Labour MP] about him.'[3]

The importance of the meetings lies not in their purpose, whatever it was, but in the fact that Kerby told Lipton about them and aroused the suspicion in Lipton, a simple old-fashioned army man, that there was something odd about Philby. Lipton was thus unconsciously primed for the role he was to play, not in pinning Philby, but in clearing him.

In keeping with his professional life, Philby's personal affairs were in tatters. Aileen was left alone most of the time with the children at the house in Heronsgate while he spent his time in London, drinking, or visiting a woman civil servant he had met. Sometimes he did not come home for days, and when he did he was usually drunk. There are accounts from their friends that suggest that Aileen at last suspected her husband's true allegiance. Patrick Seale quotes one as saying that she heard Aileen blurt out one night: 'I know you're the Third Man,' and Mrs Hazel Sporel, a friend from Istanbul, as remembering that Philby had told her that Aileen had sent a telegram to the Foreign Office saying exactly this about him.

Aileen's mother tried to rescue her daughter by buying a large Edwardian house in Crowborough on the Kent–Sussex border and moving the family there. But it was too large to look after properly, the garden was soon overgrown, and Aileen knew no one nearby. Philby only came down at weekends to see the children and when he did he and Aileen hardly communicated. She began to have accidents again, on one occasion crashing her car into a shop window. She was drinking heavily and had several spells in hospital.

She was probably too far into her own despair to notice that Philby's load had suddenly lightened – he had heard from the Russian intelligence service. 'I received, through the most ingenious of routes, a message from my Soviet friends, conjuring me to be of good cheer and presaging an early resumption of relations. It changed drastically the whole complexion of the case. I was no longer alone.'[4] This statement has been interpreted by some as an indication that what happened next, an event that a Victorian melodramatist would have entitled 'Philby Cleared', was under the secret direction of the Russians. This was not so. The 'early resumption of relations' the Russians presaged was more likely to be due to their assessment that if Philby had survived so long under suspicion, then the case against him was weak and his nerve strong, so there was no reason not to use him again.

And FBI documents obtained until the US Freedom of Information Act make it clear that, of all people, J. Edgar Hoover was primarily responsible for clearing Philby and giving him another seven valuable years as a Soviet agent. The story begins with the defection in Australia in April 1954 of Vladimir Petrov, an intelligence officer in the Soviet embassy in Canberra. By September of that year the news value of the defection had virtually run its course, but *The People* newspaper in London managed to resurrect it with a story by Petrov revealing that Burgess and Maclean were not merely two defecting diplomats – the government line until then – but long-term Soviet agents, recruited in the early 1930s, who had fled to escape arrest. The Foreign Office was forced to confirm the essential truth of the story and to publish a White Paper on the defections on 23 September 1955.

When Hoover read the White Paper he was appalled that it made no mention of any suspicion attaching to Philby, so he decided to do something about it. Motivated partly by his anti-communist zeal and partly by a sense of personal betrayal – he had been a dinner guest of Philby's in Washington – Hoover set out to plant a story in British and American newspapers suggesting that Philby was responsible for tipping off Maclean that it was time to run, that Philby was the elusive Third Man.

Hoover arranged a meeting in his office with a friendly reporter from an agency, the International News Service, and gave him all he needed for a 'hot story'. He told him that Philby had been employed by British intelligence in Washington; he was a heavy drinker; he had access to highly secret information; he had been recalled in London after the Burgess-Maclean disappearances and (here Hoover was wrong) a representative of British intelligence had come to Washington to escort him back to London.

Hoover's memorandum of the meeting continues: 'But I cautioned him that in the White Paper . . . there was no mention of Philby's name, apparently because of lack of direct proof against Philby and the fact that Philby was in contact with lawyers and threatening heavy libel suits if any paper prints his name in connection with his matter.'[5] Hoover then suggested to the reporter that the place to apply the pressure to get Philby's name into the open was in London with the British.

The seed matured quickly, because it is possible that Hoover told MI5 what he was doing. The reason for thinking this is that the editor of *Empire News*, Jack Fishman, who had a very close working relationship with MI5, now became involved. By the first week in October Fishman knew that Hoover strongly suspected Philby and was anxious to make his name public. Fishman, presumably with MI5 approval, tried to do this by persuading a Labour MP, Norman Dodds, to ask a parliamentary question in which Philby's name would be mentioned. (Since parliamentary speeches and reports of them are privileged in law, this would have avoided the libel problem.) But Dodds was dissuaded from this course by a senior Labour MP, George Wigg, who said it would be much better to ask for a Foreign Office inquiry because it was wiser 'never to frighten the rabbits when there may be much bigger game around'.

Assured by his security service contacts that there was no bigger game than Philby, Fishman switched his attack. He says:

A colleague and friend, Henry Maule, then headed the New York Daily News London bureau. I deliberately gave Maule the story to break it in America [where libel laws are laxer] knowing it would be cabled back here and quoted in the Commons. I also spoke to both Norman Dodds and Marcus Lipton [who, as we have seen, was already suspicious of Philby] about the background to my enquiries to prepare them for possible supplementary questions and debate.[6]

In New York, the *Sunday News* of 23 October named Philby as the Third Man, and on the following Tuesday Lipton rose at question time in the Commons to ask:

Has the Prime Minister made up his mind to cover up at all costs the dubious third man activities of Mr Harold Philby who was First Secretary at the Washington embassy a little time ago, and is he determined to stifle all discussion on the very great matters which were evaded in the wretched White Paper, which is an insult to the intelligence of the country?[7]

With this explosive question, nearly a month after Hoover had played the first note of a carefully orchestrated campaign to expose Philby, Philby's name was well and truly out in the open. The government quickly committed itself to make a statement and to allow a debate in the Commons.

Hoover was delighted and moved quickly to consolidate his advantage. On 2 November he cabled the FBI office in London to explain what he was doing:

Public identification of Philby as individual who may have tipped off Burgess Maclean and requests of Bureau from other government agencies for information on Philby's role in case make it necessary that Bureau furnish information on Philby to certain high US government officials of Philby's role – Hoover.[8]

It is not difficult to see what Hoover was doing. Other FBI files make it clear that American intelligence officers suspected that Philby was being protected by his brother officers in SIS and by high-ranking Foreign Office officials. If the FBI gave its dossier on Philby to high-ranking American government people up to and probably including the President, it would be difficult for the British government to resist American demands for a full-scale investigation of Philby.

But Hoover had reckoned without several peculiarly British factors which, together, wrecked his scheme. He did not allow for the anti-McCarthy feeling in Britain which regarded the pursuit of Philby as persecution. He did not allow for the rivalry between MI5 and SIS which prevented either service from taking an overview of the Philby case. For example, Menzies, in his final years as 'C' and drinking very heavily indeed, regarded the Burgess-Maclean disappearance as nothing to do with SIS. When a friend of Burgess's, Rosamond Lehmann, telephoned Menzies immediately after the two men had fled to offer him information, Menzies said he was sorry, he would love to talk to her, but he had to take his little girl to Ascot that week.[9]

And, most important of all, Hoover had no way of knowing the distaste that the Foreign Secretary, Harold Macmillan, and his advisers had for the whole secret world, and their reluctance to have anything to do with it. Macmillan's secretary, Lord Egremont, considered all intelligence agencies a waste of time and money: 'Much better if the Russians saw the Cabinet minutes twice a week. Prevent all that fucking dangerous guesswork.'[10] Macmillan himself made the right noises about SIS in public but in private had a low opinion of the intelligence it produced and thought that the Philby affair was a squabble between SIS and MI5 which they should have settled themselves without coming to him: 'I don't expect the gamekeeper to come and tell me every time he kills a fox.'[11]

The first thing he did was to get his office to produce a brief for him. Egremont asked around and was told that a Tory MP who had been in SIS, Dick Brooman-White, knew the inside story and was able to appreciate the political subtleties of the case. Brooman-White, an old friend of Philby's, produced a brief which leaned heavily in favour of Philby's innocence. Philby had not been fired because, despite what the American said, there was no evidence against him; he had simply been too friendly with Burgess.

Macmillan read it and got quickly to the heart of the matter. The problem would keep on surfacing as long as Philby remained on SIS's books. He would have to go. When SIS muttered about British justice and innocent-until-proven-guilty, Macmillan replied: 'We're not jailing the bugger, just firing him.'[12] A compromise was reached: Macmillan would issue a statement virtually clearing Philby in return for a reorganization of SIS and a 'general clean-up'. On 7 November Macmillan made a short statement to the Commons, the contents of which were true, but unwittingly wrong:

No evidence has been found that Philby was responsible for warning Burgess or Maclean. [True, no evidence had or has been found.] While in government he carried out his duties ably and conscientiously. [True.] I have no reason to conclude that Mr. Philby has at any time betrayed the interests of this country, or to identify him with the so-called 'third man', if, indeed, there was one. [True, Macmillan had no reason to conclude this.]

Philby had been in touch with SIS headquarters the moment Lipton first raised his name and knew beforehand that he was going to be cleared. He had sat out a press siege at Crowborough. (The Princess Margaret-Group Captain Townsend romance was in the news, so the reporters doorstepped Margaret at Uckfield in the morning, Townsend at Eridge in the afternoon and tried to get Philby at Crowborough, midway between Uckfield and Eridge, at lunchtime.) Now he moved to his mother's flat in Drayton Gardens for the finale. He disconnected the doorbell and buried the telephone under a pile of cushions.

A family friend, Dulcie Sassoon, remembered:

> The windows were locked and shuttered against reporters. No one could leave the place. Dora told me one reporter had been caught trying to climb down the chimney at two o'clock the previous night. I listened to Kim talking to his mother, to whom he was devoted, fulminating against the Americans, the injustice of their third degree treatment of him. He told me all about Burgess staying with him and how he eventually had to throw him out because his drink and drug habits (and I suppose others) were contaminating Kim's children.[13]

The moment Macmillan had spoken, Philby uncovered the telephone and told all callers that he would be holding a press conference the next day at 11 am. He handled it brilliantly. Relaxed, authoritative, polite, and charming, he began by handing out a prepared statement explaining why he had not said anything earlier: he was bound by the Official Secrets Act not to disclose information derived from his official position; he wanted to avoid saying anything that might prejudice the government in its conduct of international affairs; and 'the efficiency of our security services can only be reduced by publicity given to their organization, personnel and techniques.'

Then the journalists put their questions. Standing by the fireplace in his mother's living room, showing hardly a trace of a stammer, he ran rings around reporters who had no way of calling his amazing bluff. Yes, he did know Burgess and an imprudent association with him in Washington had led to his resignation from the Foreign Office. He never knew Burgess was a communist. Yes, Burgess did drink but he did not behave disgracefully. In any case, Philby said, he was not going to sling mud. 'There are fair-weather friends and foul-weather friends, and I prefer to belong to the second category.' Maclean was only a shadow on his memory. Yes, he was always on the left, 'but I have never been a communist' and 'The last time I spoke to a communist, knowing he was one, was in 1934.'

Watching Philby's performance in the old black and white television film of the day, one cannot help but admire his nerve. Was he too so overcome with admiration for his own performance that he risked a little gesture of contempt for the pitiful probing by the media? The press reporters had hurried off to meet their afternoon deadlines and Philby was being questioned for television. 'Mr Philby,' comes the disembodied voice of the journalist, 'were you the Third Man?' Philby smiles confidently and says firmly: 'No, I was not.' Then, so quickly that unless you have seen the sequence many times you can easily miss it, Philby's tongue flicks in and out of his cheek.

Two days later Marcus Lipton gave in:

> I was shouted down in the House. Within the Labour Party, many members considered Philby a progressive left-wing influence in the Foreign Office, as he was clearly not part of the old guard. Their instinct was to protect him. The head of MI5, Sir Roger Hollis, asked to see me . . . We talked in the Central Lobby of the House of Commons in full public view. Of course he wanted to know my evidence but I could not give it.[14]

So Philby was free and away. In Washington the CIA and the FBI were appalled. Hoover's plot had gone wildly wrong. The FBI was forced officially to clear Philby too. On 29 December 1955 it closed its file on him: 'Subject – Donald Stuart Maclean et al. During a recent review of all references in *BUFILES* on Harold A.R. Philby, abstracts were made and placed on 3 x 5 cards. Philby is suspected of tipping off subject that he was under investigation. From this review there does not appear any basis or justification for an investigation of Philby.'[15]

Philby did not know of Hoover's role. He thought he owed his clearance to Lord Beaverbrook:

> No one in the Government and, particularly, no one in the security service wanted to make a public statement as early as 1955. The evidence was inconclusive; they could not charge me and did not want to clear me. They were forced to take action by the ill-informed hullabaloo in the popular press and by the silly blunder of Marcus Lipton. For this monumental fiasco the Beaverbrook press bears a particularly heavy responsibility. It started the running and kept it up, blundering but relentless, in pursuance of Beaverbrook's stupid feud with Eden and the Foreign Office.[16]

In Moscow I told Philby the whole story of how Freedom of Information documents revealed that the pressure to make a public statement about him had originated with the FBI. 'You owe your clearance to J. Edgar Hoover,' I said. Philby took a swig of his whisky and mineral water. Then he allowed himself a long and satisfied chuckle.

*

Since Philby had been officially cleared his friends in SIS saw no reason why he should not be re-employed. Of course there was no question that this could be done officially: SIS had promised Macmillan that Philby would go; he could never again appear on the SIS payroll as a serving officer. But senior officers have a lot of autonomy in employing agents and there was no reason why Philby should not be fitted in as one when a vacancy occurred that suited his talents. His friends began to look around on his behalf.

In the meantime he deserved a rest, and here a friend from his days in Istanbul offered his help. This was W.E.D. Allen, a former press counsellor in the British embassy in Ankara. The Allen family firm in Ireland was to celebrate its centenary in 1957, so Allen invited Philby to come and stay in Cappagh, County Waterford, and help him write the firm's history. Philby did a competent if uninspired job and returned to London in July 1956 to find good news waiting for him: his SIS friends had found him a job.

Philby was to be an SIS agent in Beirut. SIS was taking an increasing interest in the Middle East, and to have an experienced agent in what was then the centre of intrigue for the area seemed a good idea. Even Philby's enemies were not entirely against the scheme, arguing that making Philby active again might lead him to provide the evidence necessary to prove his guilt and close the case. There was no chance, though, of Philby going under diplomatic cover – that would be too obvious and would invite criticism. So Philby's cover was to be provided by *The Observer* and *The Economist*, which were to share his services as 'stringer' (a non-staff correspondent) for £500 a year retainer, expenses and thirty shillings per hundred published words. Did SIS tell Philby's cover employers what he was really doing?

Sir Robert Mackenzie explained the difficulties.

After Philby had been cleared there were still some people who said he should be put right down. But there were others who said, in effect: 'We've got to be fair to the fellow. There's nothing concrete against him and he might really be innocent. If we're hard on him it might be bad for the morale of the service.' So when someone fixed his newspaper job for him and the editors asked formally if Philby had *really* been cleared, what could we say? We couldn't very well say: 'No, not really', and take the fellow's job away from him. So we said: 'Yes, he's clean.'[17]

In our conversations in Moscow Philby was in no doubt how he got the job. He said: 'The Beirut job was arranged for me by Nicholas Elliott and George Young [SIS colleagues]. There is some conflict here. Elliott assured me that he had cleared my cover with David Astor [then editor of *The Observer*] but Astor has since denied that he knew anything about it. You'll have to make up your own mind on this.'

Astor has said that he had 'no awareness' of Philby's on-going connection with SIS after he joined *The Observer*. 'Nor had I heard of Nicholas Elliott at that time. I was not dealing directly with MI6 but with an official from the Foreign Office. There was no mention of the Middle East or anywhere else. I was supposed to be rescuing the guy. When he finally turned up in Moscow they rushed over and apologized and said, "Very sorry we didn't warn you."'[18] This account is born out by other *Observer* staff who say that Astor was indignant at the time about how the paper had been used and had consistently said that he never knew that Philby, when working for the paper, had any SIS connections.

But George Young said: 'Nick did all the negotiations. I simply approved them. I would have thought that Astor knew. Philby was given Arab affairs because his family was connected with the Arab world and we saw no harm in his going out there. I briefed him before he left.'[19] As for *The Economist*, it was always a sore point with Donald Tyerman, the then editor, that although he personally checked on Philby with a senior Foreign Office official, Harold Caccia,* he was never told by either Caccia or *The Observer* that Philby's initial entrée had been strictly an official one.

The issue is impossible to resolve satisfactorily. Astor, who had had contact with SIS in 1939 over his interest in the German opposition to Hitler, must have believed that Philby, a former SIS officer, employed by *The Observer* at the specific request of the Foreign Office, was going to confine his activities in Beirut to mere journalism. He was mistaken; Philby did not.

*Ambassador to Washington 1956–61; Provost of Eton, 1965–77; Lord Caccia since 1965.

CONFRONTATION
IN BEIRUT
== 15 ==

Philby arrived in the Lebanon in August 1956 and went to stay with his father. St John was living at that time in Ajaltoun, a Maronite village about twenty miles from Beirut, in a white bungalow with magnificent views. He had been banished from Arabia after falling out with the young Saudi princes after the death of his patron, King Ibn Saud, and had arrived in the Lebanon with his Saudi wife, Rozy, and their two sons, Khalid and Faris.

It was a weird household. St John was in the middle of what he called 'my Pygmalion experiment', an attempt to make Rozy adapt to Western ways. He had ordered her to remove her veil; he had hired a Lebanese Christian girl to keep her company; and he had sent the boys to a neighbouring Roman Catholic school. But the experiment had not gone well. Rozy refused to leave the house, slopped in carpet slippers and ate huge amounts of sweets. She would disappear into a back room when St John had visitors and would not accompany him to village social functions. Sometimes they had lengthy shouting matches which usually ended when St John gave her a welt on her behind.

However, St John seemed delighted to have Kim with him and for the first time in years father and son had time for each other. They would sit on the verandah of the house, enjoying the crisp mountain air, and talk until an approaching chill in the atmosphere made St John, who was now seventy-one, throw a bedouin cloak over his short-sleeved shirt. Or St John would dress up in a white suit and take the whole family for a walk in the village, acknowledging the greetings of the villagers who respectfully called him Hajji, the Muslim term for a man who has made the pilgrimage to Mecca, and proudly introducing Kim to the village dignitaries. Sometimes they would go off alone to Beirut where, conscious that his son had to earn a living, St John made a point of presenting Kim to everyone who might be a source of news or influence.

These must have been happy times, because St John briefly indulged in an ageing male's fantasy. He wrote to his wife in London,

200

suggesting that she close down the Drayton Gardens flat, persuade his other children to abandon England, and all come and join him, his mistress, his other children and Kim, in one huge joint family. 'I think we might all put our heads together and plan a migration en masse to Lebanon . . . There would be about a dozen of us to lay the foundation of a Philby colony in one of the nicest countries in the world.'[1]

In this period when Kim was wondering what to do about Aileen and his children, still back in Crowborough, doubtful of his ability to make a living as a journalist, and uncertain how long it would be before MI5 returned to the attack, his father was of great help to him. Sure of his own worth and in the knowledge that others would one day recognize it, he steadied Kim, helped him regain his self-confidence and gave him the will to rebuild his life.

In November 1956, St John made his peace with the Saudi royal family and returned to Riyadh. He had planned to spend the following summer in England, and stopped off in Beirut on the way only to be met by Kim with the news that Dora had died in her sleep two nights before. St John was shattered, realizing perhaps for the first time how much he had come to depend on her, how much their shared interests had bound them together although they were physically apart.

Philby, too, was deeply grieved by his mother's death. He told me in Moscow: 'My mother literally drank herself to death. Towards the end she was drinking a bottle of gin a day. The trouble was that my father was a terribly insensitive man as far as women were concerned. He had no regard at all for their feelings. It wasn't deliberate. He just didn't understand why my mother should feel the way she did.'

St John went off to London anyway, and Philby continued to live in Ajaltoun, coming down to Beirut a couple of times a week to collect his cables from London and to do his stories. He may also have had a room somewhere in the city, because he told other correspondents that he was staying in east Beirut but could not be contacted there because he did not have a telephone, something they thought rather strange for a newspaperman. Either way, it was a lonely life, and therefore it came as no surprise to his small circle of friends when he suddenly fell desperately in love.

He was having a quiet drink in the bar of the St George's, then perhaps the best hotel in the Middle East, when the waiter handed him a note from Eleanor, the wife of the *New York Times* chief correspondent in the Middle East, Sam Pope Brewer. Brewer had met Philby when they were both covering the Spanish Civil War and had heard of Philby's appointment. He was out of town on an assignment but had told Eleanor that if Philby should turn up she should introduce herself and offer to do anything she could to help him settle in – a generous gesture he was later to regret.

Philby read the note and came over to join Eleanor. 'What touched me first about Kim was his loneliness,' Eleanor wrote later:

> He knew no one in Beirut . . . A certain old-fashioned reserve set him apart from the easy familiarity of the other journalists. He was then forty-four, of medium height, very lean, with a handsome heavily-lined face. His eyes were an intense blue. I thought that here was a man who had seen a lot of the world, who was experienced, and yet who seemed to have suffered . . . He had a gift for creating an atmosphere of such intimacy that I found myself talking freely to him. I was very impressed by his beautiful manners. We took him under our wing. On his visits to town he usually came to see us and soon became one of our closest friends.[2]

Eleanor's switch from her own impressions of Philby to the plural personal pronouns 'us' and 'our' conceals the fact that she and Kim soon became lovers. Sam Brewer was out of town a lot on assignments, and when he was away Philby and Eleanor would set off for picnics in the mountains, swimming parties, visits to markets, lunches in out-of-the-way restaurants, coffee in tiny cafés. Philby bombarded her with tiny love letters written on paper taken from cigarette boxes. In cold print they are embarrassing. 'Deeper in love than ever, my darling. x x x from your Kim,' and later the same day, 'Deeper and deeper, my darling. x x x from your Kim.'

But Eleanor, a straightforward pleasant woman from Seattle, who had travelled widely but who remained surprisingly unsophisticated, was bowled over by them. 'Like his beautiful manners, Kim's skill in writing letters was a reminder of a civilized way of living, particularly appealing to an American. They drew me into his daily life by the little incidents he described so wittily and gracefully.'[3] Eleanor had fallen for the famous Philby charm, but what did he see in her? His colleagues were surprised by the romance. They did not think her his equal in intelligence or personality, 'a slightly dull and flaccid person with a modest talent as a sculptor, an annoying habit of talking through clenched teeth, and a reputation for tottering into cocktail parties glazed of eye', was one unflattering description of her.

But, for Philby, there was more to Eleanor than that. In a very revealing letter, Philby wrote:

> You are one of the easiest, most soothing presences I have ever met. If circumstances had made it impossible for me to become your lover, I would still have wished to be a very close friend. For a week or two, in fact, I thought I was just that. Now, darling, I know you have had a bitter experience . . . But do you also know what it is like to be chivvied? I have had it at least twice; and *that* is difficult. One of the most wonderful things about you is that you have accepted me as I am – except for *araq*, and quite rightly – and that you haven't tried the common female trick of trying to turn me into the sort of man you would have liked to think you loved.[4]

Sam Brewer was no fool, and one day when Philby brought Eleanor home from a picnic in the mountains, he was waiting at the door. He told Philby that he could not prevent him from seeing Eleanor but that he was no longer welcome in the Brewer house. Philby now pushed Eleanor to get a divorce and when she left Beirut to go to Seattle to make arrangements for her elderly father's welfare, she agreed that while in the United States she would start proceedings.

Suddenly everything accelerated. On 12 December 1957 Philby received news that Aileen had died the day before of congestive heart failure, myocardial degeneration, a respiratory infection and pulmonary tuberculosis. She was only forty-seven but had gone downhill rapidly after Philby had left her. Sir Robert Mackenzie remembered meeting her when he went to dinner one night at a friend's house in Cadogan Square and discovered Aileen working there as the cook. 'I was shocked. She was obviously a very sick woman, both mentally and physically. She talked only nonsense. I wasn't surprised to learn a few months later that she had died.'[5] There seems little doubt that Aileen finally knew of Philby's treachery, the secret he had kept from her all their married life, and her drinking was one way of obliterating the knowledge. She remains the most tragic figure in this story.

Philby cabled Eleanor asking her to marry him, and when her Mexican divorce came through in July the following year he went to see Sam Brewer to tell him of their plans. It was a civilized meeting of two worldly men. Philby said: 'I've come to tell you that I've had a cable from Eleanor. She's got her divorce and I want you to be the first person to know that I'm going to marry her.' Brewer replied: 'That sounds like the best solution. What do you make of the situation in Iraq?'[6]

Civil war in the Lebanon delayed Eleanor's return. When she eventually did get back they were married in Beirut, but because of the Mexican divorce the British embassy could not recognize it. So they came to London for a second marriage on 24 January 1959, in the Holborn Register Office. She was forty-five and he forty-seven. The witnesses were Philby's former colleagues, Jack Ivens, who had worked with him in Section Five, and his old schoolfriend Tim Milne, then still a serving SIS officer and a staunch Philby supporter. Their willingness to be seen with Philby suggested that at last the clouds had lifted. Eight years after the Burgess-Maclean affair it looked as if MI5 had finally decided to leave Philby alone.

Philby presented Eleanor to his children, took her on a tour of his favourite London haunts and introduced her to all his friends. 'This is love with a capital L,' Philby told one. 'We shall take a house in the mountains; she will paint; I will write; peace and stability at last.'[7]

There is no evidence that during this period in Beirut – his first three years – Philby was very active in the intelligence world for either side, and he does not seem to have done much journalism either. He filed his first story for *The Observer* on 30 September 1956 – 'Western Oil Threat by Lebanon' – and continued to file careful if boring pieces at the rate of one or two a month. Patrick Seale, a specialist writer on the Middle East who knew Philby at the time, says: 'He showed no interest in scoops, was in no sense the newshound, did not cultivate Arab contacts, and avoided travelling if he could. His prose was literate rather than lively, bureaucratic rather than journalistic.'[8]

Nevertheless, Philby had his standards. He cared enough about his reputation as a journalist not to wish his name to appear on what he considered to be stories about trivial subjects. He wrote on politics and international affairs and he made it clear to *The Observer* that he was reluctant to file anything else, even when the stories were to appear under a pseudonym he had invented for himself. When asked by *The Observer*'s syndicated news service for a story on Arabian slave girls, a topic he should have known something about, if only from his father, he replied: 'You ask me hard things. I will try to meet your request, but the piece will have to be attributed to the unfortunate Charles Garner.'[9]

We can see now that Philby was marking time, waiting for something. Seale says of this period:

The most striking thing about Philby was that he was not doing very much. He led a pretty domesticated life. His routine was to get up late, make his way hand in hand with Eleanor to the Normandy – not the smartest hotel – to collect his mail and have a few drinks; to do a little shopping, a little cooking; take a siesta; perhaps put in an appearance at a party; return home to a bottle of vodka *citronné* cooling in the ice box.[10]

Philby was waiting to return to his real métier – espionage. His problem was that his Moscow masters could not use him again until the British did. In *My Silent War* he says of his Beirut period that the Soviet Union was interested in a wide range of Middle East phenomena and that its main priority was always the intentions of the United States and British governments in the area. He then goes on to describe how he was well placed as a journalist to have conversations with American and British officials and to assess such intentions. But, of course, the information available to him as a journalist was trivial compared with what would be available to him as an active intelligence agent. And that was the rub: having fixed a job for him as an agent in Beirut, SIS was not using him. And if SIS was not using him, he was of little use to the Russians.

Then overnight this changed. In 1960 Nicholas Elliott, the man who had fixed Philby's cover job with *The Observer* and *The Economist*, was posted to Beirut as SIS station commander. He began to push Philby to produce a steady flow of high-grade information. Suddenly Philby became one of the most active journalists in the area. He was here, there and everywhere, filing copy from Amman, Riyadh, Damascus, Sharjah, Bahrein, Baghdad, Cairo, Kuwait and Yemen. Later, when Philby had defected, the CIA compiled a breakdown of these trips and the copy they produced and decided that there was an unjustifiable discrepancy – he had visited too many places for too few journalistic results. The CIA attributed this to his work for the Russians, but it was SIS that kept him busy. There are two theories as to why.

The first is the innocuous one: Elliott thought that Philby was not being used properly and wanted to get the best out of him. The second is the conspiratorial one. In 1956, in the wake of the 'Buster' Crabb scandal,* Dick White had been moved from being head of MI5 to become chief of SIS. There, White had been alarmed to

*In April 1956 SIS mounted an operation to examine the hull of the Soviet cruiser *Ordzhonikidze* in Portsmouth Harbour, hoping to learn about its anti-submarine and mine detection equipment. But the cruiser was carrying the Soviet leaders Bulganin and Khrushchev, and the frogman SIS hired,

discover that Philby was still on SIS's books, but he did nothing about it. His first few years were spent reorganizing SIS, moving the service away from the thrills and spills of the Great Game to the more difficult but more rewarding field of intelligence analysis. By 1960 he was able to return to Philby, and after reading the file again and consulting his senior officers he decided on a plan to bring the case to a conclusion.

The idea was to force Philby out into the field, to give him the profile of an active and industrious intelligence officer and thus force the Russians to use him again. Philby would be taken into Elliott's confidence; he would be made a part of SIS operations; he would learn information so important that he would have to pass it to his Soviet control. But although some of that information would be genuine, some of it would be a plant and Western counter-intelligence would be waiting to see where it surfaced. If it could be traced back to Philby, and only to Philby, then the British authorities would at last have proof of his treachery.

It was a tricky game with many imponderables. Philby might suspect what was happening, but he could not refuse to play because that could be seen as a tacit confession. He could not go only part of the way – agree to his more active role for SIS but not pass anything to the Russians – because that would make his Soviet control begin to doubt Philby's loyalty. He could not get out of the whole thing by pleading that he was too old, recently married, in need of a quiet life, or anything like that because it was Nicholas Elliott, his old friend, his most ardent defender in SIS, who was giving him this chance to work his way back into the club.

So Philby, his old anxieties re-awakened, was forced to join the game. He must have known that sooner or later something like this would happen because he tried to take as many precautions as he could. He told me in Moscow: 'From 1951 on I began to prepare for the ultimate crisis, knowing it might come at any moment.' One precaution not revealed before was to try to change his nationality. India had a small legation in Beirut run by one Indian diplomat, Godfrey Jansen. Jansen, a friend of St John, first met Philby when he arrived for lunch one day as a substitute for his father, who was unwell. Jansen recalls:

Then, later, Philby came into the legation, by appointment, to

---

Commander Lionel Crabb, was too old and too frail. He vanished forever, (a headless body which might have been his was washed ashore some time later), the Russians complained, and Prime Minister Eden had to apologize in the Commons on 4 May 1956.

ask me whether I could provide him with an Indian passport. His British passport, he said, had come up for renewal and he was having difficulties because he and his father had been born outside the UK, in India and Ceylon respectively. I had to tell him that I couldn't help him because Indian citizenship was granted only after seven years' uninterrupted residence in India. He looked really disappointed.[11]

Philby's story of difficulties over his British citizenship cannot have been true: he left a brand-new passport behind when he defected. His real reason for wanting Indian nationality must have been either to make it more difficult for the British authorities to seize him when the 'ultimate crisis' came, or to give him the option of going to India rather than to the Soviet Union.

Those last years in Beirut were in stark contrast to the early ones. Under pressure from Elliott, short of money, away on assignments a lot, Philby had little peace and frequently sought refuge in alcohol. Then he suffered two blows. The death of his father on 30 September 1960 was the first. St John had spent the summer in London, following his usual routine of lunch and dinner at the Athenaeum and afternoons at Lord's for the cricket. In August he had gone to Moscow for the Orientalists' Congress, then returned to Britain for a brief family holiday in Falmouth before setting out for Arabia. He stopped in Beirut to stay with Kim and Eleanor for a 'fling'. This involved a round of parties at which St John held the floor, arguing until the early hours on everything from Middle Eastern politics to the purpose of life.

The last of these parties was at the flat of John H. Fistere, a former writer for *Fortune* magazine, and his equally American wife. St John was at his most sparkling and entertained a crowd of people half his age until the early hours, ending his discourse only so that he could take Kim and Eleanor to a nightclub on the way home. Next morning he found he had difficulty in breathing and Kim rushed him to hospital, where the doctors diagnosed a severe heart attack. He lost consciousness, woke only once to say: 'God, I'm bored', and died late that afternoon. He was seventy-five. Kim arranged a quiet funeral the next morning in the Muslim cemetery in the Basta quarter of Beirut, and had the tombstone inscribed: 'Greatest of Arabian explorers'.

In his death St John found the fame he had always sought. Tributes to his achievements poured in from all over the world, and in 1973 he was honoured by a full-scale biography written by Elizabeth Monroe, an emeritus fellow of St Antony's College, Oxford, and a distinguished Middle Eastern scholar. 'All through his life, [St John] saw himself as acting from the highest motives,' Monroe wrote, 'and with the right in a free country to think what he liked and say what he thought about broken British promises, or his conscientious objection to war. The flaw in him was not the creeds he preached but his immoderation in expounding them.'[12]

Kim was deeply affected by his father's death, and went on a drinking bout that lasted several days. Did he regret that he had never told St John about his true loyalties, probably because he was unsure how he would have taken it? For, despite his dissent, St John had remained sturdily British, with his *Times*, cricket scores, Honours List, his London club, and his English attitudes. 'If he had lived a little longer to learn the truth,' Philby wrote about his father, 'he would have been thunderstruck, but by no means disapproving.'[13]

Philby was still recovering from St John's death when he was dealt another knock. In April 1961, George Blake, an SIS officer who had won a lot of praise for his daring work in Berlin, was lured back to London from an Arabic language school in the Lebanon, arrested and charged under the Official Secrets Act. He had been working for the Russians all along. Blake confessed, was tried at the Old Bailey, and given the savage sentence of forty-two years' imprisonment, the longest term ever imposed under English law.*

Philby was shocked and worried. There was little danger that anything Blake had said in his confession would incriminate Philby, because the two were separately run by the Russian intelligence service and did not know of each other's true role. But Blake's exposure represented another triumph for British counter-intelligence and the length of his sentence, far greater than anyone had expected, must have startled Philby. He began to go downhill rapidly, his periods of drunkenness became more frequent, and he became so saturated with alcohol that, on occasions, two martinis would send him rolling into the gutter. His friends called less often, complaining that they could not stand Philby's incoherence and Eleanor's constant complaints about money troubles.

Public functions became a horror for Eleanor, worrying what outrage her husband would attempt next. His friends began to get used to his condition, and often a party would continue over Philby's

---

*Blake served barely five and a half years and then made a dramatic escape from Wormwood Scrubs prison, West London. He vanished, only to surface a year later in Moscow where he now lives.

prostrate figure on the floor, staring glassy-eyed at the ceiling. When it was time to go, the men would carry him to a taxi. Eleanor told friends that Kim was having terrible nightmares and would wake up shouting, apparently for help.

Their friends tried to organize social events where they could limit the couple's drinking – Eleanor was by now drinking almost as much as Philby. They would invite them for a picnic in the country, offering to pick them up and bring them home. But on the way the Philbys would announce that they wanted to pick up their mail at the Hotel Normandy, which would inevitably involve a few quick drinks at the bar. At the picnic site, Philby and Eleanor would quickly finish the wine and then Philby would make a trek to the nearest café and come back with a paper bag full of miniature bottles of spirits. He and Eleanor could drink fifty of these in an afternoon. By the time the picnic was over, they had to be carried to the car and would sleep all the way back to Beirut.

Kim sometimes took Eleanor on assignments with him, and the couple soon had a reputation around the bars of the Middle East for their capacity for drink and their boisterous horseplay. For some years after Philby's defection the barman at the Amman Club in Jordan would entertain customers with his account of how the drunken Philbys would play 'bullfights', a tablecloth for a cape, each taking a turn to be the bull and the matador.

In April 1962, Aristotle Onassis's yacht arrived off Beirut. One of the guests on board was F.W.D. Deakin, the Warden of St Antony's College, Oxford, a fellow Westminster schoolboy who had had a brilliant wartime career in Yugoslavia. He got in touch with Philby and the two spent a long evening together, reminiscing. His lasting impression was of how Philby seemed to enjoy the company of someone familiar, his reluctance to leave, and how he appeared on the point of breakdown.

Little things seemed to tip him into bouts of deep drunken depression. He had a pet fox cub, Jackie, given to him by friends when it was only a few weeks old. He house-trained her, and was delighted when he imagined he saw some human traits in her character – once he caught her lapping up some spilt whisky, and on another occasion sucking at the stem of his pipe. He took photographs of her at various ages and eventually wrote an article about her, 'The Fox That Came to Stay', for *Country Life*.

But by the time it was published on 6 December 1962, Jackie was dead. Either she fell five storeys from the parapet of the Philbys' terrace – Philby had written about her 'canters around the top of the parapet in a carefree fashion' – or she was tipped over by the concierge, who had earlier complained about the keeping of a fox in the apartment. Eleanor returned from a few days in Jordan to find Philby slumped on the terrace, barely coherent, and in a heavy depression. It took him weeks to get over the death of his pet. Patrick Seale tells of another occasion when Philby found a live mouse floundering helplessly about in the lavatory bowl. 'The secret agent who had sent men to their deaths could not bear to see it suffer and fished it out.'[14]

If ever in his career Philby's guard was down and it should have been possible to have spotted his true allegiances, then it was during this period. After he had defected, his colleagues and acquaintances scoured their memories for some little thing that Philby had let slip that, if they had been listening more carefully, would have given him away. Only the most minor hints emerged. Godfrey Jansen, back in Beirut in the early 1960s as a journalist instead of a diplomat, says that in Philby's flat one entire bookshelf was filled with the collected works of Karl Marx, 'perhaps a dozen volumes, handsomely bound in dark red with gold lettering'. But a serious foreign correspondent could argue that he needed them for his work.

One night in a taxi Philby and Jansen were talking of the battle for world power between the United States and the Soviet Union. Jansen said that since the end of the war the Soviet Union seemed more successful. Philby said quietly: 'Its success is inevitable.' Jansen says: 'His use of "inevitable", that key word in Communist jargon, a dead give away, surprised me so much that I can still remember the exact spot where he said it – just opposite the entrance to the British Bank on rue Makdisi.'[15]

One night at a party at the Fisteres', the question of nationality came up and someone asked Philby how he felt. 'I was born in India,' he said, 'brought up in various parts of the Arab world and I was at school in England. I don't feel that I have any nationality.' This shook Fistere: 'I just couldn't believe it. Kim seemed such a Britisher. It sounded as if he was denying his country.'

Another couple, Yussuf and Rosemary Sayigh, used to talk politics with Philby for hours. After he had left they spent days trying to remember anything he had said which could have indicated a pro-Russian leaning. All they could come up with was that he had once said that the Soviet medical system was good. It is all rather thin stuff, and remarkable only because of its meagreness: this is *all* anyone can remember. And all this time, depressed, drunk, hung over, Philby not only concealed his true self but also managed to continue to function as an intelligence officer. What did he get that was useful to the Russians?

Elliott was careful to limit Philby's access to that SIS information which was necessary to bait the operation that White had planned to entrap him. But Philby was experienced and enterprising. A lot of serving and former SIS officers passing through Beirut made a point of looking him up, having a drink with him, and 'talking shop'. One, Anthony Cavendish, remembers:

> More often than not I met him in the opulent bar of the St George's; alone. It seemed that Kim wanted to talk about SIS matters and personalities and therefore believed that I was more likely to be forthcoming about what I knew if there were no journalistic witnesses. I talked to him just as I would have talked to any other former colleague from the Secret Service . . . I believed that if he were still in touch with members of the Service it was right to give him the benefit of the doubt.[16]

And, according to documents obtained under the Freedom of Information Act, the CIA believed that Philby had a top-level source within the agency who revealed to him in Beirut some of its covert actions. According to the documents, the CIA was convinced that one of its own officers, Wilbur Crane Eveland, told Philby about the agency's operations in the Middle East and Africa, including plans to bring down the Syrian government late in 1956 and its efforts to rig the 1957 Lebanese election in favour of the pro-Western Chamoun regime. The CIA documents refer to a CIA interrogation of Eleanor Philby after Philby's defection. A report of this interrogation dated 1 November 1965 reads: '[Mrs Philby] said her husband had remarked that all he had to do was to have one evening with Bill Eveland in Beirut and before it was over he would know of all his operations.'[17]

Eveland, now sixty-nine, had been employed directly by the CIA's director, Allen Dulles, as a trouble-shooter in the Middle East and Africa. He has denied the accuracy of the CIA documents, insists that he was never indiscreet with Philby, and says that the mere fact that he *knew* Philby in Beirut ruined his career in the agency. One can appreciate his problem. Since SIS appeared to trust Philby sufficiently to be using him in its own operations, any CIA officer would be entitled to believe that Philby had been cleared. Eveland was probably not alone in this belief. As George Young has said of other CIA officers, 'Philby was friendly with all the Yanks in Beirut. A lot of them blabbed. He was pretty good at getting them to talk.'[18]

But this was not how Philby managed to be so prescient about the arrival of the US Marines in the Lebanon on 19 July 1958 – ostensibly to restore order after Nasserite groups rioted against Camille Chamoun's regime, but really because Washington believed

211

a communist takeover in the area might be imminent. Philby told journalists three days before that the Marines were going to land, and his colleagues remember that he spoke not like a journalist making a prediction, but as a man who knew for certain what was going to happen. It is unlikely that Philby learnt of the landing plans from Eveland because he wrote later:

> The local CIA man, whom I knew well, was dumbfounded by the intervention . . . I never met a single American Embassy official in Beirut, Damascus or Aleppo – Ambassador, Service Attaché, Consul, CIA man, or run-of-the-mill secretary – who gave the slightest credence to a red threat in either Lebanon or Syria . . . The point, of course is that JFD [John Foster Dulles, the American Secretary of State] seems to have ignored the evidence provided by his officials on the spot and this must have been deliberate. Why? Did he *need* something evil to combat, as the Puritans needed sin?[19]

He may have learned about the landings from other American sources, or from his Soviet control. But the most likely source would have been SIS, perhaps to see what Philby would do with the information.

The months staggered by and Philby held on – by a thread. Elliott's posting came to an end and he left Beirut with the Philby case still unresolved. Then two events, a defection and a piece of Zionist politics, finally put paid to Kim Philby's career as a Soviet spy.

The defection was that of Anatoliy Golitsyn, who came over to the CIA station chief in Helsinki on 22 December 1961. Golitsyn had worked as a deskman in the first chief directorate of the KGB, which conducted all aggressive intelligence operations against the Western world, and for two years had served in the NATO section of the information department. He had prepared for his defection by memorizing information and gathering clues to agents' identities that would help expose important Soviet spies in the West. He gave the British the clues to fill in the gaps about Kim Philby.

But even this by itself might not have been enough had not Flora Solomon, the Philby family's friend, the woman who had introduced Kim to Aileen, the woman who had been a witness at their wedding, decided to come forward with a vital piece of information. Solomon's motives are far from clear. As she has told it, in the early 1960s, while working for Israel, she read Philby's dispatches in *The Observer* and became angry at their anti-Israeli bias. But it is simply not true that Philby's articles showed any bias against Israel. True, he wrote favourably about Nasser, who was getting a bad press in Britain in the wake of Suez, and he believed the Palestinians had a genuine grievance, but Philby was a stringer, not a commentator, and if any of his articles were blatantly slanted against Israel, *The Observer* would not have printed them.

Nevertheless, Flora Solomon decided that she would have to do something to counter Philby, and in 1962 when she was at the Weizmann Institute of Science in Rehovot and met Lord Rothschild, she acted. She told him: 'How is it that *The Observer* uses a man like Kim? Don't they know he's a communist? You must do something.' Rothschild questioned her further and then told her he would think about it. On Solomon's return to London, Rothschild asked her if she would attend a meeting at his flat with an MI5 officer. Solomon repeated to the officer what she had told Rothschild: that in 1937 Philby had come to see her before he left for Spain and had said: 'I'm doing important work for peace. You should be doing it, too, Flora.' And that in 1938, just before Munich, Philby had taken her aside and said: 'I want to tell you that I'm in great danger.' She told the MI5 officer that she deduced from these remarks that Philby was still associated with communism, a cause he had espoused at Cambridge.

Solomon continued: 'I was now also asked to meet a member of Mossad, the Israeli Secret Service, in the belief that I might have further information to divulge and would perhaps say more to an Israeli than to MI5. The two services, I was told, operated in close harmony. Of course I knew no more and deeply resented an implication questioning my first loyalty to Britain, but I agreed to the interview nevertheless.'[20]

The puzzling part of Mrs Solomon's story is why she decided to act against Philby when she did. At first she says it was because he was writing anti-Israeli articles in *The Observer*, but when she complains to Rothschild about him she says it is because he is a communist. Since she had known this at least since 1938, why did she wait until 1962 to say anything about it? Was it politically convenient at that moment?

In an attempt to clear this up, I asked Philby in Moscow about his views on Mrs Solomon and her motives for informing on him. He was surprisingly forgiving. He said: 'Flora was an old family friend. I had known her since I was a boy. My father used to take me to see her. I met her several times when I was in the period of my fascist front. Sometimes I'd catch Flora looking at me with a wry look as if to say that she knew exactly what I was up to. She was hard left herself once, you know. Then in her later years she became very pro-Israeli and seemed to change.'

I tried to get him to say how he felt when he learnt that Solomon had betrayed him to MI5 and Mossad, but he seemed more interested in talking about Victor Rothschild's role. He said: 'Here's a little story about Rothschild for you. Make of it what you will. We were talking one day in 1946 and Victor suddenly said: "And how long have you been a member of the Communist Party, Kim?" I said: "Me, Victor!" And he said: "Just a little joke. I try it on everyone." '

SIS and MI5 now prepared a prosecutor's brief on Philby and Nicholas Elliott volunteered to return to Beirut, confront Philby with it, offer him immunity from prosecution, and get his full and uninhibited confession. As John le Carré has said, a *full* confession from Philby would have been one of the most valuable intelligence prizes on the market. Elliott arrived in Beirut on 10 January 1963, rented a private flat, telephoned Philby and invited him over. Philby turned up with his head in bandages. He had drunk too much on his birthday, he said, and had fallen and hit his head on the radiator in the bathroom of his apartment.

Elliott went straight into the attack. He outlined the case against Philby and the new evidence from Golitsyn and Solomon. Then he said: 'You took me in for years. Now I'll get the truth out of you even if I have to drag it out. I once looked up to you. My God how I despise you now. I hope you've got enough decency left to understand why.'[21] Philby was thunderstruck. When he regained his composure he confessed that he had indeed been working for the Russian intelligence service for many years. But he was not prepared to say more. Elliott made his offer of immunity from prosecution in return for a full confession and a commitment from Philby to return with him to London for an extensive debriefing. Philby asked the terms of the immunity, accepted it in principle but said he would need time to think the whole matter over. He resisted Elliott's pressure to begin writing it all down there and then, but said he would resume discussions the next day.

He returned with two typewritten pages, part of which was devoted to clearing Anthony Blunt of any suspicion of having worked with Philby, and part to naming other agents, all of whom turned out to be innocent. (Philby had clearly used the intervening period to contact his Soviet control.) There then began a prolonged battle of wills, with Elliott doing his best to persuade Philby to tell more and Philby constantly stalling for time. Elliott even agreed to dine with the Philbys one evening so as to reassure Eleanor and keep contact with Philby. But in the end, Elliott had to accept that the confrontation was inconclusive: he had no detailed confession, no evidence that would survive in a British courtroom, and Philby was flatly refusing to come back to London with him. A week after having arrived in Beirut, he returned to London virtually empty-handed.

How had Philby got away with it? I asked him the question in Moscow. 'It seemed to me that there was something strange about the whole confrontation business. You see, in November 1962, just a couple of months before Elliott arrived, I wrote to Astor at *The Observer* saying that I would like to take some home leave. I had some family affairs to attend to in Britain. I asked him if July the following year would be suitable. He wrote back saying that would certainly be all right and to go ahead and make my plans. In other words, in July 1963 I planned to be in London, within the jurisdiction of the British courts, and virtually at the service's mercy if they wanted me. Yet SIS decided to send Elliott to confront me in January in Beirut, where they had no legal standing whatsoever. What do you make of that?'

I thought about it for a moment. 'I suppose it's possible that Astor didn't tell SIS that you were coming in July, especially since he denies knowing about your cover,' I said. (Astor later told me that he does not remember receiving such a letter from Philby. 'I enlisted him – to my cost,' he said. 'But after that he kept away from me. So it's more likely that he would have written to the foreign editor. But he could have written to me. I just don't remember it.')[22]

'Of course that's possible,' Philby said. 'But Astor would not have had to tell anyone. A lot of people were suspicious of me by that time, so MI5 would have been controlling my mail [opening it in London]. They would have read my letter to Astor. No, it doesn't add up. SIS knew I was coming to London in a few months' time but deliberately decided to confront me in Beirut. Then Elliott offered me an immunity deal that was no deal at all. It was contingent on my telling all I knew about the KGB and naming names in Britain. Elliott mentioned some names to me, several of which alarmed me. It became clear to me that my immunity could be withdrawn at any time unless I named names. So for me this deal was not on.

'Now you take these two facts – the choice of Beirut for the confrontation and an immunity deal that was patently unacceptable – and you have to ask what was going on? My view, and that of my superiors here in Moscow, is that the whole thing was deliberately staged so as to push me into escaping, because the last thing the

British government wanted at that time was me in London, a security scandal and a sensational trial.'

Philby's interpretation could be right. SIS had been fighting to retain its special relationship with the CIA ever since the Burgess-Maclean affair. If Philby were brought back to Britain, arrested and tried, it would emerge that he had never been taken off SIS's books, despite what SIS had told the Americans, and that he had actually been taken on as an agent in Beirut. Moreover, at that time the Conservative government headed by Harold Macmillan, the very man who had cleared Philby, was being battered by a series of security scandals. First there was the case of George Blake; then a special tribunal had been announced on 13 November 1962 to inquire into the failure of MI5 to detect the activities of the Admiralty spy, John Vassall. In December a senior officer of the Central Office of Information had been sentenced to two years' imprisonment for passing secrets to her Yugoslav lover. And, finally, rumours of what was to become the Profumo scandal were already circulating in Fleet Street.* The Philby case could well have been the last straw for an embattled government.

It is possible to argue the opposite: that the scandal of Philby's escape was greater than if he had been caught. But this does not mesh with the fact that the British government succeeded in concealing the full extent of the scandal until 1968, when Macmillan had long since gone. The only other explanation is that Elliott had a fall-back plan: if he failed to get Philby to confess, then he was to push him into trying to run – a damning admission of guilt – and then, with the cooperation of the Lebanese authorities, grab him before he actually got away. There is some support for this theory in that on 16 January, by which time it was becoming obvious that Elliott's main mission had failed, the new SIS station chief in Beirut ordered Philby to report to him at the embassy. Since this was British territory, Philby could have been arrested and held there. He pleaded illness from his head wound and did not go.

There is another point to make about Philby's account of the immunity offer. He was careful to tell me that *several* of the names on Elliott's list of suspected moles alarmed him; that is, that the British services were correct in their suspicions of these people. If he had

---

*John Profumo, Secretary of State for War, lied to the Commons over his relationship with a good-time girl, Christine Keeler, who said that she was also the lover of the Soviet assistant naval attaché, the GRU (Military Intelligence) officer Yevgeny Ivanov. On 5 June 1963 Profumo admitted the lie and resigned.

said 'one of the names' then it would have referred to Blunt, who was exposed the following year. But the fact that he said 'several' – and declined to name them to me – sows the suspicion, justified or not, that the names which alarmed him were not all caught and remain active to this day.

Next I put it to Philby that Elliott was unsuccessful in the confrontation because Philby had been tipped off that Elliott was coming and that gave him time to prepare. Further, I said, Peter Wright believed that the tip-off came from Hollis, who knew, of course, of SIS's plans. Philby laughed. 'There was no tip-off. There was no need for one. The truth is that I had been preparing for twelve years for this. So when the day did come, what then? Le Carré talks in the introduction to your book about my "long and perilous hesitation". This is gammon. I knew exactly how to handle it. God knows I had rehearsed it often enough. Just a little stalling, just a little drinking to show nothing was afoot, just a little time to make assurances along the escape route doubly sure. Then, at a given signal, away and gone! How could they have stopped me? I had friends as well as enemies in Beirut.'

And this is how it seems to have worked. Even Eleanor Philby noticed nothing untoward in Philby's behaviour. On the afternoon of 23 January, five days after Elliott had left, as Beirut was lashed by a winter rainstorm, Philby grabbed his raincoat, telling Eleanor he would be back by six in plenty of time to change for a dinner party they were attending that night at the residence of the First Secretary at the British Embassy, Glen Balfour-Paul. Asked where he was going, Philby said to meet a contact. In Moscow Philby told me: 'Eleanor knew I was working for SIS. I'd say I was going out to meet a contact and she'd assume it was an SIS contact whereas sometimes it was a KGB one.'

That day it must have been a KGB one, for about 5 pm Philby telephoned and spoke to Harry, his youngest son, then thirteen. Eleanor was busy in the kitchen, so Harry called out: 'Daddy's going to be late. He says he'll meet you at Balfour-Paul's at eight.' Philby never turned up. Soon after midnight Eleanor rang the new SIS station chief at home but he was at the embassy attending a hastily summoned meeting about Philby. Eventually he came around to the apartment and asked Eleanor to check if anything of Philby's was missing.

Over the next few weeks Eleanor had several letters from Philby saying that he had gone off on a long reporting tour for *The Observer*, telling her where to find sums of money he had hidden around the flat, asking her not to mention the letters to his journalist colleagues

- 'I would like my scoop to be really exclusive' – and assuring her of his love. But it gradually dawned on Eleanor that Philby had gone for good, and almost certainly to Russia.

Some of his colleagues thought so too. Clare Hollingworth of *The Guardian*, who had been at the Balfour-Paul dinner party, filed a speculative story the day after Philby's disappearance, saying that he had enhanced his claim to the title of the 'Third Man' by vanishing so abruptly, presumably aboard a Soviet freighter, the *Dolmatova*, which had left Beirut homeward bound that very night. *The Guardian* did not use the story. Two days later the local English-language newspaper, *The Daily Star*, reported Philby as officially missing. Peter Kilner, a British journalist, relayed the story to Reuters in London, where it was 'spiked'. Kilner remembers discussing Philby with the correspondents for *The Times* and the *Daily Telegraph*, who were both opposed to reporting Philby's disappearance in case he really had gone off on a reporting tour or was on a 'blinder'. Later reports with more details of what had happened failed to make the British press. It seems likely that SIS arranged for the Foreign Office discreetly to ask Fleet Street editors to play down the story.

It was not until 20 March that the Foreign Office, under pressure from *The Observer*, which on 3 March had told readers that its correspondent was missing, agreed to a statement. The Lord Privy Seal, Edward Heath, said that the government had made inquiries about Philby's whereabouts but without success. Then Heath added: 'Since Mr Philby resigned from the Foreign Service in 1951, twelve years ago, he has had no access of any kind to any official information.' Philby, already home and dry in Moscow, read this report in his airmail copy of *The Times* and laughed out loud.

HOME TO A
HERO'S WELCOME
=== 16 ===

Philby arrived in the Soviet Union on 27 January 1963, just four days after he had sailed from Beirut in the Soviet freighter *Dolmatova*, which left port in a hurry at about midnight, some of its cargo abandoned on the dockside. In his Moscow apartment on 19 January 1988, Philby offered me a glass of champagne to celebrate the approaching twenty-fifth anniversary of his setting foot on Soviet soil. But when I pressed him for details of his escape he grew short-tempered. 'That's a KGB operational matter I can't discuss,' he said. 'Anyway it's unimportant. But I want you to write down exactly what happened when I did arrive.

'Let me set the scene for you. It's five o'clock in the morning. A small frontier post in mid-winter. [Probably a port on the Black Sea.] There's a table and a few chairs; a charcoal stove. Tea is brewing on the stove and the air is thick with cigarette smoke. Awaiting me are three or four militia men and a man from the service who spoke English, sent specially down from Moscow to meet me.

'After the formalities were over, I apologized for coming. I said that I had wanted to stay on in the West and continue to serve but the pressure had become too much for me. My colleague from Moscow must have seen that I was a bit emotional about it all. He put his hand on my arm and spoke to me. I can remember his exact words to this day.

'He said: "Kim, your mission has been concluded. We have a saying in our service that once counter-espionage becomes interested in you, it's the beginning of the end. We know that British counter-espionage became interested in you in 1951. It's now 1963 – twelve years. My dear Kim, what on earth are you apologizing about?" '

This moment obviously meant a lot to Philby. Perhaps he expected recriminations for not sticking it out, as Blunt had continued to do. Instead he had been met with warmth and understanding. This continued when he arrived in Moscow. The KGB took him directly to one of its own clinics for a thorough medical examination. The years of nervous tension and excessive drinking had taken their toll, and a prolonged period of drying out and vitamin injections was prescribed. Then he was moved to a small flat overlooking the river and put in the care of an old housekeeper who cooked him four large meals a day. A nurse called regularly to give him vitamin injections.

As soon as Philby was feeling better he had his first meeting with Sergei, the senior KGB officer who had run him from Moscow. According to Eleanor Philby, who met him later, Sergei was about forty, spoke fluent English with only a trace of an accent, and had an excellent sense of humour. The meeting must have been an emotional one; months later Eleanor overheard Sergei still telling Philby that the Soviet Union could never fully repay him for all that he had done.

The greetings over, Sergei got down to practicalities. The KGB was appointing a special security officer, one of Sergei's assistants, who would be responsible for Philby's safety for the rest of his life. He was to be consulted on any move Philby wanted to make. Philby protested that this was not necessary. As he told me in Moscow, Sergei and his assistant were not convinced. 'They said to me: "What would you say the odds were of the Western agencies trying something against you?" I thought for a while and said: "Oh, at least a thousand to one." And they said: "Those are odds we are not prepared to accept." So I got this security officer and I've still got one and his job would be on the line if anything should happen to me.'

Then Sergei said he had a number of flats for Philby to look at and would drive him around Moscow to see which one he preferred. In the meantime, what did he want from his apartment in Beirut? His record collection, his books, his oriental rugs and the Spanish antique table given to him by Tommy Harris. This would be no problem but might take a little time. (They finally arrived in June 1964.) His pipes? The Soviet consulate in London would send someone to Jermyn Street, buy him two, and put them in the diplomatic bag.

As far as financial matters were concerned, Philby would be paid a basic KGB salary of five hundred roubles a month (then about £200), but there would be bonuses for special work. The KGB would provide, over and above this, a sum of £4,000 a year in foreign exchange for the support of Philby's children in Britain until they were earning their own living. Philby could call on a chauffeur-driven car when he wanted one and have access to a dacha in the country when he liked. As for his personal arrangements, if his wife wanted to join him then this could be organized. All he had to do was let Sergei know.

Philby said he would write to Eleanor and ask her to come to Moscow as soon as possible. This turned out to be more difficult than he thought. Eleanor had been in touch with SIS's Beirut station from soon after Philby's disappearance and, uncertain whether Philby had gone to Moscow of his own free will, had agreed to tell SIS of any approach to her by the Russians. So when a man Philby had once introduced to her as the correspondent in Beirut of a German news agency called on her and said: 'I'm from Kim,' she refused to accompany him and told SIS as soon as she could. Later in London, when SIS showed her a file of photographs, she picked out the man.

Instead of going to Moscow from Beirut, as Philby wanted, in May Eleanor went to London. The press was there to meet her in force, hoping for some clue as to Philby's whereabouts – it was not until July that the government, buffeted by the Profumo affair, admitted that he was in Moscow. But SIS whisked her away and then began a long campaign to persuade her not to join Philby and to pump her for all she knew. They told her of Philby's treachery; they said that if she went to Moscow she might never be allowed to leave; they directed her to a doctor who prescribed Librium and who saw her once a week. 'These consultations seemed more like psychiatric sessions,' Eleanor wrote. 'His gentle but persistent questioning made me suspect he might have some Foreign Office connection.'[1]

But in the end Eleanor went. Following Philby's instructions she called at the Soviet consulate in London, where an official gave her £500 to buy some warm clothes and said everything would be arranged for her. She landed at the VIP airport of Vnukovo on 26 September 1963. Philby and Sergei were waiting, and they drove straight to Philby's new flat in a residential suburb about fifteen minutes by Metro from the centre.

By Soviet standards it was large and comfortable – four rooms, including a living room, a study, a dining room and a bedroom. The kitchen was modern and well equipped and there was a television set in the living room. The rent, including the heating and light, was thirty-five roubles a month (then about £20). Philby had arranged for a maid to come in each day for cleaning and shopping. Eleanor unpacked and then she and Philby drank a toast in Russian champagne to the first day of their new life in the Soviet Union.

Two other defectors, Guy Burgess and Donald Maclean, had already been there for twelve years. They had surfaced in 1956 when, largely due to the initiative of Richard Hughes, the Far Eastern correspondent of *The Sunday Times*, who had asked the Soviet authorities for permission to interview them, they had been produced at a press conference where they had read a prepared statement. Conflicting stories about their life had made their way back to London: they hated the Soviet Union; they were quite happy in the Soviet Union; the KGB was suspicious of them; the KGB had employed them; they wanted to visit Britain; they never wanted to set foot on British soil again.

There was more news of Burgess than Maclean. Burgess wrote freely to all his old friends and for a while even telephoned one of them, Peter Pollock, every Thursday morning. But Pollock felt he had to tell MI5 about the calls, and after a few months they ceased. Another friend, Tom Driberg, went to visit Burgess. To Driberg, Burgess confided that he had a problem: he had been unable to find any boyfriends. Driberg, who had swiftly located the chief meeting place of gay Moscow, passed on the information to Burgess, who followed it up immediately. He was soon comfortably installed in a flat on Bolshaya Pirogovskaya with a blond electrician called Tolya, the last of his lifelong succession of friends.

Burgess had not changed. At a cocktail party in the new Chinese embassy he got roaring drunk and urinated all over the fireplace. The Chinese were outraged and the incident led to a serious quarrel with Donald Maclean, whose diplomatic sensibilities were offended. The two hardly spoke after that. As the years passed Burgess spent more and more time in his flat, drinking, reading, listening to music, deep in nostalgia for the England he had left behind. After a spell in hospital, he died on 19 August 1963 from liver failure and hardening of the arteries. Maclean read the funeral oration and a brass band played the 'International'. Burgess would have appreciated Professor Kiernan's verdict on him: 'He did what he felt it right for him to do. I honour his memory.'[2]

Burgess knew Philby was in the Soviet Union because Western journalists, with whom he kept in touch, told him abut Philby's flight from Beirut, and because on 3 July, six weeks before his death, *Izvestia* announced that Philby had been granted Soviet citizenship. In fact, in a codicil to his will, Burgess left Philby his library of 4,000 books, his winter overcoats, items of his furniture, and £2,000. Some reports say that the two men met, that Philby called on Burgess for an emotional reunion as he lay dying in hospital. Others quote Burgess as saying in some dismay: 'Kim can't be in Moscow. I'd be the first person he'd contact if he were here.' I asked Philby about all this. He said: 'The truth of the matter is that Burgess was a bit of an embarrassment here. They did what they could for him, found him a place to live and tolerated his homosexuality. But he created a major problem. He wanted only one job in Russia: he wanted to be head of the English desk of the KGB. Now there was no way he was going to get such a job – all sorts of bureaucratic reasons, apart from anything else – and he wasn't happy about it.

'He and Maclean hung around Moscow for a bit doing nothing except being pursued by journalists. So the KGB decided to give them a new start, to send them off to Kuibyshev [an industrial city 550 miles south-east of Moscow]. Maclean made out okay there. He got a teaching job and was all right, but Burgess continued his crack-up.' (Burgess wrote to a friend in London describing Kuibyshev as a vision of hell. 'Can you imagine Glasgow on a Saturday night in the nineteenth century?') Philby continued: 'After a couple of years Maclean got tired of it and was longing to get back to Moscow, so he wrote directly to Molotov [the Soviet Foreign Minister] and Molotov got him a job in the ministry. He did very well there and wrote a good book, *British Foreign Policy Since Suez*. It got excellent reviews even in the West. But Burgess never managed to fit in. They let him come back to Moscow but he just kept going downhill. As I told you, they kept us apart when I arrived, to avoid recriminations. I didn't get to see him before he died. I'm sorry we didn't meet one last time. He'd been a good friend.'

Burgess's death threw Philby and Maclean together, and when Eleanor arrived the two couples met for dinner. They got on well and soon settled into a pattern of meeting two or three times a week to dine, play bridge or Scrabble, gossip about life in Moscow, or go to the theatre or ballet together. The wives would compare notes about scarce foodstuffs they had managed to find, while Philby and Maclean would talk about former colleagues in the Foreign Office. When Philby was not busy Melinda Maclean took them around Moscow so that they could familiarize themselves with the city's layout.

Sometimes they went on trips together. They went to Leningrad on the night express and Maclean showed them around, throwing in an occasional scholarly explanation of some historical feature. When Eleanor went on a visit to America, Philby toured the Baltic States with the Macleans. They spent weekends at the Macleans' dacha and went cross-country skiing with them. They put in joint orders for food from GUM, the big Moscow department store, and for luxury canned goods and liquor from a supplier in Denmark. When the Philbys did not get on with their maid – she was too bossy – it was Melinda Maclean who dropped a word to the right official and had her replaced. When they wanted to buy gifts in Britain it was Melinda Maclean who allowed them to draw on her sterling account and repay her with roubles in Moscow.

Outside the Macleans, their circle of friends was very limited. Sergei told them to keep away from diplomats and the press, and Philby was upset when, despite his precautions, a Reuters correspondent recognized him in the Ukraina Hotel and, before Philby could get away, managed to ask him how he liked life in the Soviet Union. In its story on 1 January 1965, Reuters quoted Philby as replying: 'Marvellous, absolutely wonderful.' On another occasion, lunching in a small hotel, Philby suddenly got up and left the table, saying that he had seen Larry Collins, an American journalist they had known in Beirut, enter the restaurant.

Occasionally they met Hilda Perham, an English communist who worked on the *Moscow News* and who lived in the same block of flats as Burgess, and Peter Tempest, the *Daily Worker* correspondent. When Eleanor was away Philby went to a party given by two old Bolsheviks and met 'a splendid old American girl, Jessica Smith, who first came to the Soviet Union with a Quaker relief mission in the lifetime of Lenin'. He wrote to Eleanor: 'She has just completed a tour of Siberia, where she was given the works, and had a lot of encouraging things to say about the new world coming into being there. There are no flies on her, and she had some critical things to say; that made her generally optimistic accounts of what she had seen all the more convincing.'[3]

Despite the solitary existence, Philby seemed to be settling into life in the Soviet Union reasonably well. He began to take Russian lessons from a woman professor, who came three times a week for a two-hour lesson each time. He did his homework conscientiously, and by the end of 1964, not quite two years after his arrival in Moscow, he was reasonably fluent in the language for everyday use and took pride in demonstrating it in the street. This led to puzzling encounters.

'When I first arrived in Moscow,' he told me, 'for some reason or another everyone seemed to pick on me to ask directions. After a while I got tired of trying to explain that I was a foreigner who didn't speak Russian, so I asked my teacher for the expression "Over there". From then on when anyone asked the way I'd gesture vaguely, say "Over there" in Russian and they'd go off quite happily. When I got to know the city better and my Russian was fluent, I'd very proudly launch into detailed instructions. The person asking me would then look at me in a peculiar way and immediately go and ask someone else.'

Philby ordered the first four volumes of Vernadsky's *History of Russia* from Bowes and Bowes of Cambridge and began to study them. ('Actually it is one of the worst of the standard histories in style and composition but it contains an awful lot of facts that are difficult to dig out elsewhere.')[4] He had *The Times*, the *Washington Post*, *Time* magazine, the *Herald Tribune* and *Le Monde* all sent to him by airmail. He listened to the BBC and the Voice of America. He followed reports of the assassination of John F. Kennedy, was depressed by what had happened, and moved to tears when Eleanor, in hospital in Moscow for a minor operation, told him that the doctors, nurses and patients had wept openly at the news. He was delighted when Johnson defeated Goldwater in the 1964 Presidential election: 'A big hand to the American people . . . We cannot expect miracles overnight, of course, but we can look towards slow but steady strides towards normal relations.'[5]

But Eleanor, the American used to the easy availability of consumer goods, found the absence of small things, like bobby pins or ballpoint pens, annoying. She hated the cold, the lack of variety in her social life, and after the comforts of Beirut she resented the battle for daily existence. And she felt that Philby owed her an explanation for his years of deceit.

Daily I half expected him to take me aside, throw an arm around my shoulder and say, 'My dear, it's like this. I did so-and-so all these years because I believed in such-and-such . . . These beliefs are my philosophy, my reasons for living. They explain my glad acceptance of what we are here and now experiencing – the piercing cold, the stale cabbage smells and the solitary life we lead.' But he said no such thing. For him, life in Moscow needed no justification. He just lived it. In fact he adored it – weather and all.[6]

The main difference, of course, was that Philby had his work and all that went with it – the challenges, the rewards, and, above all, the continuing warmth and approbation of his colleagues, recognized formally in 1965 when he was given the Order of Lenin and the Order of the Red Banner, the first of his many Communist decorations. In those early years he was fully occupied with his debriefing. Sergei would arrive in the morning and for hours he and Philby would be locked in his study. Eleanor heard only the murmur of voices and the click of typewriter keys.

Philby was emptying his mind of *everything* he knew about the workings of British and American intelligence. He named every officer he had ever met or knew about, every agent ever employed, every operation ever mounted. He described how each service was organized, who reported to whom and how, and the physical layout of all the service buildings. He drew charts and diagrams, described staffing and recruitment procedures, pay and pension arrangements. He wrote miniature biographies of all the senior SIS and CIA officers he knew, assessing their weaknesses and strengths. *Nothing* was considered too insignificant or trivial to be recalled and recorded. 'I emptied my memory and my emotions on to paper,' Philby told me later. 'I wrote down the full, unexpurgated story of my life as an intelligence officer. It's all in the archives somewhere.'

And all the time Sergei was there to prompt him, help his recall, probe more deeply into this or that operation and constantly reassure him of the value of his work. At the end of it all – and it never really ended, because for years afterwards Philby would remember something to add – the KGB knew more about SIS and the CIA than many a senior officer in each Western service.

Naturally both Western services had anticipated that this would happen when Philby got to Moscow, and immediately began to prepare damage assessment reports so as to mitigate the harm that Philby's information would cause. But when an intelligence officer as senior as Philby defects there is not a lot that *can* be done. Intelligence agencies are big, bureaucratic organizations employing thousands of highly trained people, many with specialist skills. The way these organizations work cannot be changed overnight; the people they employ cannot be quickly replaced; operations under way for years cannot be immediately aborted. This is why one CIA officer told me in 1968 that although the CIA knew that Philby had 'blown' whole sections of the agency and many of its senior officers, short of closing it down and starting all over again there was nothing it could do.

But Philby was debriefed in 1963–6. He worked in Washington with the CIA from 1949 to 1951, he was in the wilderness from 1951 to 1956, and employed only as an agent for SIS from 1956 to 1963. Surely one could argue that what he had to tell the KGB in his debriefing was out of date. When I put this to Philby in Moscow he strongly disagreed. 'Nonsense. It's absolute nonsense to say that intelligence knowledge is ever out of date. Even today things still come in on which I have an opinion which is valuable, an instinct, a feeling for the situation.'*

Philby's workload increased midway through his second year

---

*This is also the view of successive British governments which argue that much information regarding security and intelligence matters should remain secret forever lest it complete some Soviet spymaster's jigsaw.

in Moscow when the KGB asked him to ghost Gordon Lonsdale's memoirs. He also wrote occasional political pieces for Russian magazines, advised various KGB section heads on operations in the West and wrote political papers for the KGB giving his view on how the Soviet Union should react to international events. He told Murray Sayle in 1967: 'I was asked to write a paper on the African situation generally soon after I arrived in Moscow – one of my first jobs for the KGB here, as a matter of fact. I took a generally cautious line. By all means give these new African States a reasonable amount of financial aid on real projects. But I warned, don't get deeply involved. Well, we did. Millions of roubles down the drain . . . I was proved right. Our policy in Africa now is watch, help, but no deep involvements. Incidentally, the Chinese seem to have done even worse than we did.' (See Appendix.)

Philby was not entirely uncritical of the Soviet régime during this first period. After the fall of Khrushchev in 1964 he wrote to Eleanor saying he was disturbed that the authorities had not issued a statement explaining the why and wherefore of the change:

It is clear that the old boy was becoming increasingly difficult to deal with, and that he made quite a few mistakes. But it would be a good thing if they would publish a statement explaining where he went wrong and, incidentally, paying him tribute for his considerable achievements – notably in liberalizing Soviet life and in launching and consolidating the policy of peaceful co-existence.

And he was not above the occasional joke at the expense of some pompous Soviet official. His favourite went: 'One of our top military men went to Cairo during the Six-Day War. An Egyptian commander poured out a tale of woe about the Israeli advances and his failure to stop them. The Russian said: "Never mind, comrade. Do what we did during the Great Patriotic war. Dig in and wait for General Winter." '

The break-up of Philby's marriage had its origins in Eleanor's decision to go to the United States in the summer of 1964 to see her daughter. She was away for five months, longer than she had expected, because the American authorities seized her passport on her arrival and did not return it until after the Presidential election. Her absence threw Philby more and more into the company of the Macleans, and, since Donald Maclean had his work, it was often Melinda Maclean who went with Philby to the theatre or the ballet, or shopping, or just for a walk. Philby grew closer to her. He cooked dinners for her, gave her presents, and listened sympathetically when she told him how dissatisfied she was with her life with Maclean. When the break between Eleanor and Philby finally came, Eleanor believed she had lost her husband to Melinda. But there was more to it than that.

Firstly, the KGB never entirely trusted Eleanor. Her relations with SIS and the CIA in Beirut and then in London made Sergei consider whether Eleanor could be involved in some deep Western plot. At Sergei's urging, one of the first things that Philby did when Eleanor arrived in Moscow was to get her to write a detailed account of her experiences with British and American intelligence officials in the months when she had been alone. Eleanor tried to explain that, left to fend for herself and with no certain knowledge of Philby's whereabouts, she had been forced to depend on the British and Americans for help. Slowly, Philby's questions began to take the form of a grilling, with him asking her the same questions over and over again – one of Skardon's techniques.

Eleanor wrote later:

> Kim was patient, but unusually stubborn and persistent. It was only then that I confessed that I had had to take the British fully into my confidence and how from photographs provided by [SIS] I had identified his mysterious Russian friend who had called on me that early May morning in Beirut. That was, perhaps, the biggest mistake I made. But, as far as I was concerned, I had never kept anything from him and therefore saw no reason to do so now. My error was human, but I felt that Kim was angry. Thanks to me, his wife, the Russians had lost a valuable agent. 'What a pity,' he said. 'He was one of my greatest friends and our best man in the area. His career is finished.' The barrier between us widened.[7]

Then, when Philby and Sergei met Eleanor on her return to Moscow at the end of November 1964, they questioned her carefully about the two bottles of whisky she had brought for Kim as a present. Sergei wanted to know exactly where she had purchased the bottles. Could they have been tampered with? Philby insisted that she describe the duty-free shop at Copenhagen airport and became annoyed when Eleanor laughed at his fears that someone might try to poison him.*

And, finally, deep in the recesses of Eleanor's mind, worrying

---

*The idea that Western agencies might attempt something against Philby was not far-fetched. SIS and the CIA had certainly considered an operation against Maclean. Former CIA officer Robert Amory Jnr told me in 1967 that he had sat on a planning committee in the autumn of 1962 to consider if it

at her like a malignant tumour, was Philby's reply to a question she should never have asked him. Puzzling over Philby's interrogation of her about her contacts with the CIA and SIS, Eleanor waited her moment and then asked Philby outright: 'What is more important in your life, me and the children or the Communist Party?' He answered firmly and without a moment's hesitation: 'The Party, of course.' Eleanor was stunned. 'I had never met a truly dedicated communist before. Kim very rarely mentioned his political convictions and I had always thought we shared the same views.'[8] Later she told him bitterly that he should have married only a dedicated communist and he replied: 'You're absolutely right.'

So in the end, Eleanor went back to the West for good. She left Moscow on 18 May 1965 with a gift from Philby of his old Westminster scarf and an au revoir note asking her to remember their good times together, telling her that she was the best friend he had ever had, and promising never to forget her sweetness and goodness. She had left him a letter to be opened after she had gone, saying that if he ever had second thoughts she would be ready to return, but not to any city in which Melinda Maclean was also living. Eleanor was touched by Sergei's consideration when he saw her off with a bunch of tulips. 'If you ever want any help,' he said, 'go to the Russian embassy wherever you may be and tell them who you are. They will do everything they can for you.'[9]

Eleanor died in the United States in 1968. To the last she would not hear a bad word about Philby. Before her death she wrote:

> I remember him as a tender, intelligent and sentimental husband . . . He betrayed many people, me among them. But men are not always masters of their fate. Kim had the guts, or the weakness, to stand by a decision made thirty years ago, whatever the cost to those who loved him most, and to whom he too was deeply attached.[10]

Melinda took Eleanor's place. Philby had already had a row with Maclean, not about Melinda but about Philby's allegiances. According to Eleanor, Maclean had said that Philby was '*still* a double agent'. But this sounds unlikely, implying as it does that Philby was still working for SIS. It is more likely that Maclean referred to Philby only as 'a double agent', a term that annoyed

---

was feasible to kidnap Maclean. 'We had been passing our U-2 spy plane photographs to SIS and they asked us if we could do a photo-analysis of Maclean's apartment block. We got some better stuff from one of our early satellites and our lab men did some excellent diagrams. But, for some reason or another, that was as far as it went.'

him because it suggests that he owed equal loyalty to both sides. 'I was never a double agent,' he told me. 'I was a straight penetration agent. My loyalty was always to the Soviet Union.'

The only possibility that Maclean *did* make the remark Eleanor attributes to him would be if Maclean had learnt – either from Philby or other sources – that Philby had been in touch with SIS after arriving in Moscow, and Maclean considered this disloyal to the KGB. Philby had written to Nicholas Elliott, in friendly persuasive terms, inviting him to a meeting in some neutral place such as Helsinki to clear up any lingering misunderstandings after their confrontation in Beirut. But the letter must have been inspired by Sergei, probably to provoke Elliott into compromising himself, because it said that Elliott must on no account inform his SIS superiors. If he had succumbed to the temptation to meet Philby, Elliott would have put himself into a position to be blackmailed by the KGB, because if news of the arrangement leaked it would have been difficult for him to explain why he was secretly meeting a known enemy agent. Elliott admitted he was tempted, but he informed Dick White of Philby's approach and was forbidden to have any contact with him.

Much has been made of Philby's courtship of Melinda. The usual criticism is that the old deceiver, marooned in Moscow with no secrets left to steal, stole instead his friend's wife. Philby scoffs at such interpretations. He told me in Moscow: 'The Macleans' marriage was over in 1948, and although they tried again it didn't work. In 1951 Donald came here without her. Four months later she arrived with the children. She couldn't really explain why she had come. Sometimes she'd say that she felt the children needed a father and that it was worth yet another try. Other times she'd say that the very moment she saw Donald at the airport she knew it wasn't going to work. They never really got things together again and she was a free agent when we began our affair. There was no question of stealing her from anybody.'

With the appearance of the *Sunday Times* series on Philby in November 1967, the KGB decided that it would be a good idea for Philby's own version of these events to be published. Since Philby had written an extensive account of his life as part of his debriefing, it was not difficult to convert part of this into a manuscript. Harold Evans, editor of *The Sunday Times*, heard rumours of the book and wrote to Philby saying the newspaper might be interested in publishing it. It was for this reason that Evans sent Sayle to Moscow.

Sayle remembers: 'Evans received a telegram from Philby saying:

"Send someone with power to negotiate – Philby." But it had no address, so when Evans sent me to Moscow my first problem was to *find* Philby. Someone in Beirut had told me that Kim was passionately interested in cricket. Now the cricket scores are certainly not published in *Izvestia*, so it seemed to me a fair bet that Kim would get airmail copies of *The Times*. So I went along to the post office where foreigners get their mail and sat around all one afternoon. It wasn't easy because the militiamen kept moving me on.

'Next morning I was back again and in came an unmistakable Englishman – woollen shirt, knitted tie and a kind of sports jacket. It's got to be Kim Philby. So I went up to him and said: "Mr Philby?" He asked me what hotel I was staying at and he said he'd ring me. I went back to the hotel and sat around for a while and he rang. "Minsk Hotel," he said. "Room four-three-six. Tonight at eight." And he hung up. So I went around to the Minsk and showed the lady at the desk the number. She held up three fingers so I went up to the third floor, which seemed quite empty. There was a man in a blue suit with a bulge under his shoulder at one end of the corridor and another at the other end. With some trepidation I found the room and knocked. Inside was a small hotel room. You could see Red Square through the window. And there is Kim sitting at a table; two chairs, a briefcase, a bottle of vodka and two glasses.

'We exchanged greetings and then he said: "I'm going to assume that you're an officer of a hostile service. Let me warn you now, you wouldn't get twenty feet down the corridor." I said: "Okay Kim. Fair enough. In your position I'd be a bit suspicious also about visitors from London. But I'm a straightforward journalist. I'm an Australian, and my name is Murray Sayle and what do you want to see us about?" Then he said: "Well, sit down and have a vodka" – most conversations with Kim began with, "Have a vodka."

'What he proposed at that first meeting – and it took some hours and most of the bottle – was a very complicated deal. First of all he said he just wanted his book published. Then, later, he hinted there were terrible disclosures in the book which would greatly embarrass the CIA, SIS and so on. But he would consider not publishing the book if a deal could be worked out for the release of the Krogers, in jail in Britain for their connection with the Portland spy case.

'I later learned that the Krogers' history went back to the Rosenbergs, who'd been executed in the United States for passing atom secrets to the Russians in the Forties. Philby clearly had something to do with that, because he seemed to feel a personal responsibility to the Krogers to get them out of jail.*

'He mentioned an exchange for Gerald Brooke, an Englishman who was doing time in the Soviet Union for handing out anti-Soviet leaflets in Red Square [see Appendix].

'I said: "Look, Kim, I can talk to you about books, but I've got no authority to negotiate an exchange of prisoners with anyone. But as an outsider it occurs to me that there is only one Brooke and there are two Krogers." Kim said: "It's always like that. We have more and better spies than you have. Do you know why? Ours operate from conviction; yours work for money. That's how we catch them. Money. They've always got too much money."

'I said I'd report all this to my editor in London who would no doubt be in touch. He said: "I'd be careful of the phone if I were you. It's bugged both ends." Well, we saw quite a bit of each other after that. Talked about all sorts of things, including those two writers, Daniel and Sinyavsky, who'd been sent off to a labour camp for publishing their stuff in the West. Philby thought they'd been harshly treated.

'There was one funny incident. Kim's son John turned up from London to visit his father. One day John and I were coming out of the Hotel Komsomolski and we were accosted in the street by one of those funny money men who wanted to exchange our money on the black market. This guy was particularly insistent so finally John rounded on him and said: "You'd better watch it, mate, my old man works for the KGB." The suggestion that this foreigner's father would be working for the KGB struck the Russian money man as so uproariously funny that he couldn't follow us any more because he was doubled up with laughter.'[11]

Sayle duly wrote about his meeting with Philby (see Appendix). Philby's book was published in the West in 1968 by MacGibbon and Kee in Britain and by Grove Press in the United States. Of Graham Greene's introduction to it, Philby has said: 'I was flabbergasted when I read it. He understood what I had done and why I had done it.'[12] And, as Philby had hoped, the Krogers were exchanged in 1969 for Gerald Brooke. I asked Philby about all this. He said: 'Murray's article was first-rate, a very fair report. But soon after it was published my immediate boss in the KGB [probably Sergei] came to me waving a copy of The Sunday Times and said: "Look

---

*This would make sense if a 1963 FBI report was more than speculation. It said: 'Philby and his Russian spy chiefs even knew that the FBI planned to arrest the Rosenbergs [but] chose to sacrifice them, most probably to keep Philby's identity a secret.'

what this Western journalist has quoted you as saying about Daniel and Sinyavsky. This can't be right, can it?" And I said: "Well, yes, that's my opinion and that's what I did say." And he thought for a moment and said: "Hmm. Let's hope the chaps upstairs don't get to see it."

'Sayle was very straightforward in his dealings with me. But Evans has been . . . what's the in-phrase now? . . . a little economical with the truth in his account of our dealings over my book. I had letters from him expressing great enthusiasm for publishing it in *The Sunday Times*. Then when George Brown publicly attacked Lord Thomson for giving so much publicity to me, Evans's enthusiasm seemed to decline very quickly.' (Evans says he never intended to publish in *The Sunday Times* anything from Philby's book because he wanted nothing to contaminate the original reporting effort, he was loath to spend time verifying the book's contents, and he did not want to reward treason by paying Philby. He had opened negotiations with Philby only because 'it would be interesting to see what he was up to'.)

Philby's first five years in the Soviet Union had been busy ones. He had been welcomed by his colleagues in the Russian intelligence service, had enjoyed their respect and deference. He had been decorated and given a rewarding job. He had been debriefed, learnt Russian, travelled widely, ended one marriage and started an affair. He had become rich in roubles but poor in dollars and pounds. He had lost his close friend and colleague, Guy Burgess. He had made another friend in Donald Maclean, only to fall out with him. He had written one book, ghosted another, and seen his story splashed in the Western press. Contrary to the view in the West of the homesick, disgruntled exile, he had settled into life in Moscow almost as if he had been born there. Then everything changed for the worse.

DOUBT AND
DISILLUSIONMENT
═══ 17 ═══

In Moscow Philby told me that he never did discover what went wrong in his relationship with the KGB. It is possible that Sergei disapproved of Philby's romance with Melinda Maclean – despite his early suspicions of Eleanor, he had been shocked at the break-up of her marriage to Philby and had done his best to keep Philby and Melinda apart. Now nothing was said, but steadily Philby's workload was reduced. He lost the office and the secretary he had been given when he was working on the Lonsdale book. KGB cars with couriers bringing papers for his immediate attention no longer called at his apartment. Sergei himself called less frequently, pleading pressure of work.

'I didn't know what was happening,' Philby told me in Moscow. 'My pay still arrived regularly, but they gave me nothing to do. The KGB seemed to have no idea of my real potential. I became depressed, unhappy, and prone to doubt. Now doubt is a terrible thing. As you know, I've met Graham Greene several times over the past couple of years. They were the most rewarding meetings in our long friendship. For the first time we were able to speak frankly with each other. We were able to discuss doubt, a matter of great importance to us both – the nagging doubt we had both felt, him as a Roman Catholic and me as a communist.

'My problem was that I hadn't swallowed everything. I hadn't taken it all in. While I was busy and they needed me, this didn't seem to matter. But when they didn't use me the doubt crept in. The leadership at that time had something to do with it. The Brezhnev period was a difficult one. We all suffered under his stultifying, leaden influence.'

(Philby clearly detested Brezhnev. Our conversations took place during a period when there was a speeding up of investigations into corruption during Brezhnev's rule, 1964–82. Philby followed all this avidly, not only reading the newspapers but asking KGB callers for the latest gossip. As the investigations came closer and closer to the Brezhnev family, Philby grew more and more delighted.)

'In an effort to snap out of it,' Philby continued, 'I took to travelling. I've seen practically every corner of the Soviet Union and the Eastern bloc countries except the Soviet Far East. I also started drinking heavily again in an attempt to shut out what had become a burdensome life.'

Philby was doing more than drink heavily; he was frequently drinking himself insensible in a manner that could be described as verging on the suicidal. I know from other sources that he went on three- and four-day binges in his Moscow flat; that he often did not know night from day; that he would sometimes wake up and complain that the maid had not come to clean the flat and do the shopping, only to discover that it was 2 am; and that during his travels he would think he was in Moscow only to discover that he was in Leningrad.

His memory of this period was not the best, but he did tell me one story he remembered because, he said, it suggested that there were other people who drank more than he did. 'I visited a wine factory – as they call them – I think somewhere in Georgia. Over a few glasses, the manager told me that the heaviest drinker he had ever met was an Englishman called J.B. Priestley. He said Priestley drank brandy with wine chasers. I said: "Did he get drunk?" The manager laughed. "Drunk," he said. "He was so drunk we had to help him to bed and in the morning his hands were shaking so much that he couldn't sign the visitors' book." '

If Philby's aim was to kill himself with drink, then he might well have succeeded. His constitution was already weakened. Since his arrival in the Soviet Union in 1963 he had been in hospital four times, mainly for treatment for pneumonia, which he had twice developed in Beirut. But his last attack in May 1965 had been complicated by what the Russian doctors diagnosed as tuberculosis. Drinking heavily, eating little, smoking a lot, and depressed emotionally, he was heading for a physical breakdown from which he might well have not recovered.

Then, in a scene which could have come straight from a 'true romance' magazine, and at the age of fifty-eight, he fell desperately in love. His affair with Melinda had not gone well. There was friction with her children, and when she and Philby decided that they could no longer live together, she had nowhere else in Moscow to go, and was left with no alternative but to return to Donald.* But Philby was not the sort of man to live without a woman for long. In Moscow, his face bright with the memory

---

*Melinda remained another eight years in Moscow and then went back to the United States, where she now resides.

of it, he described how he had met his last love, turning occasionally to his wife to prompt her into telling her part of the story.

'In the late autumn of 1970 I had invited my son Tom to visit me in Moscow. George [Blake] and his wife [a Russian] were apparently a bit worried about me and wanted to cheer me up, so they asked Tom and me to join their party for an ice show. George's wife arrived with a friend called Rufa, a half-Polish, half-Russian woman. I learnt later that she'd been brought up in Russia after the early death of her father. She and her mother had had a really tough time of it.

'Well, I made up my mind twenty seconds after meeting Rufa that she was the woman I wanted to marry. In these matters I can be quite determined so I arranged a series of meetings through friends, culminating in a weekend party at a dacha. It didn't take me long to realize that the hostess disapproved of my pursuing Rufa and was doing her level best to keep us apart. I decided that drastic action was necessary.

'We were all out at a market and it was quite busy. I waited for my chance, seized Rufa by the wrist, and, using a bit of the old spy tradecraft, I escaped with her into the crowd. It was only when I had her alone that I realized we had quite a problem: she spoke no English and my Russian wasn't good enough for the sort of conversation I wanted to have with her. But I plunged in and said to her in Russian: "Look here, now. I'm putting my cards on the table. I want to marry you."

'But I didn't get much further with my proposal because she was fascinated by what was meant by the phrase "putting my cards on the table" and it took quite a while with my Russian and some sign language to explain it all. Once we got over that hurdle I managed to say, again in Russian, that I wasn't an impetuous young man. I didn't need an immediate answer. "Think it over," I said. "Take your time." '

Rufa picked up the story. 'I thought that all these meetings were coincidental but I realized then that he had planned them all. I was impressed but undecided. And he was not as patient as he has made out. When he left me at my door back at the dacha he said, quite plaintively: "Is there any hope for me?" I said what any woman would say. I said: "Perhaps." '

Philby continued. 'We arranged to meet the following week for lunch at the Metropole Hotel. I said at noon sharp because I wanted to get a table for two, no easy task in Moscow. [Most tables in Moscow restaurants are for four or more, and couples are expected to share.] Well, she turned up at twelve thirty. Her excuse was that she had been unable to remember whether our appointment was for noon or one o'clock, so she had compromised on twelve thirty.'

Rufa interrupted. 'When I arrived and saw him waiting, I knew I was late. But there he was, leaning patiently against the wall, smiling and happy to see me. There was no anger, no reproach. He was absolutely charming. My heart went out to him. I realized he had won. Now it seems as if I have known him all my life. I can't remember the time without him. I'd never married before; it's as if I had been waiting for him.'

Philby said: 'We were married two months later, on 19 December 1971 – for a wedding present the KGB gave us that dinner set over there, fine English bone china. Rufa changed my life. I realized that most of the women I had known before had been fighting a secret battle against breakdown. To meet a normal woman who loved me was an uplifting experience. My friends said I was crazy even to consider marrying her: I knew so little about her, and language was always going to be a barrier. But everything has worked out marvellously.'

Philby is a little vague on dates, but it would appear that his marriage coincided with a change in the KGB's attitude towards him. 'They suddenly began to use me again. I can only guess that it was due to some change in the KGB, probably about major-general level. Someone must have said: "Philby might be able to help here," because the papers started arriving again and in no time everything was back to what it was before. My doubt and depression vanished. I was doing interesting work, I had a marvellous wife and life was good again.'

Part of Philby's work during this period was writing papers on international affairs. Although he declined to list for me the issues on which the KGB had consulted him, we can see the technique in an issue on which they did *not* seek his view – and no doubt later wished they had: Afghanistan. 'My advice was not sought on Afghanistan. If it had been I would have advised against intervention on purely historical grounds. I would have said, look what happened to the British there, those interminable wars. So I would have said keep out at all costs.'

But it would appear that he was also still involved in intelligence operations. He would look at an operation that had gone wrong, conduct a lone inquiry, apportion blame, and make recommendations to prevent a recurrence. 'It's amazing what can go wrong even when you think you have planned for everything. There was this case in the United States. Someone threw a parcel over the wall of the

Soviet embassy. It was bulky and looked as if it could be a bomb. So the embassy staff called the police who called the FBI and the FBI duly took the parcel away. It turned out to be a batch of high-grade secret defence material which someone wanted us to have. And what was worse, there was also a letter suggesting a meeting with us and naming a rendezvous point. Of course, the FBI kept the rendezvous and arrested the person. A sad story for us, but it won't happen again.'

Sometimes he would get an assignment on the periphery of the intelligence world. After he had lectured KGB officers on motivation, he was approached in 1978 by the manager of the Soviet national ice hockey team. The team had been having a bad spell. It had lost the international championships two years running, something that had never happened before. The manager asked Philby if he could take responsibility for the team's motivation. Philby told me: 'Since it was a subject that I can claim, with all due modesty, to know something about, I agreed to do my best.' The Russian team duly beat Czechoslovakia in the final that year, and Philby was rewarded with a framed picture of the team showing him sitting alongside the manager. He hung it on his study wall in a prominent position.

In 1980 he was given a new decoration – the Order of Friendship of Peoples (Nations), introduced in 1972 for foreigners who have helped the Soviet Union. The award coincided with publication of the Russian translation of his book, *My Silent War*. Philby told me: 'It was an enormous success and sold more than two hundred thousand copies. The trouble was that I hadn't foreseen that it would sell so well. It was only in the bookshops a few days and then it was gone, out of print. So I didn't get enough copies for myself. There have been Czech and Bulgarian translations as well. That gave me a lot of Czech and Bulgarian currency to spend, so Rufa and I thought we may as well visit Prague and, perhaps later, Sofia.

'The Czechs gave us a great welcome. We had two cars, one for us and one for the bodyguards. At one stage they even gave us a private plane. The whole trip, two weeks in all, cost us only a hundred and twenty roubles. In the summer we did the same thing in Bulgaria and liked it immensely. All this had the advantage that it established with my bosses in the KGB that we could leave the Soviet Union twice a year, so we started going to Bulgaria in the summer and somewhere else in the Communist bloc in the winter.'

But his security officer had drawn the line at Philby's plan to venture further abroad. In the late 1970s he had received repeated invitations from colleagues in the Cuban intelligence service to visit

Havana. 'I was keen to go and so was Rufa, so I put it to the KGB that it would be perfectly safe. We could go by Aeroflot and once we were there the Cubans would be responsible for our safety. But they said: "What if the plane gets diverted or forced down by bad weather or something and you end up in the United States?" I thought about this for a while and then I said: "Okay. We'll go by Soviet freighter." They reluctantly agreed and that's what we did. We sailed down the Channel and I just missed seeing my old prep school at Eastbourne. The visibility wasn't quite good enough.

'We had a wonderful time in Cuba. My colleagues took us everywhere and entertained us royally. We didn't get to meet Castro but we met just about everyone else, and I ended up with a Cuban decoration. We came back the southern route via Turkey. I'd been looking forward to this part of the trip because I hoped to be able to show Istanbul to Rufa. But the whole of the Bosporus was hidden in a veil of rain.'

When he got back, Philby could not resist making a little mischief out of his trip. He began to drop hints in his letters to me and others that he had been out of the Soviet Union, remarks like – 'Just back from a few weeks abroad . . . recently returned from a few weeks in the sun.' I wrote to him saying:

David Leitch is still puzzling over your tantalizing reference to a recent return from sun and sea with long cool drinks. I told him that you make regular visits to India to watch cricket and stock up on Mrs Fern's prawn balchao . . . I'm going to India myself soon. Hope to hear from you before I leave, but if you're sunning yourself and drinking long rums, then perhaps we'll meet in Bombay. Cricket starts in September.

Philby replied on 20 February 1980:

So Leitch is puzzled by my weeks in the sun. Would he believe you if you told him I had been sipping stengahs in Diego Garcia? Too bad I couldn't join you in Bombay. Perhaps with Mrs G[andhi] back it might be possible one day (after all her father and mine were up at Cambridge together and argued at the Magpie and Stump).

I confess to a certain boredom with cricket. Of course it would be nice to spend a lazy afternoon watching Viv Richards belting them past cover. But I was happy with the county championships and the Tests, and now, what with John Player, Benson & Hedges, Schweppes, Gillette, aluminium bats, white balls, funny clothes and Uncle Kerry Packer and all, it is too confusing for a gentleman of the old school like myself. Ichabod say I.

I enclose a recipe for prawn balchao from a book authored by (I quote) AN ANGLO-INDIAN (the late Mrs J. Bartley). It is no further use to me. Since Carter's swingeing economic sanctions began to bite there is a shortage of bilambees [an Indian vegetable] hereabouts.

Since Philby knew that his letters to London would be opened and read by MI5 he was, as Maurice Oldfield told me, hoping to lure it into spending its time checking on where he had been and why. But Oldfield was wrong in his assessment that Philby had made it all up. Philby *had* been to Cuba, and if MI5 did indeed make checks and discover this, then it would naturally want to know why. Philby was thus able to turn a holiday visit into a KGB advantage.

He continued to follow happenings in Britain, especially those to do with the intelligence world, with close attention. I wrote to him in 1977 telling him of the plays, television productions, projected films and book on his life that were under way that year. He replied:

It was good of Booth [an editor at Quartet books] to pass on my message and to get your acknowledgement on return from a few weeks spent invading the privacy of trout in the Carpathians; appropriate also that your note should give a succinct account of the massive invasion of my own privacy this year. You say it all adds up to something, but you can't think what. I'll tell you what: 1977 is the centenary of the birth of Felix Dzerzhinsky, founder of the Cheka, a fitting subject for celebration through publicising FD's illustrious disciples.

I'm glad the BBC think I have been over-exposed. Their view may be traceable to a letter I wrote Erik de Mauny a year or so ago. He had written to tell me that he *might* be revisiting Moscow and *might* want a short recorded interview, to which I replied with the very word: 'over-exposure'. Yet there seems to be some lack of coordination out there, because I very recently received a BBC proposal which didn't excite me very much. Still wondering what to reply, if anything. They want me to talk about patriotism – one in the eye for me? They might do better with one of those who have defected to America, e.g. the BBC's own Smarty Cooke, Alistair of that ilk. His 'Letter from America' becomes more and more preposterous.

In 1979 I sent him Andrew Boyle's *Climate of Treason*, the book which led to the public exposure of Anthony Blunt as a one-time Soviet agent. He replied:

My conscience has been jolted twice in the last few days. First the news that you were suing the you-know-what [the CIA] for action in the Holden affair [the mysterious murder of *Sunday Times* foreign correspondent David Holden in Cairo in December 1977] reminded me that your letter of June 15 was still lying without answer in my files. Second, I received your *Climate*, with the explicit reminder of my want of courtesy. Actually, I could not have answered you before your departure for India and Australia as your letter did not reach me until July 15. So then, of course, not knowing how long you would be away or whether the *ST* would ever appear again, I dithered, got caught up in travel myself, then in a major house redecoration and repair, and so on. *Peccavi*, but I hope for forgiveness.

So AB [Andrew Boyle] exploded his petard at last, if only by remote control; one bull's eye, one outer and a lot of random splinters causing random injury. Quite like Ulster. Alexander Chancellor [of *The Spectator*] asked me to review the book but I had to decline. It would have been great fun but a serious review would have led me into a swamp of impermissible indiscretion. As Wittgenstein so truly observed: *Wovon man nicht sprechen kann, darüber muss man schweigen.* ['Whereof one cannot speak, thereof one must be silent'.]

I thought *The Observer* death-bed interview with Goronwy [Rees, a friend of Burgess and Blunt who was himself under suspicion at one time of being a Soviet agent] in the worse possible taste; doubtless you spotted the yawning gap in G's final testament. It would probably take me months to dig up the BBC book review here, so could I be brazen enough to ask you for a photocopy. I know I don't deserve it, but Malcolm [Muggeridge] on me is always a delight.

Philby learnt from the BBC overseas service of Mrs Thatcher's statement to the Commons on 15 November 1979 revealing that Blunt, after being given immunity from prosecution, had confessed in 1964 to having been a Soviet agent. He told me in Moscow: 'I was appalled. I am at a loss to know why she did it. MI5 must have been horrified. It was totally counter-productive. At a stroke it wiped out the whole idea and purpose of immunity from prosecution. Blunt had an immunity deal which, of course, included secrecy. The British government broke that deal. What spy would now believe anyone in Britain who offered him immunity in return for cooperation?

'Anyway, soon after Mrs Thatcher's announcement blowing Blunt, a man walked into the Soviet consulate in London, and handed over a package. He asked if it could be sent to Kim Philby in Moscow. He could have posted it. Mail addressed simply "Philby, Moscow" finds me without difficulty. But I supposed he wanted to make absolutely sure that this parcel reached me.

'When I opened it I found a fine engraving of a column in Rome, that of the Emperor Marcus Aurelius Antoninus, the Antony who had done battle against the Germans. That's it on the wall over there. It was so like Blunt to have done something like that. I pondered for a while as to whether I should acknowledge having received it. There were all sorts of reasons why I didn't. When I learnt that he had died [on 26 March 1983] I was sorry that I hadn't. But I've got the engraving to remind me of him and the battles we fought against the Germans.'

A few weeks earlier, on 6 March, Donald Maclean had died in Moscow. Now only Philby was left. Although he had fallen out with Maclean he kept in touch with what he was doing and with news of anything that happened to him. He told me in Moscow: 'After Mrs Thatcher's announcement about Blunt, the British journalists here wanted some comment from Maclean. Maclean had made the mistake a long while ago of having his telephone number listed, so the press knew where he lived. They descended on him en masse and when he didn't answer the bell, they tried to force open his door with crowbars. It took us a while to get the KGB around to drive them away.'

But Blake had long since replaced Maclean in Philby's social life. In the summer months Philby and Rufa would spend weekends with Blake and his Russian wife Ida, at the Blakes' dacha, an hour's train ride from Moscow. Blake's son Mischa, born in 1971, was particularly fond of his 'Uncle Kim'. I knew of this relationship before I went to Moscow so I asked Philby: 'Do you still see George Blake?' He said: 'Not so often. I haven't seen him for some time. He has a different job. But his son is seventeen now and very bright. We have five grades of marks in the Soviet Union. Five is the best, one the worst. Blake's son gets fives and fours all the time.' (I later learnt that there was more to the infrequent meetings of the two men than Philby had told me. Blake, a more retiring personality than Philby, objected to Philby's continuing contacts with the West. The two men argued and they drifted apart.)

I tried to get Philby to tell me how Blake brought off his amazing escape from Wormwood Scrubs prison in West London, and made his way to Moscow. He said: 'I know how Blake got away but I can't say anything about it because it involves KGB operational matters.' I said: 'Not even who sprang him? Can't you end the rumours? Was it the IRA? The Committee of One Hundred [a militant section of the Campaign for Nuclear Disarmament]? Sean Bourke [an Irish adventurer who had been in jail with Blake and who claimed credit for Blake's escape]?' Philby interjected: 'You've left out SIS. Maybe British intelligence sprang him.'

I said: 'But why would SIS spring him? They put him in jail in the first place. Or did they spring him to keep the promise they made to him of a light sentence in return for his cooperation? Were they shocked that he got forty-two years?' Philby's temper was becoming short. 'All I can say about Blake is that his escape involved a great individual achievement by Blake himself. Blake himself played a major role.'

Philby kept up with all the latest spy fiction, especially John le Carré's books. He wrote to me asking why David Cornwell chose le Carré for his pen-name and inquiring whether Cornwell had ever made any personal attacks on him in my presence. I replied saying that he had not, and that I had only heard of him speak of Philby with professional neutrality. He returned to this subject after reading a new le Carré novel:

Meanwhile Smiley rides again, a little wearily, perhaps, but that is natural for a contemporary of mine. You write that Cornwell's attitude to me is neutral. Maybe he is a mite schizophrenic; his introduction to your book was generously described by H.T.R. Dacre as a 'flatulent puff', and in a recent *Observer* I am a 'bent voluptuary'. The first word is C's very own; the second a crib from H.T.R. Ho, ho!

He arranged through the KGB for Soviet consulate staff to video-tape television programmes that interested him, using a KGB record-er to watch them, since he did not have one of his own. After watching a French programme during which the guests discussed the Granada television play *Philby, Burgess and Maclean*, by Ian Curteis, Philby wrote:

I saw the French TV film featuring [Patrick] Seale, [David] Leitch, H.T.R. [Hugh Trevor-Roper] and Co. Seale (slightly oleaginous) had an obvious advantage in his bilingualism; L. ran him reason-ably close, but poor old Hugh was an also-ran, his French about as rusty as my own. Best of all, I think, was the Frenchman, fat, voluble and lucid. He also spoke very good French.

On one of his twice-yearly trips outside the Soviet Union, Philby went to East Berlin, where Litzi, his first wife and fellow Com-munist, had made her home after the war. Litzi, who had married

Honigmann after her divorce from Philby, had done very well there in the film business, specializing in dubbing films from English into German and vice-versa. In 1966 she had divorced Honigmann (who was then director of DISTEL, a leading satirical cabaret), reverted to the name of Friedmann, and had gone to live on her own in a comfortable flat in Karlshorst, a suburb of East Berlin. A Communist since she was eighteen, she had a good income and freedom to travel to the West once a year. Today, even as a grandmother of seventy-eight she retains her youthful attractions – sharp intelligence, a love of life, and a sparkling vivaciousness.

So I asked Philby if he had taken the opportunity of his visit to East Berlin to call on Litzi. He hesitated before replying, then seemed evasive. 'I didn't,' he said. 'I didn't know she was divorced and I didn't want to embarrass her. And anyway, that period of my life is so long ago, almost like another world with other people.' This seemed strange. One would have thought that Philby, a sentimental man, would have liked to have one more meeting with the woman who had confirmed him in his communism, the woman with whom he had shared so much when they were both young, and when they had risked their lives for their beliefs. I decided that back in London I would make further inquiries about Litzi.

The results were surprising. Litzi had left the Communist bloc and settled in the West. She had done this mainly for personal reasons, but there were political ones too. Her daughter had married a German working in East Berlin at the Academy of Science and he had later moved to Strasbourg to do research work on the explorer-scientist Friedrich Humboldt. Litzi missed her daughter and her grandchildren and moved to Austria in 1984 to be closer to her family. But she also told friends that she had become frustrated with the slowness of reform in East Germany and decided to leave. As she told me, 'I had a permit to visit Austria for one week and simply did not return.' Did Philby know that Litzi had gone to the West and was he embarrassed to admit it? He died before I could ask him.

In September 1986 Graham Greene visited Moscow and met Philby. They had been writing to each other since 1969. Philby had opened the correspondence after seeing a letter from Greene in *The Times* complaining about the imprisonment of the Soviet writers Daniel and Sinyavsky for publishing their work abroad. Greene said he had decided as a protest to forbid publication of his work in the Soviet Union, and added that he would not visit the USSR 'as long as new conditions are not brought about.' Soon afterwards Greene received a letter from Philby saying that he approved of Greene's decision. He hoped that conditions in the USSR might soon change, 'not only because what you did is just and honourable, but because it might result for us in some unexpected gratification, some meal together, for instance, when we could talk like old times . . .'

Greene answered and they exchanged a letter or two a year for the next seventeen years. Greene sent Philby all his books – they occupied the bookshelf immediately behind Philby's desk. He also sent him the manuscript of *The Human Factor*, Greene's novel about an SIS agent who defects to Moscow, to check it for authenticity. Philby, no doubt looking around his own pleasant apartment, said that the man's flat in Moscow was too drab, but Greene stuck to his description. The letters were mostly personal and nostalgic. 'If there was anything political in it, I knew that Kim would know that I would pass it on to Maurice Oldfield [then head of SIS], so it was either information or disinformation.'[1]

Greene's visit in 1986, his first for twenty-five years, was at the invitation of the Soviet Writers' Union, prompted, no doubt, by Philby. Five months later Greene returned, this time for the international peace forum in Moscow. He went again in September 1987, when he toured remote Siberian cities, and again in February 1988, shortly before Philby's death. He saw Philby on every occasion. 'When I went to meet Kim for the first time after all those years, he said, "No questions, Graham." I said, "I've only one question. How's your Russian?" And we drank and conversed about the past. And then I saw him again with one or two others in the dacha of a painter living outside Moscow and then a third time I saw him at a dinner with the Union of Writers. Finally we had a private dinner. I went by myself to his flat but I won't say anything about that.'[2]

Rufa, the host at these dinner parties, had been afraid of meeting Greene. 'I had the impression that he was a man of sarcastic character. But this was entirely wrong. In fact he was a very charming man who laughs a lot and whose eyes are filled with childish naivety. I liked him very much.'[3] Rufa's mother helped with the entertaining, which reminded Greene that, 'I once had a letter in which Philby said that unlike most Englishmen he was very fond of his mother-in-law.'

Philby recalled his meetings with Greene with great pleasure. 'Graham is big-time here,' Philby told me. 'I listened to one of his speeches at that peace forum. He said that he saw approaching an historic alliance between Communism and the Roman Catholic Church, the two marching shoulder-to-shoulder against poverty and repression. And he said he expected to see in his lifetime a Russian ambassador at the Vatican. As you can imagine that went down very well and he was interrupted with spontaneous applause, the only speaker so honoured.

'The contrast with Britain is amazing – you know *The Times* won't publish his letters any more. Here he is the great British writer and everybody wanted to interview him. They've made an hour-long television programme about him – my contribution alone lasts ten minutes. He hardly had a moment to himself all the time he was here. I remember sitting somewhere with him when he was being interviewed by two very intense Soviet radio people. There was a microphone on either side of his face and a seemingly endless barrage of questions. First this microphone, then that one. I could see Graham wriggling with what I thought was impatience. Then suddenly he said: "That's it. Now I've got to go and piss." It was the only answer of his they didn't broadcast.'

Philby's library grew larger. Once a week he cleared his post box – a major event in his routine – and collected books he had ordered. His tastes were catholic. 'I read the Raj Quartet because of my interest in India and thought [Paul] Scott an excellent novelist. I read everything John Erickson writes, one of the few historians with an understanding of the Soviet Union. But he was let down by his editors or his proof-readers in his last book. There are lots of mis-spellings of place names, especially Hungarian ones. I thought I'd write and tell him but I haven't got around to it yet.'

He kept up to date with British politics. Mrs Thatcher appalled him, but one sensed he had a certain grudging admiration for the strength of her beliefs – and he clearly had a soft spot for her husband, Denis. 'Mrs Thatcher has that most essential ingredient for any successful politician: luck,' he told me. 'The good news is that I think she has finally woken up to President Reagan. All those speeches of hers on domestic finance – "You cannot run a household by always borrowing money. You cannot run a country by always borrowing money." She thought Reagan was of a like mind, and I think it has come as something of a disappointment to her to realize that he has let her down. Her consolation is that she now realizes that she can play a part on the world economic stage. As for Denis, he delighted me with what he said on his seventieth birthday. Some unctuous reporter asked him how he had made it so far, and he snapped back: "Gin and cigarettes." '

But for Philby himself, whisky and cigarettes were beginning to take their toll on his health. In the winter of 1986, aged seventy-two, he had to go into hospital again. He had been sleeping badly – 'I get up and eat a huge piece of chocolate cake; it's the only thing that will get me back to sleep again' – his pulse was irregular and he felt tired all the time. His doctors diagnosed arhythmia (an uneven heartbeat), but there was another symptom that worried them: since his return from Cuba, Philby had had two or three brief blackouts; once he had fallen unconscious in his bathroom. He came home from hospital complaining how difficult it had been to get a drink there, and rebellious about being ordered to cut his smoking to ten cigarettes a day. But he laughed at Graham Greene's joke: 'Kim, we've both got an incurable disease; it's called age.'

THE FINAL COUP
18

The last years of Philby's life slipped easily by. He had come to terms with the fact that his major work for the KGB was over but was pleased that the service still used him. 'I still try to keep a nine-to-five day,' he told me. 'But the office is understanding, and the pace not too demanding. They bring me something around and they say: "Can you do this for us?" And I look at it and say: "Yes, it'll be ready by Thursday." And they say: "So soon. Please don't tire yourself." ' In his last days he had been working on a new training syllabus for young KGB officers.

He would start this work in the morning after a light breakfast of tea and toast. Then he would go to his study, read his copy of *The Times* and tackle the crossword puzzle. He usually had at least one week's supply of *The Times* on his desk and preferred to work through the copies in order, but something seemed to have gone wrong with the postal system – either the Russian or the British – in recent years and Philby was annoyed about it. 'I get my *Times* from Embassy newsagents at Notting Hill,' he said. 'It used to take a while to get here but it always came in order. But now it comes in any old order and all scrunched up. I have to iron it to flatten it out.'

He would knock off work at about 2 pm and eat his main meal of the day with Rufa. Sometimes he would stop work earlier and cook the meal himself. Always a good cook, his speciality was Indian dishes. He asked my wife, who had brought him some spices: 'How long do you cook your rice? I do mine for exactly thirteen minutes.' If they did not eat an Indian dish, the Philbys' meal would probably consist of a Russian soup, smoked fish, or a stew with boiled rice, pickled cucumbers and whatever fruit was in season, except apples, to which Philby was violently allergic.

In the afternoon he would read and write letters. In the evening he would drink two or three double whiskys – usually Red Label Johnnie Walker taken with Russian mineral water. His evening meal would be a light one, sometimes only a Russian dairy dish, halfway between buttermilk and yoghurt. Sometimes Rufa would go to the cinema, alone or with friends. Philby, not very interested in films, would listen to music or read.

Rufa, who certainly does not look her fifty-five years, dresses well, choosing the best of Moscow fashion to complement her reddish hair. Her figure is on the full side but she defends this by saying: 'The latest medical research in the Soviet Union suggests that women with Rubensesque figures are ill less often than thinner women.' In company, Philby and his wife certainly seemed a happy couple. He treated her with elaborate courtesy, paid her flowery compliments, and frequently said how much he depended on her. She was very protective of him, watching his alcohol intake and complaining about his smoking. The only cause of possible friction that I detected was that Rufa had a tendency to interrupt Philby's best stories, not an unusual marital problem. Then he would chide her gently: 'Now then, darling, who's telling this story? You or me?'

In Russian-speaking company they tended to speak Russian with each other. When I was there they spoke English but Rufa would occasionally turn to Philby for help with an English word. They said that at home they usually spoke English, unless Philby's mother-in-law was present, in which case they interspersed a lot of Russian. I was in no position to judge just how good Philby's Russian was, but I heard him hold conversations with Vladimir, his KGB bodyguard, and on one occasion, when I was telling him something, he listened with the other ear to Vladimir telling Rufa in Russian about the progress of the corruption inquiry that looked like involving the Brezhnev family. I got the impression that his Russian was adequate for everyday purposes, but that if he wanted to hold a conversation that involved subtleties he would have to use English.

Philby was an expansive host. He liked taking visitors to a Georgian restaurant where he was well known. 'Tonight's on the KGB,' he said one day during my visit. 'We'll eat out. A car will pick you up at the hotel at seven.' It did, and then we collected the Philbys and drove to the restaurant. Vladimir checked out the arrangements before we went in and ushered us to a private dining room. Philby wore a pin-striped suit, with old-fashioned red braces. The menu included black and red caviar followed by shashlik, kebabs and roast lamb, all washed down with six hundred grams of vodka and four bottles of Georgian red.

I mentioned that the shashlik and kebabs probably recalled his time in Turkey. Philby, relaxed and cheerful, said: 'Ah, that reminds me of what I had been meaning to tell you about Mount Ararat.

You've seen all this stuff in books and articles about a photograph I had on the wall in Beirut, a framed photograph of Mount Ararat, taken during my time in Turkey. You had something about it in the Insight book, about the double humps of the mountain and how the little hump in my picture is on the wrong side. You made a big thing of it. It's only like that when you look at it from the Russian side, you said, and went on, like a lot of others, to see something significant in this. I remember someone wrote it was a symbol of my enigmatic status. Well, the truth of the matter is that the Soviet border is some distance from the foot of Ararat and you can photograph the mountain from the "wrong" side and still be in Turkish territory. So much for spy stories.'

Earlier that day I had told Philby about a rumour in publishing circles that Anthony Cave Brown, the British author who lives in the United States, was planning a biography of Philby, that he hoped to see Philby in Moscow, but that this would be difficult to arrange and could cost as much as ten thousand dollars. Philby had obviously been thinking about this, because at dinner he raised the matter, got me to repeat the rumour, and then said: 'I hope this won't be taken to mean that the ten thousand dollars would be for me. For one thing I don't need money. You have to understand that this is a cash society. There is no credit, no steadily getting into debt. God knows what would happen to the Western economies if all that personal indebtedness was suddenly called in. Here you can safely spend what you've got. I have no sense of financial anxiety because I know exactly where I stand financially for the rest of my life.'

Philby paused for a drink, and it occurred to me that he had had money worries most of his early life and so had his father. Suddenly I could well understand the appeal for Philby of a society where he knew exactly where he stood financially for the rest of his life. As if he had read my thoughts he continued: 'But suppose, just suppose, that I needed ten thousand dollars. Really *needed* it. Where do you think I would get it from? Precisely. From the KGB, from our people. That's the sort of service it is. Peter Wright's quarrel about his pension is something that could never have happened with us. Never.'

I asked him what he thought of Wright's book and suddenly saw a flash of the former Philby, the upright British civil servant. 'I can't accept Wright's version of the so-called Wilson plot.* If there was a

*Harold Wilson, Prime Minister 1964–70 and 1974–6, believed there was an MI5 plot to overthrow his government.

plot against the Prime Minister then it must have been a group of officers acting on their own. Neither of the DGs [Director Generals of SIS and MI5] would ever have countenanced anything like that. If they had heard about it they would have squashed it instantly. They are the servants of the Prime Minister, not him theirs.' (Writing this I remember Philby saying 'ours' instead of 'theirs', and thought at the time what an interesting slip it was that Philby, just for an instant, thought himself back in SIS. But my note says 'theirs' and perhaps I was mistaken.)

I said: 'You can discuss that in your next book.' Philby said: 'I'm not writing a new book. I have nothing more to say about the whole business, except the technical details, and they're in the archives somewhere. I'm bored and fed up with the whole story. Clearly the Western press remains fascinated, though.They're always pressing their correspondents in Moscow for interviews with me.' He stopped, took a glass of vodka, then smiled and continued: 'We know this because we read their messages.'

As the evening wore on we moved to international affairs. He was annoyed about something he had read in the American press. 'The West is always going on about the repeated claims of the Soviet Union to want to dominate the world. I can't remember any Soviet leader ever saying that. Eugene Rostow [the American political commentator] has cautioned against haste in ratifying the INF treaty. He says that the West must wait six months until we know whether Gorbachev means what he says or whether his words conceal an aim to control Western Europe, China and Japan.

'Now for an otherwise first-class intellectual to say something like that is ridiculous. What he claims is a sheer impossibility. We have enough problems of our own without taking on other people's. Likewise, all the talk of the Soviet Union being a threat to Western Europe since the end of the war is a myth. In 1945 the USSR was exhausted. The United States had the atomic bomb. What would we have had to gain by deliberately attacking Western Europe? No one wants to be incinerated.'

I said: 'Well, how do you explain Afghanistan?' Philby said: 'You have to try to understand our point of view. We got on well with the king and his successor. The Afghanis knew where their bread was buttered. Then came the 1977 revolution. It was called a communist revolution but there were really two rival groups. We gave them economic help and arms. In 1979 President Noor Mohammad came to Moscow and was given the red carpet treatment. He went back and was murdered.

'This introduced a period of uncertainty. How were we to handle the split between the two parties and get the country on an even keel again? We decided to go in and hold the country down for a bit until we could restore order. Were we invited? I can't say. There were no doubt some elements in Kabul which did want it. But there was also more than a suspicion that Amin [Hafizullah Amin, president after Noor Mohammad] was dickering with the American embassy.

'Now there was no way we would tolerate the Americans on our doorstep there. You could argue that they are already on our doorstep in Turkey. That's so but we didn't want them on our doorstep in Afghanistan as well. Of course, we shall never know what would have happened if we had not gone in. But now we are anxious to pull out as soon as we can without a massacre of our friends there. Our intervention has had a bad effect on our standing in the Third World and the Arab world. Our government has said that we will pull out by the end of this year [1988]. My own opinion is that it will take a bit longer than that. We need agreement with the United States and Pakistan and we need absolute honesty in those agreements.'

'And then what?' I asked him. 'Would you like to look ahead and tell me what the Soviet Union will be up to in the forthcoming years?'

'Certainly. As soon as we have got out of Afghanistan we will settle our border troubles with China. We are still wondering what's going on over there, but we know that the Chinese are disappointed by the outcome of the opening to the United States. There was a lot of excitement in America about the business possibilities in China. All those millions of people. But in all the excitement, no one stopped to ask how the Chinese were going to pay for all those goods. Now the excitement has died down and the Chinese sense it. So all that stands in the way of better relations between us and the Chinese is Afghanistan and Vietnam.

'I've told you about Afghanistan, but Vietnam remains a big problem. The Vietnamese are extremely mysterious people. They fight superbly – ask the Pentagon. Now you'd think that people who can run a war so well would be able to run and expand their economy. But for reasons we don't fully understand they seem to have difficulties in this area. But we need to address ourselves to this because it is an essential part of an eventual agreement with China.'

On the way home in the car, Philby, sitting in the front seat, asked the KGB driver to turn down the car radio. 'I can't stand loud music,' he said. 'And it's becoming increasingly difficult to get away from it. Can you believe that Muzak has reached the Soviet Union? I was in a lift the other day and there was this dreadful music surrounding me.

Do you know the only place now that you can hear real silence and get away from the ghastly din of modern music is in Siberia? You take a tent and some provisions and walk out into the wilderness and there, at last, you can hear silence. And as for pop music! Well, you may have read that there has been a bit of youthful unrest here. It has been largely caused by hooligans inflamed by bourgeois rock music.'

I had kept for our last meeting all the most difficult questions. The Philbys had invited us for a farewell party but Philby, sensing this, suggested that we should arrive at his apartment at 6 pm, 'so we can get some work done before dinner'. We sat in his study, him on one side of his desk, me on the other. 'Let's begin with patriotism,' I said. 'Didn't you feel any for Britain?'

Philby said: 'Patriotism is a very complex emotion. Take the Russians. They have a great love for their country, but over the years, many have emigrated and made new lives for themselves – although most claim to miss Mother Russia. Incidentally, I think there should be free emigration from the Soviet Union. I think the authorities would be surprised how few Soviet citizens would go and how many would later want to come back. But this is only my personal opinion.

'Millions of people fight and die for their country, yet millions leave to found new nations. As you know, I'm from such ancestry myself, the Filbys, coming originally from Denmark. So it's simplistic to ask why I felt no patriotism for Britain. Which Britain? I'm intrigued when Mrs Thatcher says: "I passionately love my country." Which country is she talking about? Finchley and Dulwich? Or Glasgow and Liverpool? I don't believe that anything I did harmed my own Britain at all. In fact, I think my work for the KGB *served* the bulk of the British people. And that is not only my view. Trevor-Roper [Lord Dacre] wrote that he thought I had never done England any harm.* As I've said, in my terms that is certainly true, but I was surprised and touched that he thought it was so in his terms, the terms of an old-fashioned high Tory.'

'That may be one view,' I said, 'but what about the view of another of your old colleagues, Malcolm Muggeridge?'

*Lord Dacre actually wrote that until 1944 Philby did not have much opportunity or need to do Britain any harm and that later the contest with the USSR was one in which local battles could be lost without disaster.

'Malcolm has this mad theory that I had always been pro-nazi and that I switched sides when I realized that the Germans were going to lose the war. This is just Malcolm going against the stream. The first article he wrote about me after I had gone to Moscow was reasonably friendly. But other people were doing the same, so he thought that it was an opportune moment to take the opposite stance. I foresaw years ago that he would end up in the Catholic Church. But he was great company and I still feel a genuine affection for him. If you see him, say: "Hello, you old rascal" for me.'

'So you'd do it all again?'

'Absolutely.'

'No regrets?'

'None in the sense that no course of action is ever entirely right or entirely wrong. So, trying to strike a balance in my life I would say that the right I've done is greater than the wrong I've done. I accept that many would disagree with me.'

'It's hard to believe that you have no regrets at all,' I persisted.

'Of course I regret what happened to my relationship with friends,' he admitted. 'People like Tommy Harris must have been very angry with me and quite rightly so. I regret that. And I regret that professionally I could have done better. I made mistakes and I paid for them.'

I said: 'Let's stick to friends and personal betrayal. I've met people who say that they can forgive your political betrayals but they cannot forgive your personal ones. So what about those, the people you left behind; the family and friends who took you at face value? How did you feel about them? Didn't one write to you from Beirut saying: "All the time you must have been secretly laughing at us"?'

Philby said: 'Yes, that was the American, Miles Copeland. But that wasn't true. I wasn't laughing at them. I have always operated at two levels, a personal level and a political one. When the two have come in conflict I have had to put politics first. This conflict can be very painful. I don't like deceiving people, especially friends, and contrary to what others think, I feel very badly about it. But then decent soldiers feel badly about the necessity of killing in wartime.'

'The other charge is that your political development must have been frozen in the Thirties; that only a man who had not thought about politics since then could still be a communist.'

Philby said: 'I know the argument: I have failed to adjust my views in the light of developments that occurred after I had made my commitment. My only objection to Trevor-Roper's book on me is that he said I had become a political fossil. But is the Archbishop of Canterbury a fossil because he remains all his life an Anglican? I have told you about my doubts, and there have been ups and downs. The Brezhnev period was stultifying. But Andropov was a fine man and a fine leader and it was a great tragedy that he died so soon. In Gorbachev I have a leader who has justified my years of faith. Anyway, when it became clear that things were going wrong in the Soviet Union,* my choices were limited. Have a look at what I said in my book about the choices open to me.'

What Philby wrote was:

> First, I could give up politics altogether. This I knew to be quite impossible . . . Second, I could continue political activity on a totally different basis. But where was I to go? The politics of the Baldwin-Chamberlain era struck me then, as they strike me now, as much more than the politics of folly. The folly was evil. I saw the road leading me into the political position of the querulous outcast, of the Koestler-Crankshaw-Muggeridge variety, railing at the movement that had let *me* down, at the God that had failed *me*. This seemed a ghastly fate, however lucrative it might have been.
>
> The third course of action open to me was to stick it out, in the confident faith that the principles of the Revolution would outlive the aberrations of individuals, however enormous. It was the course I chose, guided partly by reason, partly by instinct. Graham Greene, in a book appropriately called *The Confidential Agent*, imagines a scene in which the heroine asks the hero if his leaders are any better than the others. 'No. Of course not,' he replies. 'But I still prefer the people they lead – even if they lead them all wrong.' 'The poor, right or wrong,' she scoffed. 'It's no worse – is it? – of course it may be the wrong side. Only history can tell that.' The passage throws some light on my attitude at the depths of the Stalin cult. But now I have no doubt about the verdict of history.[1]

I said: 'Le Carré talks about the ambivalence of your position. In the introduction to our book he writes of you: "He enjoyed the establishment; he enjoyed its camaraderie, its inside track, its institutional warmth." That seems to me to be fairly accurate.'

'There is no ambivalence whatsoever,' Philby retorted. 'Once duty demanded that I should pose as an acquiescent member of the Establishment, I made the best of it. Of course there are

---

*Stalin's ruthless elimination of colleagues who disagreed with him and the forced collectivization of agriculture which resulted in the deaths of millions of Soviet citizens.

aspects of the Establishment which anyone would enjoy. But there is much, much more. What about the millions outside the Establishment, those millions whom the Establishment manipulates with such off-handed ease?'

'From the way you speak of Britain, I gather it holds nothing for you any more?'

'Oh, I'd love to go back there for a visit to see my grandchildren. But if given only one choice, I'd prefer to go to France. I had some very happy times there. And, of course, the England that exists today would be a foreign country to me.'

'There must be something of England that you miss?' I interrupted.

Philby thought for a while and then said: 'Colman's mustard and Lea and Perrins sauce. You can bring me some next time you come.' Then he continued: 'Don't you see? The Soviet Union is my home, and although life here has its difficulties I never want to live anywhere else. I get great pleasure from the dramatic change in seasons. I even get pleasure in the search for scarce goods. I *like* it here.'

'But you're a privileged citizen. You're a general in the KGB.'

Philby said: 'Strictly speaking I have no military rank. But I do have the *privileges* of a general. The only one that is really important to me is first-class medical treatment available very quickly. I know that this should not be, that a privilege like this should be everyone's right, but frankly, having been ill, I would find this privilege very difficult to relinquish.'*

Over dinner we tidied up some loose ends. I asked Philby for a full list of his decorations. He went back to his study and produced most of them: the Order of Lenin, the Order of the Red Banner, the Order of Friendship of Peoples (Nations), the 100th Anniversary of the Birth of Lenin (military version), the medal for Victory over Germany, and Hungarian, Bulgarian and Cuban decorations. The

*There is independent evidence that Philby was indifferent to some of his other privileges. One of his British relatives recalls a party Philby organized to see the Bolshoi. As they were standing in the snow afterwards with the temperature at minus 15 centigrade, desperately trying to get a taxi, an Englishwoman in the party said: 'For God's sake, Kim. You're a bloody general in the KGB. You're entitled to a chauffeur-driven car. Why don't you use it sometimes?'

Order of the Golden Dagger (Hungarian) is the most spectacular and is as its name implies. But Philby was most proud of the Order of Lenin. 'It's the equivalent of a K[nighthood], you know,' he told me. 'Of course there are different sorts of Ks, but the Order of Lenin is equivalent to one of the better ones.'

Then I had a series of questions to ask on behalf of other people. What did he think of Maurice Oldfield? 'I never had the slightest suspicion that he had any homosexual tendencies – if indeed he had. I was shocked and surprised at the way Mrs Thatcher treated him. I described him in my book as "formidable" and indeed he was.' Had he met Edward L. Howard? Philby looked bewildered. I explained that Howard was a former CIA officer who had defected to the Soviet Union in 1985. 'Never heard of him,' Philby said. Which world leader, apart from his own, did he most admire? He said David Lange, the Prime Minister of New Zealand. 'He had the courage to ban nuclear ships from New Zealand waters. Now we have no reason to target New Zealand with our intercontinental missiles and indeed we have ceased to do so. I'm sorry I cannot say the same about Australia.'

We had a last whisky. 'Is there anything we haven't touched on?' I said.

Philby thought for a moment. 'Ah, yes,' he said. 'One bone I want to pick with you – that line in your book: "Philby has no home, no woman, no faith." Well, you've seen my flat. You can make up your own mind about that. And if "home" is not meant literally, then I can tell you that behind and around this place is the biggest home in the world, more than eight million square miles of it. No woman? Many a man would envy me my marriage to a woman such as Rufa. No faith? Come, come, Phillip; only a fool would deny me my faith.'

Philby had asked me to keep him informed about progress to publish my conversations with him. When he appeared in the Soviet television programme about Graham Greene I became worried that this might be a prelude to further television appearances and sent him a telegram saying that *The Sunday Times* would begin to serialize my articles on 20 March – 'providing you postpone your blossoming television career'. He replied by telegram on 21 February saying: 'Television totally terminated.'

On 28 February he replied to a letter I had sent asking him to tell me the dedication in the Peter Wright book which Graham Greene had given him. It was one of the thousand things I had forgotten to ask. His letter read:

> My dear Phillip,
>
> I am writing in haste and discombobulation. We have had our distinguished Catholic friend [Greene] on and off our hands for the past few days; and what with the usual telephonic and transport foul-ups we are a bit on edge! I have told him nothing about the future, and he has gladly promised to repulse any journalists who may ask him about me.
>
> The dedication you ask me about runs, 'For Kim and Rufina with affectionate greetings from Graham and Yvonne, Sept 9, '87'. His Yvonne is as fair as yours is dark, so we have to call them blond Y. and brunette Y. to distinguish who we are talking about. One more damned complication in an already confused life.
>
> We loved the family pix. [I had sent him photographs of a dinner party with his son John and John's wife Jo.] John looks suspiciously bonhomous as if he had been at the soda water. We were also touched by the thank-you card from the brunette Y. Although registered it took sixteen days from post office to post office . . . Josephine [his daughter] sent me a shirt last summer or autumn and it still has not arrived. But it was not registered.
>
> Congratulations on placing your material so soon. I have not tried the great dish yet [a book I had given him about the Profumo affair] – too many noises off-stage. And you will have gathered from my awful typing that I am all of a dither. So now to a simple supper and early to bed.
>
> Kindest regards to you all,
> Kim.

I sent him another telegram listing the foreign newspapers and magazines which were serializing the articles and received a brief reply from him saying: 'Congratulations. Astonishing.' But I learnt later that he was not entirely happy with what I had written. He had two major complaints. The first was that I had implied that Maurice Dobb had recruited him and *The Sunday Times* had called Dobb a 'Talent spotter for the KGB'. Philby said that it was disgraceful to say such things about a man who was dead and no longer around to defend himself. He repeated what he had said to me: that Dobb had done nothing more than to send him to 'a perfectly legal organization in Paris'. The second was that the way I had written the account of his getaway from Beirut implied that the British had let him go, and this detracted from his achievement in escaping.

Since I had already planned a new biography of Philby, I made a note of areas that needed to be re-examined and began arrangements to go to Moscow again at the end of May. On 11 May came the news that Philby was dead. He had gone into hospital a fortnight before, but was improving and hoping to return home. On the night of 10 May he had telephoned Rufa, who had visited him earlier that evening, to see that she had arrived back at their apartment – the KGB car had been late. He sounded fine, but the next morning the hospital telephoned her to say that he had died peacefully at 2 am.

My first thought was that he had known when he saw me that he was going to die soon and that our talks had been in the nature of a last testament. I remembered what he had said when we had discussed how I would publish our conversations – 'I'll leave it entirely to you, but as far as I am concerned, the sooner the better.'

On the other hand, when we had talked about his health he had gone into some detail about his arhythmia, how it could be easily treated, and how his doctors had told him that 'as long as I keep out of draughts and do no heavy lifting – which suits me fine – then I'll be okay for a few years yet.' And he certainly did not behave like a man under sentence of death. He was so free from stress that the famous stammer was almost non-existent; just an occasional hesitation once or twice in an evening, and certainly nothing like the crippling speech impediment described by others who knew him. And he told me: 'These recent times have been the happiest of my life.' I can only conclude that if he did have some premonition of his death then it did not derive from his knowledge of any immediate illness.

Philby's funeral took place under clear skies on Friday 13 May. It began in Dzerzhinsky Square, where his body had lain in state in the KGB annexe alongside the main building throughout Thursday. (This was to allow Philby's service colleagues who did not want to be seen at the graveside to pay their respects.) The line of mourners took two hours to pass the coffin, open at the top in the Soviet manner, draped in red and piled high with red carnations. From there, the cortège moved to Kuntsevo military cemetery in the western suburbs of Moscow, reserved for high-ranking officers and distinguished Soviet citizens.

To Chopin's march, the cortège, led by KGB border guards, proceeded to the grave, at the end of a line of graves of Soviet generals. The coffin was placed on a velvet-covered concrete plinth surrounded by thirteen wreaths, all with cards saying simply that they were from 'Your comrades in arms'. His medals and decorations were set out on a red cushion at the head of the coffin. Four KGB officers spoke. They all echoed the glowing obituary issued by the news agency Tass the previous day, the theme of which was that Philby's career had been marked by 'his tireless struggle in the cause of peace and a brighter future'.

The guard of honour fired three shots and a brass band played the Soviet national anthem. Among the mourners were Rufa and Philby's mother-in-law, his son John and his daughter Josephine who had flown to Moscow from London on Thursday, and many of his Russian and other friends and acquaintances, including his former colleague, George Blake. Philby's headstone has his photograph (a Soviet custom), one gold star, and an inscription in Russian which translated says simply: 'Kim Philby, 1.01.1912–11.05.1988'.

If the Russians treated Philby as a Soviet hero, then the West contributed to his status by reporting his death in a manner worthy of a major international statesman. British newspapers and television stations carried long obituaries, articles, assessments of his career, and reaction from former Western intelligence colleagues. Some of these reactions were amazing. From his home in Tasmania, Peter Wright, the former MI5 officer whose career was devoted to catching spies, paid tribute to Philby as 'an outstanding man in the intelligence world . . . who would undoubtedly have become the leading officer in British intelligence.' Wright said: 'I believe that if it had not been for the defection of Burgess and Maclean there would have been a very good chance that Philby would never have been discovered.'[2]

For every former officer who celebrated Philby's death, who opened a bottle of champagne, or who said that he hoped Philby died in the same sort of agony he had caused other people, there were others prepared to say something flattering about him. Malcolm Muggeridge said: 'I know Kim behaved abominably, but there was a good streak in him. I'm convinced that the key to the whole affair was his father. Kim could never be the towering figure his father was. So he compensated for it by defying him, and all he stood for, in a most appalling manner.' (This is a 180-degree turn from Muggeridge's view expressed to me when we met at the BBC on 31 October 1979. Then he said: '[Philby] liked to think he was following in his father's footsteps. Russia was his Arabia and Stalin his Ibn Saud.')

Lord Dacre said: 'Philby was the most successful spy in England. If it had not been for Burgess and Maclean being caught I think he would have been chief of the Secret Service. It is difficult personally to forgive such a betrayal.'[3] Miles Copeland said: 'I differ from my British colleagues who hated him. How could I hate him for being a double agent when we were doing the same thing to the other side? I am truly sorry that the old bastard is dead. He was one of the best intelligence officers this century. The way he kept one step ahead of the hounds was masterful. I wish we had some like him operating for us.'[4]

But Dr Christopher Andrew said that the men who recruited Philby were subsequently killed, and the three heads of Soviet intelligence for whom he worked in the 1930s – Genrikh Yagoda, Nikolai Yezhov, and Lavrenti Beria – 'are now described in the Soviet Union as criminals of an unusually unpleasant kind.' He added: 'Philby deluded himself into believing he was serving an elite force but he refused to admit to himself or to others the nature of the organisation which he joined.'[5] Philby's wartime colleague, Robert Cecil, said: 'When I think of Philby I think of those commandants of concentration camps. They were merciless in killing people, yet they would be concerned for their wife's migraine – they lived a complete double life.'[6] And a former director of the CIA, Richard Helms, said: 'He was a traitor to his country and the free world. I do not shed any crocodile tears over his demise. I don't know that the damage that he did can ever be actually calculated.'[7]

Philby's death stirred old controversies, largely to do with the question: why does Philby exercise such a hold on our imagination? Anthony Hartley in the *Sunday Telegraph* writing before Philby's death but after the *Sunday Times* articles, thought it astonishing, even sinister, that thirty years after Philby's defection the British public and the media still found him fascinating. He thought the answer had to do with some weakness in our society:

> Fifty years ago, if anyone had been a confessed German agent or displayed sympathy for one, he would have been professionally ruined and socially ostracised. Not so today. We can all be 'understanding' about Russian spies without anyone batting an eyelid, though it is hard to imagine a similar situation in France or the United States. What has happened in British society? Do we no longer blame those who damage our society? Is patriotism a meaningless word? . . . Perhaps it is time for us to realise that this intense preoccupation with a secret world does us no good. To brood continually over who betrayed whom forty years ago is morbid and unhealthy.[8]

Patrick Seale of *The Observer*, writing from a different political viewpoint, nevertheless agreed that there was something odd about our obsessive interest in Philby: 'Britain's prurient interest in him, which is scarcely comprehensible to foreigners, must be largely due to the fact that in a deferential, class-ridden society, he exposed unmentionable things in the ruling class.'[9]

Personally, I do not find the intense interest in Philby at all surprising. Let us consider what effect Philby, just by being there in Moscow, had on Britain. He forced us to examine our attitudes to patriotism, treachery, class, and political conviction. This examination took place not only in newspaper articles and in learned journals but through books, drama, film and fiction. Philby forced us to think about the duty of the citizen to the State and to look at ourselves and wonder if we too, given the right circumstances, could be traitors.

Treachery is far from easy to define, even legally, and often depends on timing and who is using the term. Were the Yankee rebels who fought for American independence traitors? Were the Frenchmen who secretly aided the rebels in Algeria? Was Oliver North or the pro-Contra faction in the US government? Or, closer to home, were Englishmen who supported Ian Smith in Rhodesia traitors to the British Crown? As V.G. Kiernan has pointed out, when the Tory Party was blocking the way to Home Rule for Ireland, Randolph Churchill coined the slogan, 'Ulster will fight and Ulster will be right' – a call for insurrection that was technically treason. A Russian defector is considered a hero in the West and a traitor by his fellow Russians.

The truth is that treachery is an elastic concept and in Philby's case has more to do with betrayal of class interests than with betrayal of country. No one pretends that if Philby had been the son of an accountant, a grey recruit from a north London grammar school and a red brick university, his treachery would still be under discussion nearly half a century later.

No, the fascination in Philby lies not in his act of betrayal but in who he was and why he did it. The enigma is that he was a pillar of the establishment he was supposed to be protecting. George Blake, said to have sent more agents to their deaths, does not hold the same interest because he was not part of the ruling class in the first place, whereas if Mrs Thatcher had been around in Philby's day to ask if he were 'one of us', the answer would have been a resounding yes. Even worse, Philby betrayed for no material gain. As Sir Robert Mackenzie said when I told him in 1967 that we were writing a book on Philby, 'Make it clear – and this is important – that Philby didn't *sell* his country's secrets. He gave them away. He didn't do it for money. He never got a penny. He did it for his ideals.'

A man prepared to risk all for his ideals is a rare and dangerous man. And one of the reasons for the fear Philby arouses in the British ruling class is, at the time he decided to take that first risk, he was not alone. When Anthony Blunt was exposed, Philip Toynbee said that when he had been in charge of the Oxford

Communist Party in 1938 he would have regarded it as the highest honour to be asked to perform any service at all for Soviet Russia. He was not asked. As Geoffrey Wheatcroft comments, 'There are, one imagines, a fair number of very eminent Englishmen today at the end of distinguished careers who hear the names of Blunt and Philby and think, "There but for the Grace of Stalin . . . " '10

Philby has explained how he set out along his road to Moscow and in the context of the 1930s his was not an outlandish decision. As Murray Sayle has written, 'As to Communism *vs* Fascism or Stalin *vs* Hitler, Kim in 1933 certainly made the same choice the whole democratic or bourgeois world made only a few years later.'11 What most cannot accept is that he remained stubbornly faithful to his decision all his life.

Wheatcroft argues eloquently that Philby and his ilk were power-worshippers. He says they must have known the nature of the murderous dictatorship of Lenin and Stalin and yet they continued to believe in it. Why? He says that, like any religious faith, communism required a suspension of belief, but that blind credulity could not be the whole answer because men as intelligent as Philby, Burgess, Blunt and their like could not fail to notice the truth. Wheatcroft concludes: 'Lord Dacre once said in this context that young intellectuals pretend to love liberty but what they really worship is power. Their disillusionment begins when they realise that people like themselves are likely to be the first victims of power. Until then, at some conscious or semi-conscious level, they revered Stalin's Russia not despite the Terror but because of it.'12

But Philby has answered this charge. He had chosen his side as a young man; whether it was the right side or not only history would tell. In the meantime when it became obvious to him that things on his side were going badly wrong, his choices were limited. He could not give up politics – politics alone gave his life meaning – and he recoiled from reaction. He chose to stick it out, hoping that the principles of the Revolution would survive the crimes of individuals, however enormous. He had his doubts as to whether he would live to see this, but he died confident that he had.

This is not the whole story of Philby. A complex man has many faces. The role Philby chose for himself involved not only treachery but personal and intimate deception of family and friends. He has said that he found this very painful but absolutely necessary and that he was such a political animal that he was able to put politics above human relations. We fell out when I said I could not shed blood for a political ideal and he said he admired people who could. David Astor, for one, says that this total division of Philby's life indicated an abnormal personality and that it is therefore impossible to discuss Philby using ordinary terms.

Philby explained his personal betrayals by citing necessity. But is it possible that Philby's personality was one actually *attracted* by deceit? Sayle, who met him in Moscow in 1967, believes this to be the case:

> Was what attracted him the nature of the job itself, the idea of having a secret self, inaccessible even to his friends, his wives and their former husbands and, as the agent of one intelligence agency inside another, a doubly secret self? Was it not so much the cause, the vision of a twenty-one-year-old, never re-examined during a busy spy's life, but the love of deceit and, by extension, of spying itself that kept him at his dead-letter drops and secret inks all those lonely years?[13]

Philby has denied this – 'Contrary to what people think, I don't enjoy deceiving friends' – but it is true that in the intelligence world, where deceit and the manipulation of people are an essential part of the job, intelligence officers take a pride, if not pleasure, in the creation of their secret self – and sometimes end up never quite knowing who they really are.

Philby certainly enjoyed his work and his notoriety – for a denizen of the secret world he must have had the highest profile of any spy in history. I sent him a letter once in which I referred to those months in 1967 – when we were battling to uncover his story and to get it published, and he was trying to get his own manuscript accepted in the West – as 'the Philby days'. He replied saying: 'What you call "the Philby days" are known in my circle here as "*The Sunday Times* days". They seem a long way off now, but what a good time we all had until that clown, the Foreign Secretary [George Brown], interfered.'

The problem about coming to a decision on Philby is that a government policy that wants him and all his fellows to stay perpetually in the dark is never going to help us to understand him. It is a strange state of affairs that in a democracy a citizen who wants seriously to consider the moral problems of espionage is more likely to find the material to do so in the fiction of Graham Greene, John le Carré and Len Deighton than in books written either from inside the system (largely pasteurized) or from the outside (largely speculation) or, for the British, on revelations of maverick members of the American intelligence community.

Yes, Philby was a traitor. But traitor to what, remains open to debate. Yes, he caused the deaths of many men sent on operations against the Soviet bloc during the Cold War. But they were ill-conceived and always hopeless operations, mounted by men equally prepared to shed blood for a political cause. Yes, he clung to his beliefs throughout the worst excesses of Stalinism. He has explained this, and even if one does not accept his explanation, there is another. Sayle wrote: 'The more I saw of Kim, the less he looked like New Soviet man, and the more he came over as a stubborn, old-fashioned English eccentric, sticking to his rusty guns and be damned to the lot of you . . .'[14]

Yes, Philby put politics before personal relationships. There are people, sad though it may be, who follow the same priorities, and we call them generals, public servants, prime ministers – and load them with honours. But he made a total commitment when he was only twenty-one and he had the strength of purpose to stick to it for the rest of his life. How many of us can claim to have done that? He had the courage to risk all for his convictions and he got away with it. He was a man of his time and place who took part in momentous historical events and had no small part in shaping their outcome.

And when the day came for him to go home to Moscow, he went without looking back. He made a new life in the Soviet Union and, after ups and downs that he had the courage to admit to, he died happy, fulfilled and unracked by guilt – his final coup. We are deluding ourselves and will have learnt less than nothing from the affair if we persist in thinking otherwise.

Appendix

Murray Sayle's report of his meeting with Kim Philby, as published in *The Sunday Times*, London, 17 December 1967.

My first direct contact with Philby was a telephone call to my room at the Leningradskaya Hotel in Moscow, one of those marvellously ugly wedding-cake buildings in the Stalin Gothic style of the 'fifties.

I picked up the telephone and heard a strange choking sound, as if someone at the other end was trying to say something. Then the unknown caller hung up. The same thing happened five minutes later – a ring, the same sound, a click and silence. The third time, I picked up the telephone and said, on the off-chance, 'Mr Philby?' 'Speaking!' said Philby, quite distinctly this time, and after a few seconds of preliminaries, we arranged to meet in Room 436 at the Minsk Hotel on Gorky Boulevard (the 'Broadway of Moscow'), at 8 o'clock the same night.

I knocked, the door opened, and there was Philby, smiling with hand outstretched. I went in and took off my snow-powdered hat, and coat. The room was completely bare except for two chairs and a table on which stood a briefcase, a bottle of vodka and two glasses. The table stood by a window with a breath-taking view over Moscow, red stars shining on the ghostly white walls and spires of the Kremlin in the distance.

'This is a tough dynamic city,' said Philby. 'This society is going somewhere. Care for a drink?'

I accepted his offer and we sat down. Philby was dressed in sports coat and grey flannels; he is a courteous man, smiles a great deal, and his well-cut grey hair and ruddy complexion suggest vitality and enjoyment of life. He speaks exactly as a senior British civil servant would about his present employers— 'my superiors' he says, 'my colleagues,' and very early in our conversation he explained 'I am a serving officer of the KGB as you probably know.' He made no secret of his KGB employment and told me at one stage he had been on the telephone with his employers.

After Philby said that he worked for the KGB I took the opportunity to make my position clear: I did not propose to conduct a formal interview in the sense of asking him a set of questions, but that I held myself free to write an account of our meeting at some subsequent time; and that I did not think there was any point in our debating the merits or otherwise of Communism, or in my offering him any comments on the career he had chosen. He said in reply that he would assume that it was possible that I worked for some Western Intelligence service. (He subsequently said: 'I naturally took precautions against any rough stuff – you would not have got ten yards down the street.') But he seemed, at the time, quite relaxed.

We met subsequently at a number of restaurants nominated by Philby. During these long Russian meals vodka, wine and brandy flowed freely, and Philby talked lengthily, even compulsively. He is clearly a sociable type of drinker and he seems to have an iron head; I could detect no change in his alertness or joviality as the waiters arrived with relays of 300 grammes of vodka or 600 grammes of Armenian brandy.

The conversations which follow took place in no particular order, and I present them without further comment of my own.

Gerald Brooke and the Krogers. Philby raised this subject himself, spontaneously. 'There was an interesting suggestion in *The Economist*,' he said. 'The idea was that I would be prepared to withdraw my manuscript if the Krogers were exchanged for Brooke. If that were in fact a condition of the Krogers being released, of course I would withdraw my book.'

I asked, 'Is that a message for someone? Do you want that passed on?' Philby replied, 'No, it was just an idea I had.' I asked, 'Why are you so anxious to make this exchange with the Krogers?'

Philby: 'Our position is that the Krogers are innocent of the charges on which they were convicted. They were personal, not political friends of Gordon Lonsdale. We don't dispute that people like Gordon and Colonel Abel were our agents, highly skilled professionals, but we cannot agree that the Krogers were the top-level agents they are being represented as, or indeed our agents at all except in the sense of being friends of Lonsdale's.'

I asked, 'Did you write Lonsdale's memoirs?'

Philby: 'Gordon is a very talented fellow but he is no literary man. I looked over his manuscript.' Continuing on the Krogers, he said, 'We hear that they are deteriorating in prison. Kroger, we are informed, is covered in eczema. The conditions they are being held under are inhumanly severe.'

I said, 'I suppose a very close eye is being kept on them after Blake's escape.'

Philby: 'Perhaps. In any event, we consider this exchange could well take place. Now, look at the other side. It's a pity about Brooke, he really was a silly fellow. He got involved with the NTS (the people's 'Labour Front', a venerable Russian refugee organisation) and they gave him a list of people to contact who were supposed to be working inside the Soviet Union. We have penetrated what is left of the NTS so thoroughly that the very first person he contacted was a KGB man. All this came out at Brooke's trial and is well known in the West.'

I said, 'There seems to be a feeling in the West that Brooke was more or less innocently handing out anti-Communist literature and was grabbed by your people in order to exchange him off for the Krogers.'

Philby: 'Well, check it out with any of your Russian-speaking colleagues here in Moscow.' (I did: Philby's version of Brooke's activities seemed to square with the reports of people who attended his trial.)

Philby continued: 'Now, the NTS really belongs to the CIA. It used to be financed by the SIS but it was handed over to the CIA. This certainly makes Brooke some sort of Western agent, doesn't it? It's up to you and the Americans to decide who wants him back.'

I said: 'Are you helping things along by ill-treating Brooke, as you are reported to be doing in the West?' Philby: 'In the first place Brooke is our prisoner and we are treating him in accordance with Soviet laws, not your laws. He is being treated like any other prisoner would be in his position. After all, he is in prison. You don't expect to get all this (indicating a table spread with vodka, caviare and wine) in prison. Prisons tend to be unpleasant places. That's why I always took good care to keep out.'

I asked, 'Does this suggestion that you would withdraw your book if the Krogers were exchanged come from your superiors?' Philby: 'No, it is my own idea. I feel I would like to do whatever I can personally to get these people out. Perhaps two for one seems a bad bargain in the West, but we will just have to face the fact that the Western side always comes out worst in this type of exchange, for the simple reason that we have more, and better agents than you have. We get Colonel Abel, a first-class man, for Garry Powers, who was only a pilot, for the simple reason that you have no one as good over here for us to catch.'

Himself: 'I love life, women and children, food and drink, I have all that and I want other people to be able to enjoy it all to the full, too,' said Philby. I asked him how he felt about leaving his own family. 'I suppose I am really two people' he said. 'I am a private person and a political person. Of course, if there is a conflict, the political person comes first.' I said this sounded one of the bleakest, saddest things I had heard anyone say for a long time. He shrugged his shoulders. I asked how he reacted to the charge that he was a traitor. 'To betray, you must first belong' he said. 'I never belonged. I have followed exactly the same line the whole of my adult life. The fight against fascism and the fight against imperialism were fundamentally the same fight.'

Daniel and Sinyavsky, the imprisoned writers: 'I was completely against it, I thought the whole thing was a regrettable reversion to the old spirit. Of course, they were guilty as charged, smuggling their criticism of the Soviet Union abroad to be published. They should have got a week in jail, or perhaps a public censure from their colleagues in the Writers' Union. What's the point of sending them to a labour camp? But you have to make some allowances for what these Russians have been through at the hands of foreign invaders – they're sensitive on the area of their own people getting involved with foreigners. You can understand even if you don't agree. The old spirit survives here and there, but you'll have to admit, these sentences were against the whole direction things have been taking here.'

His book: 'My book is about 80,000 words long. No more than eight pages are political, in the sense of discussing the merits of Communism. Of course, many young people became Communists in the early 'thirties: the question in my case is why I remained one, and saw it through to the end, through the Stalin period and everything else. I make my position clear on these matters. The main part of my book is an account of my work with the SIS, CIA and FBI in my years in the West. I name the colleagues I was involved with, but not in an unkindly way. I hope just setting down the facts. I think the truth should come out.'

I said, 'Your superiors must think this publication will help the Soviet side.' Philby: 'Of course: I am a serving officer of the KGB. Naturally, I say nothing about my work for the KGB in my book, and my history becomes rather general after about 1955 – I have to think about protecting our own operations after that date.'

The KGB: 'Undoubtedly ours is the best intelligence service there has ever been. Some really tremendous triumphs. We have of course many advantages . . . We have a tradition of foresight and patience laid down by that brilliant man Feliks Dzerzhinsky (who founded the Cheka, forerunner of the KGB). When I first started to work for the Soviet Union, for example, I used to meet my contact once a week for two whole years when absolutely nothing happened at all. We were patiently waiting for an opportunity.'

Africa: 'One of the happiest days of my life was the fall of Kwame Nkrumah – not that I have anything against the poor chap personally, but I think we made some serious mistakes there.

'I was asked to write a paper on the African situation generally soon after I arrived in Moscow – one of my first jobs for the KGB here, as a matter of fact. I took a generally cautious line. By all means give these new African states a reasonable amount of financial aid on real projects. But I warned, don't get deeply involved . . . Well, we did. Millions of roubles down the drain. I was sorry to see Nkrumah followed by the people who are in there now, but at any rate I was proved right. Our policy in Africa now is watch, help but no deep involvements. Incidentally, the Chinese seem to have done even worse than we did.'

Source Notes

Introduction

1 Copeland to Bruce Page, David Leitch and Phillip Knightley, Nov. 1967, quoted in *Philby: The Spy Who Betrayed a Generation* (London: André Deutsch, 1968), p. 327. References here are to the Penguin edition, 1969.

2 Robert Porter, 'Hollis and Philby: The Shadows Stir', *Sunday Telegraph*, 3 April 1988.

3 Christopher Wilson, 'The Spy Begging to Come in from the Cold', *Daily Express*, 23 March 1988.

4 Anastasia Toufexis, 'Philby Talks: Tales from the Master Mole', *Time* magazine, 4 April 1988.

5 Harold Evans, *Good Times, Bad Times* (London: Weidenfeld & Nicolson, 1983), p. 45.

6 ibid., p. 47.

7 P. Knightley, *The Second Oldest Profession: The Spy As Bureaucrat, Patriot, Fantasist and Whore* (London: André Deutsch, 1986).

8 Oldfield in interview with author, 13 July 1979.

1 In the Shadow of the Great Explorer

1 Patrick Seale and Maureen McConville, *Philby: The Long Road To Moscow* (London: Hamish Hamilton, 1973), p. 3.

2 Elizabeth Monroe, *Philby of Arabia* (London: Faber & Faber, 1973), p. 35.

3 *Elizabethan*, March 1987.

4 Seale & McConville, p. 8.

5 Interview with author, 14 May 1988.

6 Seale & McConville, p. 12.

2 The Never-ending First of May

1 V.G. Kiernan, 'V.G. Kiernan on Treason', *London Review of Books*, 25 June 1987, p. 3.

2 Kim Philby, *My Silent War* (London: MacGibbon & Kee, 1968), p. xvii.

3 ibid.

4 Recalled by Harry Pollitt, quoted in Andrew Boyle, *The Climate of*

Treason (London: Hutchinson, 1979), p. 77.

5 Kiernan, *LRB*.

6 Donald Maclean reviewing R.D. Charques, *Contemporary Literature and Social Revolution*, in *Cambridge Left*, Winter 1933–4, p. ii.

7 Information from Kitson Clark to Hugo Young, Nov. 1967, for Page, Leitch, Knightley, unpublished.

8 Kiernan, *LRB*.

9 Page, Leitch, Knightley, *Philby* (Penguin edition), pp. 73–4.

10 Boyle, op. cit., p. 104.

3 A Bloody Initiation

1 Information to Page, Leitch, Knightley from Gedye in 1967, and see E.H. Cookridge, *The Third Man* (London: Arthur Barker, 1968), p. 24.

2 Cookridge, op. cit., pp. 34–5.

3 Naomi Mitchison, *Vienna Diary* (London: Gollancz, 1934), p. 78.

4 Information from Alice Honigmann, née Kohlman, to Ritchie McEwen in East Berlin, Nov. 1967, for Page, Leitch, Knightley, unpublished.

5 Monroe, *Philby of Arabia*, p. 209.

6 Philby, *My Silent War*, p. xix.

7 Christopher Andrew, 'More Unreliable Memoirs from "General" Philby', *Daily Telegraph*, 15 April 1988, p. 20.

4 God Save the Führer

1 Anthony Cave Brown, '*C*' (London: Macmillan, 1988), pp. 676–83.

2 Letter to the *Independent*, 16 May 1988.

3 Page, Leitch, Knightley, *Philby* (Penguin edition) p. 86.

4 Quoted in Page, Leitch, Knightley, *Philby* (Penguin edition) p. 108.

5 Seale & McConville, op. cit., p. 78.

6 Information from Chance to Page, Leitch, Knightley, Nov. 1967, unpublished.

7 PRO/FO, 1936, C 3917/3917/8, quoted in Seale & McConville, op. cit., pp. 78–9.

8 Philby, *My Silent War*, p. xv.

9 Seale & McConville, op. cit., p. 81.

5 Working on the Fascist Front

1 George Orwell, *Homage to Catalonia* (Penguin edition, 1966), p. 240.

2 Herbert Matthews, *The Education of a Correspondent* (New York: Harcourt Brace, 1946), pp. 67–8.

3 Information from Marsans to Adam Hopkins, for Page, Leitch, Knightley, Nov. 1967, unpublished.
4 Seale & McConville, op. cit., p. 94.
5 Philby, *My Silent War*, p. xxv.
6 De Caux to Deakin, *Times* archives.
7 *Times* Parliamentary Report, 6 April 1938.
8 Sir Geoffrey Thompson, *Front Line Diplomat* (London: Hutchinson, 1959), p. 130.
9 *Times*, 5 May 1937, p. 16d.
10 William Foss & Cecil Gerahty, *The Spanish Arena* (London: John Gifford, 1938), p. 434.
11 Seale & McConville, op. cit., p. 90.
12 See Luis Bolín, *Spain, the Vital Years* (London: Cassell, 1967).
13 Letter from Philby to author, 26 August 1973.
14 *Guernica* (1937), Museum of Modern Art, New York City.
15 Seale & McConville, op. cit., p. 100.
16 Gedye, quoted in ibid., p. 103.
17 Hart to Page, Leitch, Knightley, August 1967, unpublished.
18 Information from Marsans to Hopkins, for Page, Leitch, Knightley, Nov. 1967, unpublished.

6 Invited to Play

1 *Times*, 24 Oct. 1939.
2 Information from O.D. Gallagher, 1973.
3 Letter to author, 7 August 1968.
4 Letter from Philby to author, 26 August 1973.
5 Middleton in letter to author, 10 March 1975.
6 *Times*, 17 Nov. 1939.
7 Philby in letter to author, 26 August 1973.
8 See Robert Cecil, 'The Cambridge Comintern', in C. Andrew and D. Dilks (ed.), *The Missing Dimension* (London: Macmillan, 1984).
9 Malcolm Muggeridge, interview with author, November 1981.
10 Seale & McConville, op. cit., p. 135.
11 PRO FO/371/24589E710/25 of 16 Feb. 1940, quoted in Monroe, op. cit., pp. 226–7.
12 Seale & McConville, op. cit., p. 131.

7 *This* is the Secret Service?

1 C. Andrew, *Secret Service* (London: Heinemann, 1985), p. 47.
2 Major Stephen Alley in interview with Page, Leitch, Knightley, August 1967, unpublished.
3 'The Profession of Intelligence', part 1, BBC Radio 4, 5 March 1980.

4 Petition from Frank Greite in Parkhurst Prison, 12 Sept. 1921: PRO WO/32/4898/ERE 9077.
5 S.T. Felstead, *German Spies at Bay* (London: Hutchinson, 1920), p. 135.
6 Brigadier-General W.H.H. Waters, *Secret and Confidential* (London: John Murray, 1926), p. 65.
7 'The Profession of Intelligence', part 2, BBC Radio 4, 12 March 1980.
8 ibid.
9 ibid.
10 Nicholson in interview with author, 1967.
11 Page, Leitch, Knightley, *Philby* (Penguin edition), p. 145.
12 Hugh Trevor-Roper, *The Philby Affair* (London: William Kimber, 1968), p. 73.
13 'The Profession of Intelligence', part 2, BBC Radio 4, 12 March 1980.
14 Kenneth de Courcy in letter to author, 16 May 1981.
15 'The Profession of Intelligence', part 3, BBC Radio 4, 27 Jan. 1982.

8 Crushing the Common Enemy

1 Philby, *My Silent War*, p. 34.
2 Information from 'Spanish diplomat admits spying in US and London', *Times*, 21 Sept. 1978.
3 Trevor-Roper, op. cit., p. 78.
4 Otto John, letter to *Sunday Times*, 27 May 1988, unpublished.
5 Evidence of Petrov to the Australian Royal Commission, 1955, cited in Boyle, op. cit., p. 216.
6 Peter Calvocoressi, *Top Secret Ultra* (London: Hutchinson, 1979), p. 94.
7 Respectively, Nicholson in interview with author, 1967; Thomas O'Toole, 'World War II – Some Additional Postscripts Come to Light', *International Herald Tribune* (Paris), 14 Sept. 1978; and interview with Alex Mitchell for Page, Leitch, Knightley, 1967, unpublished.
8 Calvocoressi, op. cit., pp. 94–5.
9 ibid., p. 94.
10 C. Andrew, 'How the Russians Cracked Enigma', *Daily Telegraph*, 20 January 1988.
11 PRO/ADM/223/289.
12 Calvocoressi quoted in Peterborough, *Daily Telegraph*, 28 Dec. 1987.
13 Waldemar Werther, quoted in Rohwer & Jackel (ed.), *Die Funkaufklarung und ihre Rolle im Zweiten Weltkrieg* (Stuttgart: Motorbuch, 1979), p. 65.

9 Masterstroke for Moscow

1 Malcolm Muggeridge, 'Book Review of a Very Limited Edition', *Esquire*, May 1966, p. 84.
2 Kerby in interview with Hopkins for Page, Leitch, Knightley, November 1967, unpublished.
3 Mackenzie in interview with author, 1967.
4 Miss M. Kennard Davis, in interview for Page, Leitch, Knightley, 1967, unpublished.
5 Seale & McConville, op. cit., p. 172.
6 Philby in interview in 'Positions', Soviet TV programme, 26 February 1988.
7 Philby, *My Silent War*, p. ix.
8 ibid., pp. 63–4.
9 Cable, Foreign Office to Ambassador Algiers, 6 April 1944. Eden papers, SOE/44/17/192 Birmingham University. Philby, *My Silent War*, p. 73.
10 ibid., p. 73.
11 Robert Cecil, 'Cambridge Comintern', Andrew & Dilks (ed.), op. cit., p 179.
12 ibid., p. 180, and Cecil in interview with author, 31 Jan. 1984.

10 The Murder of a Nasty Piece of Work

1 See Nigel West, 'The Hollis Affair and That Spy Called Elli', *Times*, 23 Oct. 1981.
2 Philby, *My Silent War*, p. 90.
3 Reed in interview with author, July 1988.

11 Groomed for 'C'

1 Anthony Cave Brown, *'C'*
2 The late Col. Vivian, quoted in Seale & McConville, op. cit., p. 181.
3 Cave Brown, op. cit., p. 694.
4 Muggeridge talking to Knightley, Oct. 1979.
5 Page, Leitch, Knightley, *Philby* (Penguin edition), p. 27.
6 Philby, *My Silent War*, p. 99.
7 ibid., p. 107.
8 Trevor-Roper, op. cit., p. 21.
9 ibid., p. 42.

12 The Washington Penetration

1 Philby, *My Silent War*, p. 112.
2 Letter from Philby to author, 27 March 1984.

3 ibid.
4 Letters from Philby to Leonard Mosley, Feb. and April 1977, quoted in Mosley, *Dulles* (London: Hodder & Stoughton, 1978), pp. 489–95.
5 Lyman Kirkpatrick in interview with author, 1967.
6 Philby, *My Silent War*, p. 115.
7 Enver Hoxha, *The Anglo-American Threat to Albania* (Tirana: 8 Nentöri, 1982), p. 430.
8 David C. Martin, *Wilderness of Mirrors* (New York: Ballantine, 1981), p. 57.
9 Harry Rositzke in interview with author, 1981.
10 Philby, *My Silent War*, p. 121.
11 Rositzke in interview with author, Nov. 1981.
12 Muslin in interview with author, Nov. 1981.
13 Nikolai Yakovlev *CIA Target: the USSR* (Moscow: Progress Publishers, 1982), pp. 104–5.
14 Quoted in Seale & McConville, op. cit., p. 208.
15 ibid.
16 Mackenzie in interview with author, Nov. 1967.
17 Rositzke in interview with author, Nov. 1981.
18 Thompson interviewed by Page, Leitch, Knightley, 1967, unpublished.
19 Seale & McConville, op. cit., pp. 209–10.
20 Martin, op. cit., p. 50.

13 Terminated with Prejudice

1 Philby, *My Silent War*, p. 128.
2 Page, Leitch, Knightley, *Philby* (Penguin edition), p. 252.
3 Philby, *My Silent War*, p. 128.
4 Robert Cecil, 'Legends Spies Tell', *Encounter*, April 1978, p.16.
5 Joseph C. Goulden, *Korea, the Untold Story of the War* (New York: Times Books, 1982), p. 417.
6 Philby, *My Silent War*, p. 129.
7 'The Profession of Intelligence', part 3, BBC Radio 4, 27 Jan. 1982.
8 Philby, *My Silent War*, pp. 129–30.
9 ibid., p. 130.
10 Cecil, 'Cambridge Comintern', Andrew and Dilks (ed.), op. cit., p. 193.
11 M. Straight, *After a Long Silence* (London: Collins, 1983), p. 251.
12 Cecil, in Andrew & Dilks (ed.), op. cit., p. 195.
13 'The Trial of Roger Hollis', London Weekend Television, 3 April 1988.
14 Philby, *My Silent War*, p. 131.
15 Martin, op. cit., p. 56.

16 ibid., p. 57.
17 Lamphere in interview with author, Nov. 1981.
18 Seale & McConville, op. cit., p. 217.

14 Hoover Bungles, Philby Cleared

1 Page, Leitch, Knightley, *Philby* (Penguin edition), p. 279.
2 Philby, *My Silent War*, p. 143.
3 Captain Henry Kerby, in interview with Adam Hopkins for Page, Leitch, Knightley, 1968, unpublished.
4 Philby, *My Silent War*, p. 146.
5 FBI archives, Washington DC, 29 Sept. 1955.
6 Letter from Fishman to *Sunday Times*, unpublished, 13 Feb. 1977.
7 *Times* Parliamentary Report, 26 Oct. 1955.
8 FBI archives, Washington DC, 2 November 1955.
9 Rosamund Lehmann interview with Page, Leitch, Knightley, 1967, unpublished.
10 Lord Egremont, in interview with Hugo Young for Page, Leitch, Knightley, 1967, unpublished.
11 Page, Leitch, Knightley, *Philby* (Penguin edition), p. 301.
12 Lord Egremont interviewed by Hugo Young.
13 Letter to author from Dulcie Sassoon, 22 Oct. 1967.
14 Quoted in Seale & McConville, op. cit., p. 231.
15 FBI archives, Washington DC, 29 Dec. 1955.
16 Philby, *My Silent War*, p. 151.
17 Mackenzie in interview with author, 1967.
18 *Sunday Times*, 20 March 1988.
19 ibid.

15 Confrontation in Beirut

1 Monroe, op. cit., p. 287.
2 Eleanor Philby, *Kim Philby: The Spy I Loved* (London: Hamish Hamilton, 1968), pp. 28–9.
3 ibid., p. 30.
4 ibid., pp. 31–3.
5 Mackenzie in interview with author, 1967.
6 Eleanor Philby, op. cit., p. 39.
7 Seale & McConville, op. cit., p. 243.
8 Patrick Seale, 'The Shy Philby I Knew', *Observer*, 15 May 1988, p. 3.
9 Seale & McConville, op. cit., p. 238.
10 Seale in *Observer*, 15 May 1988.
11 Letter from Jansen to author, 20 July 1988.
12 Monroe, op. cit., p. 296.

13 Philby, *My Silent War*, p. 99.
14 Seale in *Observer*, 15 May 1988.
15 Letter from Jansen to author, 20 July 1988.
16 Anthony Cavendish in interview with author.
17 George Young quoted in *Sunday Times*, 15 May 1988.
18 ibid.
19 Philby in letter to Mosley, op. cit., p. 493.
20 Flora Solomon, *Baku to Baker Street* (London: Collins, 1984), pp. 226, 169 and 172 respectively.
21 Boyle, op. cit., pp. 436–47.
22 Astor in interview with author, August 1988.

16 Home to a Hero's Welcome

1 Eleanor Philby, op. cit., p. 57.
2 Kiernan, *LRB*, 25 June 1987.
3 Eleanor Philby, op. cit., p. 151.
4 ibid., p. 131.
5 ibid., p. 148.
6 ibid., p. 95.
7 ibid., p.77.
8 ibid., p. 78.
9 ibid., p. 174.
10 ibid., postscript.
11 Murray Sayle in interview with author, 1984.
12 Philby interviewed in 'Positions', Soviet TV programme, 26 February 1988.

17 Doubt and Disillusionment

1 'Graham Greene and Philby in Secret Moscow Meetings', *Sunday Telegraph*, 10 May 1987.
2 ibid.
3 Rufa Philby interviewed in 'Positions', Soviet TV programme, 26 February 1988.

18 The Final Coup

1 Philby, *My Silent War*, p. xviii.
2 *Sydney Morning Herald*, 13 May 1988.
3 *Times*, 12 May 1988.
4 *Daily Express*, 12 May 1988 and *Times*, 12 May 1988.
5 *Times*, 12 May 1988.
6 *Daily Express*, 12 May 1988.
7 BBC Radio news, 12 May 1988.
8 *Sunday Telegraph*, 3 April 1988.

9 *Observer*, 15 May 1988.
10 *Spectator*, 28 May 1988.
11 ibid., 21 May 1988.
12 ibid., 28 May 1988.
13 ibid., 21 May 1988.
14 ibid.

Bibliography

Andrew, C., *Secret Service* (London, Heinemann, 1985).

Andrew, C. and Dilkes, D. (ed.) *The Missing Dimension* (London: Macmillan, 1984).

Boyle, Andrew, *The Climate of Treason* (London: Hutchinson, 1979).

Brown, Anthony Cave, *'C': The Secret Life of Sir Stewart Menzies* (New York: Macmillan, 1987).

Calvocoressi, Peter, *Top Secret Ultra* (London: Hutchinson, 1979).

Caute, David, *The Fellow Travellers* (London: Weidenfeld and Nicolson, 1973).

Cookridge, E.H., *The Third Man* (London: Arthur Barker, 1968).

Evans, Harold, *Good Times, Bad Times* (London: Weidenfeld and Nicolson, 1983).

Freeman, S. and Penrose B., *Conspiracy of Silence* (London: Grafton Books, 1986).

Glees, Anthony, *The Secrets of the Service* (London: Jonathan Cape, 1987).

Knightley, Phillip, *The First Casualty* (London: André Deutsch, 1975).

Knightley, Phillip, *The Second Oldest Profession* (London: André Deutsch, 1986).

Martin, David C., *Wilderness of Mirrors* (New York: Ballantine, 1981).

Mitchison, Naomi, *Vienna Diary* (London: Gollancz, 1934).

Monroe, Elizabeth, *Philby of Arabia* (London: Faber and Faber, 1973).

Mosley, Leonard, *Dulles* (London: Hodder & Stoughton, 1978).

Page, B. Leitch, D. and Knightley, P., *Philby the Spy Who Betrayed a Generation* (London: André Deutsch, 1968).

Philby, Eleanor, *Kim Philby, the Spy I Loved* (London: Hamish Hamilton, 1968).

Philby, Kim, *My Silent War* (London: MacGibbon and Kee, 1968).

Ranelagh, John, *The Agency* (London: Weidenfeld and Nicolson, 1986).

Seale, Patrick and McConville, Maureen, *Philby, the Long Road to Moscow* (London: Hamish Hamilton, 1973).

Solomon, Flora, *Baku to Baker Street* (London: Collins, 1984).

Trevor-Roper, Hugh, *The Philby Affair* (London: William Kimber, 1968).

West, Nigel, *Friends* (London: Weidenfeld and Nicolson, 1988).

Yakovlev, Nikolai, *CIA Target: the USSR* (Moscow: Progress Publishers, 1982).

Index

All these books are available at your local bookshop or newsagent, or can be ordered direct from the publisher. Indicate the number of copies required and fill in the form below.

Send to: **CS Department, Pan Books Ltd., P.O. Box 40, Basingstoke, Hants. RG21 2YT.**

or phone: 0256 469551 (Ansaphone), quoting title, author and Credit Card number.

Please enclose a remittance* to the value of the cover price plus: 60p for the first book plus 30p per copy for each additional book ordered to a maximum charge of £2.40 to cover postage and packing.

*Payment may be made in sterling by UK personal cheque, postal order, sterling draft or international money order, made payable to Pan Books Ltd.

Alternatively by Barclaycard/Access:

Card No.

Signature:

Applicable only in the UK and Republic of Ireland.

While every effort is made to keep prices low, it is sometimes necessary to increase prices at short notice. Pan Books reserve the right to show on covers and charge new retail prices which may differ from those advertised in the text or elsewhere.

NAME AND ADDRESS IN BLOCK LETTERS PLEASE:

Name————————————————————————

Address—————————————————————————

3/87